UNKNOWN TONGUES

UNKNOWN TONGUES

Black Women's Political Activism in the Antebellum Era, 1830–1860

Gayle T. Tate

Michigan State University Press
East Lansing

♾ The paper used in this publication meets the minimum requirements of
ANSI/NISO Z39.48-1992 (R 1997) (Permanence of Paper).

Michigan State University Press
East Lansing, Michigan 48823-5245

Printed and bound in the United States of America.

09 08 07 06 05 04 03 1 2 3 4 5 6 7 8 9 10

LIBRARY OF CONGRESS CATALOGING-IN-PUBLICATION DATA

Tate, Gayle T.
    Unknown tongues : black women's political activism in the antebellum
era, 1830–1860 / Gayle T. Tate.
        p. cm. — (Black American and diasporic studies series)
    Includes bibliographcial references and index.
                                ISBN 0-87013-653-4
(pbk. : alk. paper)
    1. African American women—Northeastern States—Political activity—
History—19th century.   2. African American women—Northeastern
States—Economic conditions—19th century.   3. Free African Americans—
Northeastern States—Politics and government—19th century.   4. Women
slaves—Political activity—History—19th century.   5. Social movements—
Northeastern States—History—19th century.   6. City and town life—
Northeastern States—History—19th century.   7. Industrialization—Social
aspects—Northeastern States—History—19th century.   8. Black nationalism
—Northeastern States—History—19th century.   9. Northeastern
States—Politics and government—19th century.   10. Northeastern States—
Race relations.   I. Title.   II. Series.
E185.9 .T38 2003
974'.00496073'0082—dc21

                                                        2002155167

Cover design by Heather Truelove Aiston
Book design by Bookcomp, Inc.

Cover art: Elizabeth Catlett, *The Black Woman Speaks*, 1970, polychromed
tropical wood, 41 cm. © Elizabeth Catlett/Licensed by VAGA, New York,
New York.

Visit Michigan State University Press on the World Wide Web at:
    www.msupress.msu.edu

In memory of
Lucille Carter Tate

and the memories of
Juanita T. Glasgow,
George L. Glasgow,
and Ethel Lee Willie

and to
Olive Ramos,
my early teachers

Contents

Acknowledgments

THIS PROJECT GREW OUT OF AN EARLIER STUDY OF ANTEBELLUM black women's political philosophies that I undertook as a Rockefeller Humanities Fellow at the City College of New York. Venus Green, the other award recipient, listened to more of this project that she could ever hope to enjoy and her support and encouragement through the years has meant a great deal to me. As the project took shape, I presented working papers at conferences on various aspects of black women's political theory and praxis and benefited enormously from the comments and criticism that I receive from conference scholars, most particularly, those attendees at the Association for the Study of Afro-American Life and History annual meetings. Their questions and suggestions enabled me to formulate and reformulate my theoretical underpinnings on black women's political activism. I also owe debts of gratitude to my friends and colleagues, Edward Ramsamy and Kavitha Ramachandran, who rigorously examine varying notions and ideas of black women's consciousness with me. Those intense discussions, often highly spirited discourse, inspire me more that they could possibly know.

Equally, the completed manuscript was enhanced immeasurably by a broad array of scholars, supporters, and friends. Darlene Clark Hine, Georgia A. Persons, V. P. Franklin, Juliet E. K. Walker, James B. Stewart, and Hanes Walton Jr., meticulously read the manuscript and their criticism, wise counsel, and knowledge of politics, history, and labor mark these pages. My dear friend, Sheila Jean Walker, known by friends and students alike for her ruthless red pen, critically read several versions of the manuscript and I hope that I did her thoughts on theoretical issues, and queries and criticism on black antebellum life justice.

Among those that read portions of the manuscript, I owe an intellectual debt to Rosalyn Terborg-Penn, Elton Beckett, Gloria Burroughs, Lillie Johnson Edwards, Adriane M. Livingston, Melva D. Burke, Geraldyne Pemberton-Diallo, and Nancy Flowers Fairley, who carefully read drafts of chapters and made many helpful suggestions.

Librarians and archivists were my lifeline in making this study possible. Librarian Yvete LeRoy shared research materials that informed my work. My thanks, in particular, to the staff at the Historical Society of Pennsylvania, The Library Company of Philadelphia, Howard University's Moorland-Spingarn Research Center, Queensboro Public Library, and the Schomburg Center for Research in Black Culture, who located extant materials and made additional suggestions about sources while, at the same time, they had to be wondering if I were taking up residency there.

Many thanks to my circle of supporters, Ernest M. Tate Jr., Eartha Tate, Kenya Tate Dewdney, Rosalind White, Kenneth Hamilton, Gwen Parker Ames, and Yvette Mayo who never failed to inquire about the project and offer words of encouragement. I am also grateful to Barbara Jo Mitchell, who, with a great deal of skill and patience, kept me current on available computer software critical to my research. Janice Gray also provided technical support.

It has been wonderful working with Curtis Stokes, Senior Editor of the Black American and Diasporic Studies series at MSUP, and I thank him for his critical insights on black women's history, as well as his detailed comments on black political leadership, as he patiently moved the project, along with project editor Kristine Blakeslee and the rest of the MSU Press staff, from its incipient stages to completion.

A very special word of appreciation goes to Cheryl Wall, Clement A. Price, Ronald L. Becker, Howard McGary, Melvin L. Gary, and B. J. Walker of Rutgers University who sustained my work while they helped me navigate an increasingly difficult academic process with expertise, tenacity, and compassion. In so many ways they were a common source of joy, inspiration, and support.

Introduction

Theoretical Perspectives on Black Women's Political Activism

"Slavery is the combination of all crime. It is War."
Lucy Stanton, abolitionist, 1850

In the winter of 1850, Lucy Stanton, soon to become the first black woman to complete four years of college, stepped to the podium at Oberlin College to deliver her graduation speech, "A Plea for the Oppressed." Although ostensibly designed to elicit support for the abolitionist movement, which Stanton feared was losing steam, saying that "the Anti-Slavery pulse beats faintly," the speech emphasized the continuity of repression in the lives of bonded and free African Americans and the counterforce of resistance that blacks employed to challenge the caste system. Slavery, abolitionism, and nascent capitalism—the material realities of black life—strengthened the link between slaves and free blacks, a racial memory of common identities and struggle. It was in keeping with this common bond of oppression and resistance that Stanton made a passionate plea for abolitionists, black abolitionists in particular, to redouble their efforts to emancipate the slaves, for "the freedom of the slave and the gaining of our rights, social and political, are inseparably connected."[1]

With her graduation speech, Lucy Stanton began her journey of commitment to the antislavery cause. Other black abolitionists, such as Martin R. Delaney, were already taking note of her rising prominence, saying, "she bids fair to become a woman of much usefulness in society."[2] Similar to other black female abolitionists, Stanton articulated the oppression that circumscribed the lives of both Southern slaves and free Northern blacks: "The colored man is still crushed by the weight of oppression." Although she maintained that others were critical to advancing the struggle for black liberation, "let all the friends of humanity plead for those

1

who may not plead their own cause," she held that a consciousness common to both slaves and free blacks and collective action defined the dialectics of the struggle to be waged against the repressive forces of Southern slavery and Northern exclusionary practices.[3] Despite the differences in the regional terrain that determined the political praxis of slaves and free blacks, they were "inseparably connected," both being subjected to the material realities of an oppressed people.

INSEPARABLY CONNECTED

The struggle for racial equality was a common theme among black abolitionists, but gender, race, and resistance centered the thinking of black female abolitionists. By repositioning gender in the abolitionist discourse, black female activists were not only illuminating the exploitation of female slaves but protesting their own marginalization in society as well. At the heart of Stanton's speech was the plight of slave women and the myriad complexities of their lives that centered on the exploitation of their labor power. Here Stanton subtly intertwines the productive and reproductive capacity of slave women by focusing on slave women and their children in the larger context of resistance. "She returns weary and sick at heart from the labors of the field; the child's beaming smile of welcome half banishes the misery of her lot. Would she not die for it?"[4]

In constructing her message of slavery and oppression around the exploitation of black women, racial oppression, and the oppositional consciousness of resistance—all of the forces that shaped her own political consciousness and social identity—Stanton hoped to galvanize her audience, particularly its female members, into mass action to join forces in challenging the institution of slavery. "Woman, I turn to thee . . . Where wilt thou find objects more needing sympathy than among the slaves!"[5] This emphasis on the plight of slave women in protest speeches places young Stanton in the tradition of black female abolitionists, starting with Maria W. Stewart, who, with her talent for pithy analysis, had begun to introduce the concept of black female unity into the abolitionist movement in the early 1830s. In deconstructing slave women's experiences as the center of abolitionist discourse, black female abolitionists were constructing political bridges of identity and community to slave women as well as developing the crosscurrents of struggle. For black women, Patricia Hill Collins posits, this "interdependence of thought and action" is viewed as one continuous motion. It is from this vantage

point that Stanton's boldly charged statement took on a more confrontational style and illuminated the exploitation of black women's
labor power as well as its oppositional force of resistance: "Slavery is the
combination of all crime. It is War."[6] For Stanton and other black female
abolitionists who would give the movement new momentum, nothing
short of direct mass action would suffice.

THIS BOOK IS A STUDY of black women's political activism from its
incipient stage in slavery to its organizational stage of development by
free black antebellum women in northeastern industrial cities. These two
stages coexisted between 1830 and 1860, as black women created two
sites of resistance for community empowerment. Slave women, for example, laid the foundation of a "culture of resistance" that empowered the
slave community to survive and resist slavery. Free black women's migration to industrializing cities in the same period stimulated the black
protest movement's emphasis on community cohesiveness, organizational development, and political agitation.

The study's focus is on the evolution of black women's political development, the utilization of their labor power and "labor will" as modes
and means of resistance in slavery, and the transformation of that resistance as black women migrated to cities and began to redefine themselves
in freedom. These two stages of black women's political development in
the antebellum era evince the origins of the politicalization of black
women, on the one hand, and the political maturation of free black antebellum women, on the other. In effect, enslaved and free black women,
by initiating localized struggles, were attempting to create a substantial
base of power for the powerless. Both groups of black women needed
each other: enslaved women needed the rhetoric and ongoing momentum of protest, and free black women relied on slave women's resistance
in broadening the discourse and scope of abolitionism. Fueling both
stages of simultaneous development, and indeed providing the linkages
between the two groups, were the aforementioned slavery, abolitionism,
and nascent capitalism.

From 1830 to 1860, black women's political struggle was as much
centered on the commodity production of slavery and nascent capitalism
in industrializing cities as it was on the questions of emancipation, sexism, and civil rights for free blacks. Certainly, the prominence of slavery,
an ever-present factor in antebellum life that circumscribed the lives of
slave women as well as free black women, created the contextual struggle as both groups of women devised political strategies to strike a blow

against the system. Despite the transregional terrain of struggle, in which enslaved women created political spaces of survival and resistance in plantation communities and free black women honed their skills as political and social activists in northeastern urban centers, black women were "inseparably connected" in the complex racial and gender web of oppression that ensnared them all.

Unknown Tongues examines the transformative nature of black women's political activism and the attendant forces that contributed to its evolution. Black women's political activism in the antebellum era, a part of the "invisible politics" of African Americans, never took place in the mainstream electoral arena. Rather, it was on the tentative terrain of oppressed people fighting for a political space where black activist women can claim their freedom. This study, like most gender-based, ethnic, or labor studies, explores "politics from the ground up" and, in a larger sense, an integral component of the evolving black protest movement studies of the mid-nineteenth century. I have benefited from such pioneering scholarship as Deborah Gray White's *Ar'n't I a Woman?*, Jacqueline Jones's *Labor of Love, Labor of Sorrow,* Dorothy Sterling's *We Are Your Sisters,* Wilma King's *Stolen Childhood,* and Carla L. Peterson's *"Doers of the Word."* I have also benefited enormously from Hanes Walton Jr.'s *Invisible Politics* and Minion K. C. Morrison's *Black Political Mobilization.* In contrast with some of these works, I offer a political interpretation of black women's labor activity with its beginnings in slave communities and its maturation in industrial centers. The centrality of black women's labor activity in slave communities was their labor will, which was black women's attempt to claim agency over their labor activity, transforming labor centers of oppression (that is, farms and plantations) into sites of resistance. I argue that this appropriation of the tools of oppression and their transformation into instruments of resistance constitute both the means of resistance of female slaves and the incipient stage of the political activism of black women.

This political interpretation of ongoing historical retrievals is what Donna Haraway describes quite accurately as "a partial perspective" of a given historical time. But it may be timely not only in advancing the discourse on the role of female slaves, as well as the nature and beginnings of black woman's political activism, but also in contributing to the larger political dialogue on the constitution of sustained resistance shaping activism at different historical moments of oppressed peoples. I do not occlude, however, the stultifying labors of cash crop commodity production and their being what Carla Peterson notes as "sources of horrifying pain, generators of unspeakable terrors"; but I place this labor activity—more specifically female slaves' labor will—as a mobilizing agent within the slave community. As political resources in that community, slave women centered their daily experiences on "shared targets and objects of hostility held responsible for grievances, hardship, and suffering."[7]

SHAPING THE STRUGGLE OF BLACK WOMEN

Although black women's political development is essentially an American by-product with its origins in Southern slavery, much of it emerged from a cultural context rooted in the amalgamation of African traditions, beliefs, and values intrinsic to slave communities. These slave communities created a transatlantic slave culture and an oppositional force of resistance in which female slaves played a pivotal role. Nurtured and sustained by slave women, these slave communities became sites of resistance and cultural responses to oppression.

Although scholars have discussed the development of the transatlantic slave culture that emerged in New World societies, female slaves often do not get pride of place. Noted scholars Sterling Stuckey, Gayraud S. Wilmore, John W. Blassingame, and Philip D. Morgan describe the disparate African elements of religion, music, folktales, and the socialization process of family and community life that gave rise to the vibrant transatlantic slave culture.[8] However, female slaves were the ones who facilitated the family and community cohesion that undergirded the development of slave culture and communities. As these slave communities developed, strongly reinforced by planters to facilitate plantation commodity production, they became survival mechanisms that slaves used as they forged a cultural buffer against the ravages of the system.

African religious belief systems were the principal coagulants for slave community culture. As John Mason points out, in many instances slaves were constructing parallel realities: the outer face that confronted the material world and the inner face that communicated with the Supreme Deity in this strange new environment. As slaves infused their African religious belief systems with evangelical Protestantism, this amalgamation became both a way of staying connected to the Supreme Deity and a wellspring of survival. Albert Raboteau, Gayraud S. Wilmore, Sterling Stuckey, and Theophilus Smith note the prominence of these disparate systems in slave communities, contending that through time the syncretism of disparate African religious systems with evangelical Protestantism augured the beginnings of African American Christianity among the slaves. Historian Peter H. Wood observes that syncretism created a religious dilemma for many slaves. "Torn between the remembered belief systems of their ancestors and the dominant religion of their masters, they combined these two worlds in a process of evolution that took many generations."[9] The amalgam of African religious belief systems, the emergence of African-Christianity, the steadfastness of those of the Islamic faith, and African traditions formed the contours of slave resiliency. In this transadaptive religious process, which some slaveholders favored, hoping to encourage tractability among the slaves, slaves found a dominant source of resistance.

Although some scholars tangentially include black female slaves as a part of this cultural adaptive process, it is more compelling to argue that, as culture bearers, they were the centripetal force shaping the cultural dynamics within slave communities and, ultimately, an environmental context of resistance. Historians Rosalyn Terborg-Penn and Elizabeth Fox-Genovese, as well as political scientist Michelle D. Wright, have located the centrality of slave women's resistance as emanating from their African-derived traditions. For the most part, slave women's worldview informed the utilization of their labor will and power and, although grounded in the contemporary political and economic confluences that shaped their world, was derived from an African-centered ontology that emphasized universal affinity and humanist consciousness.[10] This worldview became integral to the politicalization of the slave community.

Slave women's roles as culture bearers were multifaceted and complex, contributing to a broad range of responses to their material realities. In some ways, female slaves were still traumatized by the loss of their homeland in Africa, the disruption of their pivotal roles in family and agricultural life, and the international and domestic slave trade that daily encompassed their lives. At the same time, their survival mechanisms against slavery dictated the creation of a cultural space where memories, traditions, and values were given symbolic and substantive meaning of psychological faith and freedom in the New World. The passing on of African culture, as well as the transformation of that culture in the new environment, was a retaliatory measure of protest and resistance against the brutalities of a slave system that denied the very essence of their humanity.

The location of female slaves in slave communities, which also localized the community's political and social resources, reinforced their position as agents of cultural change. Both Deborah Gray White and Michelle

D. Wright contend that the gender-specific roles of female slaves—that is, childcare, household sufficiency and agricultural production, and domestic duties within the slave quarters—confined them to plantation life, reinforcing African familial values. As Peter H. Wood notes, "These emerging family networks played an important role in transmitting cultural patterns and conserving African values." Wright states that the "boundary limitations" of female slaves, which confined them to plantation life, were in sharp contrast with the intraplantation mobility common to male slaves.[11] Slave women were critically placed in the slave community; reinforced by their traditional economic and gender-specific roles and, ironically, the slaveholders' desire to stabilize and increase the slave population, female slaves became invaluable transmitters of cultural traditions, including cultural resistance.

The initial stage of black women's political activism was what Patricia Hill Collins refers to as the "culture of resistance" sustained in slave communities. Resistance was intertwined in the numerous roles of slave women's labor activity, voluntary and involuntary, which Nancy A. Naples identifies as the blurred distinctions between mothering, political action, and labor activity, providing the groundings for a culture of resistance.[12] This resistance, then, was incorporated into slave women's everyday existence, which included socializing children in regard to the basics of survival, working as essential laborers in cash crop commodity production, and nurturing and politicizing the slave community on those issues vital to their collective survival and resistance.

Slave women's relations of resistance were community-based relationships with their husbands, children, and other members of the slave community. As historian Thomas L. Webber observes, the community was perceived as having an obligatory collective identity and consciousness. "Even in many of the larger quarters it would be a futile exercise to attempt to determine where the ties and reciprocal obligations of family, peer group, and congregation end and those of community begin." This sense of community was particularly impressed upon slave girls. Historian Brenda Stevenson argues that the act of slave mothers passing on to slave girls the lessons of collective survival and responsibility "were revolutionary lessons in a society where social relations were predicated on the inherent equality of Blacks."[13]

In forging a culture of resistance, slave women were evincing the early signs of black political behavior. Political scientist Hanes Walton Jr. defines black political behavior as a composite force emanating from the black experience: "Black political behavior is a function of individual

and systemic forces, of 'inner' and 'outer' forces, of intrapsychic and societal realities, of things seen and unseen, of sociopsychological and material forces, of micro and macro influences . . . Moreover, one or the other
might not be readily discernable in some situations."[14]

Female slaves influenced and sustained much of the political climate
that permeated slave communities, fostering the daily resistance and
episodic rebellions that destabilized the legitimacy of the slave institution
among the slaves. Internally, they nurtured a slave community against the
traumas of slavery, providing a supportive environment for protest and
resistance as they strove to combat the system's external intangible and
material forces. While the psychological, social, and sexual exploitation
of slaves was rife within the system, slave communities were also controlled by the political and economic forces of the Southern regional
economy. Such factors precipitated the buying and selling of slaves, the
invidious corporal punishment for all plantation infractions, and the economic well-being of the master, all contributing to the stress in slave communities. In challenging that oppression, slave women forged female
collectives and developed enduring networks of communication amid the
changing slave participants as they galvanized a community in resistance.

Slave women's "politics of resistance" was inculcated in their agricultural production. Their labor activity was principally driven by the
international and domestic political and economic forces that shaped the
market economy of the plantation South. The disparate geoeconomic
forces of the global slave trade, the financial collusion between Northern
financiers and Southern planters, and the cash crop commodity production on plantations were all intertwined in maintaining the institution of
slavery and, axiomatically, slave women's labor production. Although
slave women functioned as domestic servants, working in household sufficiency production, the overwhelming majority were principally agriculturalists. As agriculturalists, using expertise honed in African agrarian
societies, slave women did arduous labor on plantations, producing such
raw materials as cotton, sugar, wheat, corn, rice, and tobacco for domestic and international markets.

As slave women engaged in agricultural labor, they utilized their pivotal roles within cash crop commodity production to create empowerment centers in the fields. Initially, women drew strength from exercising
their expertise as agriculturalists, honed through centuries in Africa, reaf-
firming their sense of labor activity. On medium-sized and large plantations, slave-community members functioned as labor units in the fields,
providing support for slow workers. Black women were also empowered

by working alongside black men and performing the same labor tasks. As one ex-slave woman recalls, "I have done ever thing on a farm what a man does 'cept cut wheat."[15]

These labor arrangements in Southern slavery were predicated entirely on planters' pecuniary interests. Despite prevailing gender-based customs, particularly in agricultural labor, slaveholders could easily ignore atypical labor arrangements for female slaves in their intense drive for wealth accumulation. Breaking all Southern gender-based customs for white middle- and upper-class women, slaveholders assigned female slaves both household work and arduous agricultural labor on plantations. High among the slaveholders' priorities were their profit margin, their never-ending land and cotton speculations, and their desire to possess the aristocratic trappings that were the outward manifestations of ease—all taking precedence over Southern gender-based labor traditions. Thus the planters' greed and avarice, as well as their perennial need to maintain patriarchal domination and control, placed slave women at the source of their empowerment.

The invisibleness of agricultural production as slave women's empowerment center was submerged in the relations of power and domination of the slaves that determined plantation life. The patriarchal structure—in creating a race, sex, and class base of power, control, and domination for white men—obfuscated slave women's resistance at the nexus of production. What emerged instead from this province of white male domination was a romantic ideal of Southern traditions and culture that served to buttress the slave institution and the development of the planter aristocracy. Convinced of their white superiority and correspondingly the gender, race, and class subordination of slaves, planters "assumed racial inferiority form[ed] the basis for exploitation, control and psychic oppression."[16]

Although slave women derived a source of empowerment from agricultural labor, the delusional equality of labor with black men placed the entire community in jeopardy. Scholar-activist Angela Y. Davis contends that precisely this coeval relation between male and female slaves made slave women vulnerable to rape by the master. Planters were in a quagmire. Having, unwittingly, empowered slave women in this "deformed equality of equal oppression," the planters now sought to reclaim their domination and control by not only making slave women vulnerable to predatory acts of violence but simultaneously striking a blow against the entire slave community, reinforcing the powerlessness of slave women as well as the community.[17]

Resistance, however, was a dynamic force in slave communities, and acts of aggression against the slave community, though illuminating powerlessness of the slaves, at the same time strengthened the community's cohesiveness against a common enemy. Charles Tilly reminds us that "defensive mobilization" strategies develop among the powerless when "a threat from outside induces the members of a group to pool their resources to fight off the enemy." This "defensive mobilization" developed among the slaves because the raping of female slaves was a long-standing grievance that the entire community shared as they planned devious ways of retribution. Peter H. Wood states that the "inhuman treatment" that slaves experienced frequently led to violence. "Overseers were beaten to death by angry workhands in the fields; masters and their families were poisoned by desperate servants in the kitchen."[18]

Slave women extended their empowerment centers by using their labor power to alter conditions within the slave community. By shifting their roles from involuntary workers to voluntary laborers, female slaves created an oppositional force of resistance and protest against the system. By engaging in such traditional African gender-specific activities in the slave community as cooking, sewing, planting gardens, cleaning, and laundry and by working at these labors long after the field work was done, slave women created space for community sustenance and hope.[19]

As slave women went about the business of caretaking, they were daily transforming their labor power into a continuous political activity. Jacqueline Jones, Deborah Gray White, Michelle D. Wright, and Brenda Stevenson have discussed the significance of the voluntary labor that slave women performed in taking care of their families and other slave-community members. Jones argues, for example, that by volunteering their labor to sustain their families, the action of slave women "amounted to a political act of protest against the callousness of owners, mistresses, and overseers."[20]

But this "political act of protest" goes to the core of slave women's resistance. Slave women, by employing "a conscious use of self," were reshaping and shifting their labor power into a proactive labor will. This labor will was the driving consciousness by which slave women claimed agency over their lives. Thus labor will became the transformative power of black women's labor activity, enabling them to shape an incipient political consciousness within slave communities. Labor will proved to be the agency of their labor activity for the purpose of survival, nurturance, and resistance in the slave community; to nurture and sustain a culture of resistance through agricultural production and gender-specific tasks; and to employ overt and covert activities against the slave system.

This conscious use of their labor will reinforced their protest and resistance against slavery and empowered other slave-community members in acts of defiance.

Dialectically, slave women appropriated their labor power, despite its exploitation by slaveholders, as instruments in the protracted struggle of liberation. In reconstructing their labor power into an oppositional force of resistance, slave women provided the infrastructure and framework of resistance in slave communities. This arena of struggle, the slave quarters, became a contested terrain on the plantation between the world that slaveholders inhabited to affirm their power and a place where slaves harbored and developed emancipatory strategies. Slave women's employment of their labor will shifts the spectrum of resistance in the slave community from episodic acts of defiance and rebellions to a protracted struggle to destabilize the slave system.

Within the plantation system, slave women created autonomous spaces where they could activate their labor will as a protest mechanism in stimulating broad-based community resistance. They played the role of "nexus women," weaving the disparate elements of communities into a cohesive unit so that both resources and resistance could be maximized over a protracted period of time. This pragmatic strategy allowed for the material realities of slave life, such as slaves being bought and sold, the reestablishment of new "fictive kin" relationships, and the ability to sustain the interconnectiveness of all of the community members. Slave women as nexus women may be similar to Karen Brodkin Sacks's white working-class "centerwomen," although they are more likely comparable to the black women in the civil rights movement who Belinda Robnett describes as functioning as "bridge leaders."[21]

Slave women demonstrated formal and informal leadership in slave communities and were valued for their myriad roles in the community's infrastructure. The evaluative system that slaves used to measure leadership paid attention to those who supported the community on a daily basis, creating "healing spaces" for survival as well as sustaining sacred linkages to the cosmos. Chery Townsend Gilkes argues that dual systems of leadership emerged in the slave community with slave women, for example, who were recognized spiritual leaders and possessed considerable influence within the community. John W. Blassingame also acknowledges that at the top of the slave hierarchy were those slaves who were supportive of other slaves. Although he emphasizes male slaves in his discussion, clearly female slaves, providing intrinsic components of community survival, exercised formal and informal leadership roles.[22]

For slave women, their empowerment process engendered a configurative effect: in transforming the slave community they were in the act
of transforming themselves as well. White argues that female labor collectives were instrumental in shaping a female consciousness among their
members.[23] Slave women's labor will, combined with their labor power,
was reinforced on a daily basis in female labor collectives and by the
women planting the ideas of freedom among the children. Both the
female labor collectives, which consisted of an intergenerational cadre of
women, and slave women's roles in creating an environment of mental
resistance for their children contoured their roles as nexus women. The
intergenerational female labor collective offered opportunities for slave
women to elevate their own levels of awareness about their common
oppression and to embrace a mutual work ethic of obligations and
responsibilities.

Invariably, this intergenerational bonding supported slave women in
inculcating a resistance ethic among their children. Historian Wilma
King notes that slave mothers started early with planting seeds of resistance among their children.[24] While they were teaching their children to
survive the rigors of slavery, they were simultaneously encouraging them
to resist the ravages of the system, imploring them to run away if they
got an opportunity. Embedded in the survival tenets that slave women
forged for their children were family and community bonds of love and
trust, and, while appearing to appease the planter class, they were internally subverting the system. Thus it was in the context of the immediate
material realities of oppression, as well as the larger geoeconomic forces
of domination and control, that slave women asserted their sociopolitical agency in the slave community, a protracted struggle of freedom and
liberation in a hostile world.

SHIFTING TERRAINS OF STRUGGLE

The other stage of black women's political activism, the organizational
stage of development, took place on the uneven terrain of northeastern
industrial cities, where black women negotiated the harsh material realities of industrial capitalism. As social, political, and economic factors
converged to stimulate Northern industrialization in the 1820s and
1830s, they provided an external catalyst for black women's political
consciousness. In part, free black women's consciousness and resistance
turned as much on the economic and social marginalization of black

women in industrializing cities as it did on their economic activity in black urban communities. Noticeably, the relation of enslaved and free black women to the Southern and Northern market economies, respectively, held similarities of process. Just as the exigencies of the Southern regional economy shaped the labor of female slaves and ultimately their resistance in slave communities, nascent capitalism stimulated free black women's economic activity, which in turn served as a springboard to their political consciousness and resistance.

In the new dawn of freedom, whether black women were runaways, recently emancipated slaves, or moving from indentured servitude to freedom, the migration to the industrial cities of Philadelphia, Boston, and New York City transformed their lives. These black women came out of servitude with a developing racial and labor consciousness, a commitment to family and community, and an ongoing advocacy of individual and collective protest as intrinsic components of struggle. Black women were attracted to these industrial cities seeking anonymity, safe harbor, jobs, and a chance to rekindle family and community relationships that had been severed during slavery. Certainly, the individual process of defining their new freedom was tied to the exhilaration of freedom. For many of these women, removing the shackles of enslavement was an arduous process that would take a lifetime.

Key socioeconomic factors quickly dimmed freedom for these black female workers as they adapted to urbanization and industrialization. As industrial capitalism developed, its manufacturing centers in northeastern U.S. cities and in England depended on the raw materials from slave labor, especially cotton during the antebellum era, which were then transformed into finished goods for interregional and overseas markets. The growth in textile and other factories, as northeastern cities changed from artisan to factory production, created a corresponding need for aggregate labor resources.[25] Newly arrived European immigrant laborers, native-born whites, and black migrants from the South were placed in intense economic competition with each other for available employment. As successive waves of European immigrant workers arrived in major cities to compete with blacks for menial jobs, the economic competition increased, despite the fact that many white workers were now being routinized into factory production.

Black women, denied factory jobs because of racial and sexual discrimination, became a unique component of this reserve pool of laborers, and, as they struggled to make a living, the intersection of race, class, and gender in the urban marketplace formed the contextual oppression of their daily lives. This period may demarcate Evelyn Brooks Higginbotham's analysis of the metalanguage of race, in which the emerging issues of gender, race, and class of black female workers under industrial capitalism was obfuscated under the racial umbrella.[26] Although antebellum cities offered blacks greater freedom, jobs, and, especially for fugitives, a certain anonymity, the infusion of racial, sexual, and class discrimination into industrial capitalism was rapidly solidifying an impoverished class of free black women. Urban areas proved to be hostile environments for free black women and, while providing the affluent classes with a steady pool of household workers, afforded them marginal living conditions. For black women, these hostile environments not only circumscribed their economic plight as workers but their liberating strategies as well. While contextualizing the multifaceted nature of their oppression, black women had to simultaneously "reproduce political identities through their everyday lives."[27]

Black women's labor power was placed in a quagmire amid the shifting spectrum of industrialization. These workers were also thwarted by their inability to establish cross-racial ties with white female workers. White female workers' refusal to work alongside black women denied black women factory jobs.[28] White female workers also protested against the presence of black women in the workplace, thereby denying black women opportunities to alter their economic circumstances. Although white female workers frequently shared the same economic plight with black women, they were not willing to risk their white-skinned privileges to form female working-class coalitions. The marginalization of black female workers in the urban economy; the pervasiveness of sexual, racial, and class discrimination; and the inability to receive support from white female workers nurtured and in time strengthened the racial solidarity of black women.

Black female laborers found themselves tied to the economic marketplace tangentially, largely as household workers, which marginalized their participation in the labor force. Historian Sharon Harley describes how black female workers in Philadelphia were circumscribed in the urban marketplace by being relegated to the bottommost tier of the economic ladder: "They were banish[ed] to the galleys of menial labor." According to economist Julianne Malveaux, free black women inherited the legacy of slavery, which made their labor experiences distinctively different from those of white women. "Though the occupational position of black women has its roots in slavery, black women have continued to be segregated occupationally and in different ways than are white women."[29]

The conditions that black women as free laborers endured in the marketplace did not vary significantly from their prior condition of servitude. African American women were placed in a paradoxical situation: as slaves they had formed the nucleus of the slave labor force, but as free laborers they played an invisible reserved labor role in the new capitalist state. Confined chiefly to domestic service in the antebellum era, although their numbers diminished as they were replaced by Irish women in the 1840s and 1850s, black women worked as dayworkers, part-time domestics, cooks, laundrywomen, miscellaneous domestics, and "maids for all seasons" to supplement family income.[30]

Black female workers constituted the majority of black workers in industrial cities, and their numerical numbers as household workers strengthened their labor demands. Graham Russell Hodges argues in his study of blacks in New York and eastern New Jersey that not only did black women constitute the majority of black workers in New York, but their continuous pressure to be paid a fair wage for their services was a bone of contention between them and their employers: "Black New York's wage force in the 1820s remained primarily female, a characteristic that did not lend itself to deference. To the dismay of employers, the faithful servant became a distant memory. Restlessness and freedom of spirit undermined presumptions of deference and loyalty to paternalist masters. Higher wages for their services, increased demand, and republican pride combined to create a 'love for incessant change.'"[31]

Free black women used their labor power to demand better working conditions for themselves. One domestic worker, Hannah, negotiated with her employer the right to keep her children with her while she worked, and another household worker, Tamar, would work only if her daughter were hired as well.[32] Largely trapped between marginal economic opportunities and domestic jobs that native white women shunned, free black women fought for the dignity of their labor. Still, psychologically and socially, their enhanced self-confidence and earning power proved to be transformative components in their becoming economically viable members of black families and community life. Increasingly, black women's economic activity, in cities where black males experienced high rates of unemployment, proved essential to the family's survival and the sustainability of the black community. Relative to the black woman's economic role, which did not change materially, her economic status and influence in the family and community appreciated, ultimately becoming a springboard for the community-based activism of black women.

In community life, black women's praxis in struggle was forged by their linkages to black nationalism. With its philosophical emphasis on racial solidarity and self-reliance, black nationalism spearheaded black community institutional development. Black women, alongside black men, as well as in female collectives, participated in the founding of the black church, the mutual benevolent societies, the black press, and the national black convention movement—all emerging from this nationalist ethos. This early institutional formation in black communities was based on a social protest model, which Anthony Oberschall views as conflict model mobilization, where there is "the process of forming crowds, groups, associations, and organizations for the pursuit of collective goals." For black women, the ideology was also expanded to thwart sexism. "African American women also viewed black nationalism as a developing praxis by which they could counter gender oppression and promote collective female consciousness."[33]

In constructing the political and social identities of urban black communities, black women were creating structures that resisted domination and control. These urban communities, though diverse and heterogeneous, were infused with themes of common struggle. Hanes Walton Jr. comments that "the black community develops institutions and ideas that create a sense of belonging based on racial consciousness and a common cultural heritage."[34] The culture of work that centered black female entrepreneurs in the community was also key to the dissemination of information about community issues and meetings. Social organizations and ad hoc groups were other avenues of disseminating information and mobilizing the community around critical issues. With community activism, black women localized international and national struggle and became informal leaders in community life.

Still, this journey of political and social activism was no easy task, and black women's activism invited criticism from black men who touted middle-class notions of womanhood and from whites who provided black women with a marginalized existence. The "cult of true womanhood," which had been elevated to middle-class status principally to keep industrial capitalism a white male preserve, circumscribed the lives of black women. The cult's relegation of all women to the home flew in the face of black women's lives. The material realities of their lives, which necessitated work and struggle, dictated a defiance of middle-class conventions and societal constraints. Black women would find, however, that larger spheres of religious and political activism always bowed to male domination and control. But having defied gender norms in carving our their economic space, black women expanded their political space to include a broad-based infrastructure that would propel them into deeper issues of community activism, evangelicalism, and abolitionism as venues for social change.

Antebellum organizations, associations, and societies were the outgrowth of black women's developing political consciousness and community activism. But as Bert Klandermans indicates in his examination of social movement participation, structures alone are insufficient in promoting individual activism.[35] Free black female activists, continuing or paralleling the role of slave women within the slave community, became nexus women, recruiting targeted members as well as other community members to organizations and community participation. Household workers, for example, who worked away from home would be encouraged to work on a specific project that had a limited time frame. Independent entrepreneurs and middle-class women could more readily participate in long-term or ongoing community initiatives. To induce community residents to take potential risks, particularly in the areas of abolition and civil rights, female collectives with their "consciousness-raising" sessions became activist vehicles. The numerous sacred female collectives, or "prayer bands," where black women strengthened their spiritual commitment, were the training grounds for many black female evangelists.

Black female evangelism and the shaping of "gospel politics" were fostered by the holiness revivals, spiritual awakenings, and camp meetings that swept the Northeast in the nineteenth century, as well as by the emphasis on evangelical Christianity in urban black communities. Undoubtedly, the male domination of black religious institutions, which excluded black women from formal positions of authority and leadership, was a major contributing factor as well. Because the black church merged sacred and secular concerns and was the recognized arena for honing leadership skills, alternative arenas, such as female prayer bands and itinerant preaching, had to be established by black female evangelists if they wanted their voices heard.

Black female evangelists transcended the typical avenues of black religious leadership by wrapping themselves in the validation powers of a higher spiritual authority. Bettye Collier-Thomas notes that "many pioneering black and white women contended for the right to preach. Early women preachers such as Elizabeth, Jarena Lee, Zilpha Elaw, Amanda Berry Smith and Julia Foote succeeded in developing ministries without ordination." These activists, as Carla L. Peterson contends, were "insisting on their right to preach the gospel, to lecture, to write on such topics ᴵᴳs evangelicalism, abolitionism, moral reform, temperance, and ᴵᴳs rights."[36] As gospel pioneers, believing that they were "called ᴵᴳod" to preach, black female evangelists made the world their prosᴵᴳᴵytizing arena. Tempered yet undaunted by conventional gender norms and the ecclesiastical sexism within the black church, these itinerant preachers spread the gospel throughout the nation and in several European countries. Preaching to black and white audiences, enslaved and free, these evangelists had a widespread influence on believers. Empowered by the word of God, black female evangelists challenged the black male church hierarchy, gender discrimination, racism, and slavery. Defying conventional norms and expostulating that God, not men, determined justice and equality, most of these early black female evangelists became abolitionists.

Black female abolitionists fostered sites of protest, resistance, and insurgency in urban black communities. One of their primary roles was to politicize communities through a network of social organizations and cultural institutions where the twin goals of abolitionism—the emancipation of the slaves and the uplift of black communities—were articulated sentiments.[37] Abolitionism was also fostered by the oral and written reports given by black abolitionists who were returning from the international and national "field of protest": "Black abolitionists, carrying out their organizing activities, traveled widely and met frequently with their wealthy and powerful patrons. Such people returned to the black community bursting with the news of their travels."[38] The Forten women of Philadelphia, Maria W. Stewart of Boston and then New York City, and Isabella and Holmes Snowden of Boston were all abolitionists shaping political views and opinions among blacks.

Black female abolitionists nurtured the connection between the slave and free black communities in a common struggle for liberation. Despite the massive attempts by blacks to stabilize their lives, slavery and their own tenuous free status heightened their sense of insecurity. Fugitives hiding in cities or passing through on their way to Canada, or bounty hunters in hot pursuit, or the fear of free blacks being captured and re-enslaved—all contributed to an environmental resistance in black communities. Mass direct action in the form of dramatic slave rescues, of which black women were major players, also fed the abolitionist cause, empowering the communities that sensed they were under siege.

Black female abolitionists employed a number of strategies of resistance that fed the larger black protest movement. Employing both open and subversive political resistance—two complementary directions of political praxis—black female abolitionists participated in the founding of predominantly black as well as interracial antislavery societies, while at the same time participating in all phases of Underground Railroad activities in black communities. This political duality—of maintaining a surface level of seemingly benign labor activity yet concerted civil disobedience while simultaneously deepening their level of political consciousness and praxis in subversive activism—characterized much of the political activism of free black women during the antebellum era. The complexities of this political duality of black women's activism, contoured by their material lives, is addressed in subsequent chapters.

PART 1

Critical Passages

CHAPTER 1

A Long Ways from Home

The Context for Oppression and Resistance

> I was beginning to plan for freedom, and was forever on the alert
> for a chance to escape and join my sister. I was then twelve years
> old, and often talked the matter over with my mother and canvassed
> the probabilities of both of us getting away.
>
> LUCY ANN DELANEY, ex-slave, 1891

By THE TIME AFRICAN WOMEN BECAME CAPTIVES OF EUROPEAN
slavers aboard ships bound for New World plantation societies, they
were already mired in the geoeconomic forces of the transoceanic slave
trade. Their journey as commodities began at the inchoate stages of the
trade, where Africans were bought, captured, or kidnapped from the
African tribes in the inland savanna regions or those dotting the Atlantic
coastal areas where trafficking was especially brisk; marched to massive
detention centers; and readied for transport to the Americas. By the sev-
enteenth and eighteenth centuries, African women, as commodities, were
enmeshed at multiple points of entry in the burgeoning global enterprise
in significant numbers. Having varied roles in indigenous African societies, depending on the region, class, status, and mode of economic activity, African women were leaders, warriors, healers, laborers, or traders,
but it was their principal role as agriculturalists that made them so critical to plantation labor systems in the Americas.[1] Their domination in
agricultural production in Africa—most particularly soil cultivation,
planting, pruning, weeding, and harvesting—and the corresponding factor of the labor shortages on developing plantations in the Americas
increased African women's value as commodities of exchange essential
to the slave system's expansion and profitability.

This disruption of space, time, familial and social relationships, and
culture was intrinsic to the depersonalization of African women's lives.

This depersonalization experience was exacerbated by the ordeal of captivity and provided the spark for continued resistance, for African women had countered the capture of slaves for market with resistance at the inception of the trade in their villages, on the marches, and aboard slave ships during the transoceanic crossing to the West Indies and the Americas. Historians John Hope Franklin and Alfred A. Moss Jr. comment that "the Africans offered stiff resistance to their capture, sale, and transportation to the unknown."[2] Resistance strategies varied: many desperate men and women displayed singular acts of raw courage by attacking their captors, whereas others conspired to wait for an opportune moment to wage a struggle. This notion of employing diverse resistance strategies against enslavement would be carried over to their experience of brutality and oppression in New World societies.

Vincent Bakpetu Thompson points to the innumerable factors that shaped and precipitated African resistance: "Among the factors that weighed heavily in forms of resistance were the following: the resentment by Africans of the brutal manner of their capture; their storage like animals in a pen in barracoons during the waiting period before the transatlantic voyage began; and the unsatisfactory conditions of the middle passage engendered by overcrowding and inhuman treatment by the crew . . . There was also the overriding fact that their liberty had been curtailed."[3]

In a very real political and historical sense, though African American women had their genesis in Africa, slavery located their sociopolitical agency in New World societies. In the antebellum plantation economy, African women's labor production and resistance would become increasingly intertwined as they were transplanted and took root as an amalgam of worldviews, religion, terrain, marital status, and antipathies against enslavement and plantation labor conditions. Despite the rigors of plantation labor and the obstacles to resistance, black women, working in female collectives, would assert their labor will to mitigate the harshness of agricultural production while simultaneously enlarging the social and physical boundaries of their workspace to build survival units that would sustain a culture of resistance. This culture of resistance would mark the incipient stage of black women's political development in the New World.

SLAVE WOMEN AND COMMODITY PRODUCTION

"I wuz a slave fer years. I done all kind o' wuk 'bout de house an' fields," commented one female ex-slave as she reflected on her slave experiences.[4]

The Southern plantation economy depended for its viability on such sustaining factors as the transmigration of slaves, the persistence of the domestic slave trade, and the total domination and control of slave labor power. Manual technology; the labor-intensive commodity production for profit; the ownership of land, equipment, and slaves; and the partnership between Northern financiers and Southern planters were all predominant characteristics that primed the plantation system. Through time, the ideological construction that emerged in the form of slave laws and statutes, the social values and traditions of the planter aristocracy, and the racial attitudes concerning the inferiority of African peoples served to rationalize the exploitation of slave labor and perpetuate the resiliency of the institution.[5] The goal of sound plantation management was to maximize the efficiency of slave commodity production, ensure a generous profit, acquire more land and slaves, and maintain an air of Southern aristocracy.

Driving this plantation culture, which typified the Southern aristocratic oligarchy, were the fervor and passion with which the planter class, middle-class slaveholders, and small farmers strove to accumulate wealth and the racial, caste, and sexist ideologies embedded in that striving.[6] To effect their financial goals, which served as a gateway to the pseudoaristocratic lifestyle that dominated much of the southeastern coast, planters maintained strict discipline and control of their slaves, exercised harsh measures against slaves for perceived or real transgressions, and perpetuated the physical intimidation and brutality of slaves. As historian Jacqueline Jones observes, "American slavery was an economic and political system by which a group of whites extracted as much labor as possible from blacks . . . through the use or threat of force."[7]

Race, class, and sexual relations were all intertwined within the plantation system and reinforced the patriarchal system as well as the inherent notion of planters of their right to own chattel property. Slaves belonged to a class of laborers who were circumscribed by the exploitative complexities of race and caste, with black women bearing the additional burden of sexual exploitation. Although Africans proved advantageous to planters because their skin color immediately set them apart from white society and because of their estrangement from their homeland, it was because whites immediately perceived them as "outsiders" that contributed significantly to their enslavement and racial subordination. Slavery created a racial caste system by separating blacks from the rest of the society, denigrating their labor power, and circumscribing their behavior with racial proscriptions that relegated them to an inferior status. Coeval with the institution of slavery was the patriarchal structure of Southern society, which reinforced the racial subordination of free blacks and the oppression of all women, ensuring a total system of domination and control. After freedom, the perceptions of racial caste, slavery, and the subordination of black women were frequently interchangeable in the American psyche.

The variables of race, class, and sex were also intrinsic to the lives of female slaves and blurred distinctions regarding the conventional division of labor based on sex. As agriculturalists, slave women were purchased for their brawn, muscle, and childbearing capacities, thus ensuring a continuous source of capital for the planter. Hence, slave women were purchased to perform both general labor and sex-specific tasks in the plantation economy. What remained for the planters to determine was how much labor in both categories could be performed by slave women to ensure the maximization of profits. This atypical functioning by slave women made them unique in the plantation economy. Because black male slaves and white women performed work on the plantation according to gender-based labor patterns in society, slave women constituted the only plantation group assigned both sex-based and non-sex-based labor. For slave women, cross-gender workloads were the norm; traditional gender roles were flexible; and economic profit diminished all gender customs, traditions, and considerations.[8]

Planters, in effect, held few compunctions in enforcing conventional gender traditions with regard to their female slaves and concentrated more on plantation profits. As Austin Steward explained in his account of his slave experience, "It was usual for men and women to work side by side and women were compelled to do as much as the men."[9] Slave women also recalled their work experiences. "You could, any day see a woman, a whole lot of 'em making on a road. Could look up and see ten women up over dar on the hill plowing and look over the other way and see ten more."[10] This egalitarian relation between black men and women in the productive process also produced egalitarian domestic relationships. This "deformed equality of equal oppression," Angela Y. Davis observes, meant that economic, power, and control factors were not the determinants of these slave relationships. Rather, these relationships tended to reinforce the dignity of both partners by providing sustenance, support, and nurturance under shared oppression.[11]

The centrality of black women to the slave economy was contingent on the dual exploitation of both their productive and their reproductive capacities. Dorothy Sterling comments on this dual exploitation by noting that "a slave woman was both the nucleus of a labor force and the producer of wealth that increased rapidly."[12] One of the primary sources of capital and commodity production in the operation of the plantation system was in the economic and sexual exploitation of slave women's labor and reproductive capacities. Yet ironically, in order for the system to be effective, slave women had to be circumscribed by their powerlessness and, conversely, the master's power. In these relations of power, the powerlessness of black women under slavery had to be in inverse proportion to the economic primacy of their labor. Claire Robertson notes that the patriarchal structure of the plantation economy, typifying the larger white male-dominated society, devalued female slave laborers, and this devaluation led to them being sold more frequently than men.[13] At the intersection of slave women's powerlessness and the dual exploitation of their labor and their reproductive capacity lay the economic profit of the slave system. Inherent in this duality, in which black women owned neither their labor nor their progeny, were the triple foci of racial, caste, and sexual oppression of slave women.

In a patriarchal structure, in which all gender roles and conventional behavior were determined by white men and profit was the end goal, these white masters proved to be just as comfortable in assigning female slaves the same tasks as those assigned male slaves as they were in giving them household chores. Hence, domination and control by the white male patriarchy and the white male's ability to determine gender relations within the society reinforced his drive for wealth accumulation. The same patriarchal domination and control were evident in the raping of black women, which reinforced not only the male planter's absolute power and authority over slave women but also demonstrated the total powerlessness of the slave community.[14] One male slave, James Curry, recalled the treatment of both his mother and other female slaves. "My mother was treated very cruelly. Oh! I cannot tell you how dreadful her treatment was while she was a young girl. It is not proper to be written; but the treatment of females in slavery is very dreadful."[15] Sometimes rape engendered empowerment. When Celia, a fourteen-year-old slave, was raped by her new master, Robert Newsome, en route to his home, she was powerless. In 1855, however, after years of sexual abuse, she murdered him in her slave cabin. Black women were raped because, in the planters' greed or quest for power over their commodities, they had not only assigned black female labor beyond the gender sphere but also unwittingly reinforced black women's sense of their labor power as agricultural workers, and rape was an effort to diminish that sense of power.[16] Nevertheless, slave women empowered themselves and the community by forming coalitions of resistance with male and female slaves.

The primacy of black female slaves in cash crop commodity production and subsistence cultivation in the American southland reinforced both their African agricultural expertise and their role in the New World plantation economy. Despite the variations in the socioeconomic structure of African societies, African women were primarily agriculturalists, and these skills proved to be essential to the survival and profitability of Southern planters. Black women's agricultural skills had been developed, honed, and mastered in Africa, where African women cultivated grains, indigo, millet, cotton, peanuts, and rice, as well as made dyes and spun cloth for household consumption and large entrepôt markets.[17] Robert Harms notes that as cultivators of the land, even when men controlled the planting cycles of the crops, African women "had great autonomy in agricultural production and reaped the benefits of any surplus they produced."[18] Women were also able to utilize their agricultural products for a variety of enterprises. Carol P. MacCormack, in examining agricultural production in Sherbro societies, states that African women "may market produce directly, and use the surplus for consumption, exchange, or investment."[19] Still, there were other skills employed by African women in their daily work lives, depending on the societies and the economic means of commodity production. According to Martin Klein's study of Sudanic societies, "women also freely participated in industrial activities such as mining, salt making, and textile production."[20] Most large markets, however, particularly in West Africa, were dominated by women who both produced and traded food. African women were not just pivotal centers in cash crop commodity production but also engaged in the processing of foods and in the marketing, trading, and distribution of cash crops.

In the transplantation of African women to the American ecosystem of slavery, their human potentiality was stifled by confining them solely to the labor necessary for slave commodity production and their reproductive capacities as women. Sterling Stuckey notes the importance of the skills possessed by Africans that were integral to Southern plantation production: "The prevailing historical wisdom about the state of African skills in the era of the slave trade must be reconsidered in light of growing evidence that Africans were perhaps second to none in cotton and rice cultivation, in fishing and animal husbandry, in weaving and blacksmithing—areas of importance in the workshop and field of the plantation south."[21]

Although female slaves were critical to household sufficiency production in both the colonial and the antebellum eras, their primary
role as agriculturalists was central to the plantation economy. Because
approximately 89 percent of black women labored as agriculturalists and
were employed in every phase of cash crop production, they did much of
the intensive labor as soil cultivationists on Southern lands, creating a
source of wealth and profit for the planter class.[22] As one former female
slave recalled, "What did I do? I spun an' cooked, an' waited, an' plowed;
dere weren't nothin' I didn't do."[23] Performing the arduous, labor-
intensive work in the fields, black men and women prepared the land for
planting and engaged in the planting and cultivation of the soil, the harvesting of crops, and the final phase of preparing the crops for consumption and distribution for regional, national, and international
markets. Typifying a home country—colony relation, the raw materials
of "cotton, tobacco, tar, resin, turpentine, wheat, pork, and molasses"
were delivered to manufacturing centers in Northern U.S. cities and in
Europe to be manufactured into finished products and sold to consumers
as well as to planters for Southern slave consumption.[24]

Slave women's labor and the marketing of slave products connected
the ecosystem of slavery and the nascent capitalist system emerging in
northeastern cities. The relation between Southern planters and Northern financiers, an opportunity for both to prosper from slave commodity production, was determined by the exploitation of slave labor and the
maintenance of the institution of slavery. Slave commodity production
financed industrial factory development in northeastern U.S. cities as well
as in European industrial centers. The slave production of raw materials
proved to be a much needed stimulus for domestic and international
industrialization. Northern capitalists underwrote the planters' new land
acquisitions, slave purchases, and seasonal personal and business expenditures. When the agricultural cycle was completed and crops had been
harvested, these financiers served as intermediaries, providing credit
advances and the transshipment of slaves and slave products to domestic and foreign markets.[25] Primarily used in the developing manufacturing centers, these finished products were sold in regional, national, and
international markets.

By the early 1800s, cotton production supplanted the volume of
other raw materials grown in the South. The more popular long-staple
cotton, or "sea island" cotton, soon became the impetus for the rise in
cotton textile mills in New England and in England. In 1859, Stephen
Colwell estimated conservatively that New York City businesspeople,

operating as the intermediaries between the production and transshipment of cotton, made $200 million annually on the cotton trade, and the cotton trade created fortunes for both Northern financiers and Southern planters.[26] Monies derived from cotton production stimulated industrial development in all of the northeastern cities. Taking part in the slave system at multiple levels, Northern financiers owned plantations and slaves, they participated in the illicit and legal slave trade, and their financial support of the planter class undergirded the institution of slavery.

Black abolitionists who traveled abroad commented on the signs of British manufacturing prosperity as a result of the cotton imported from the United States. Sarah Parker Remond, a black abolitionist on an international abolitionist tour in England, discussed the linkage between the cotton production of slaves and the manufacturing process in the British industrial center of Manchester: "I think of those eighty thousand cotton plantations on which was grown the one hundred and twenty-five millions of dollars worth of cotton which supplies your market, and I remember that not one cent of that money ever reached the hands of the labourers."[27] With their labor and agricultural skills, black women constituted a conjunctive force between Southern slave labor and Northern capital.

THE DIALECTICS OF LABOR POWER

Whatever the political-historical moment, the centrality of black women's experiences in American society has been configured by the economic and social relation of black women to the mode and means of commodity production. Black women's labor power, initially centered in the slave experiences of black women, formed the context for their oppression. Armaci Adams, an ex-slave from Virginia, remembered that "dey wuked me lak a dog an' beat me somepin turrible."[28] "Work, work, work," recalled Hannah Davidson, an ex-slave from Kentucky, "I been so exhausted working, I was like an inchworm crawling along a roof. I worked until I thought another lick would kill me."[29] Davidson's poignant memories depict the constancy of black women's slave labors, principally as agriculturalists and household workers, that defy time, venue, and shifting modes of production.

It is not surprising, then, that much of the construction of the collective identity of black women has been located in their labor activity as female slaves and the institutional complexities of slavery as a market economy and culture. Such factors as the bondage of black women, their economic ties to the white male patriarchy, and the utilization of their labor power and resources to provide a climate of survival and resistance within the slave community were all labor activities. Intertwined in these labor activities were the forces that circumscribed slave women's oppression as well as the transforming vehicles of survival and resistance. Under the aegis of plantation production, all of these factors operated in tandem, creating the dialectics of female slave labor power.

As slave women worked to create wealth for the planter class, they collectively utilized the same labor power to form an oppositional consciousness of resistance to alter the oppressive conditions within the slave community. Dialectically, slave women were seeking to transform their environment of oppression and the devaluation of their personhood into one of resistance and collective identity. Driving the oppositional consciousness of slave women was their labor will, the agency of their labor for the purpose of survival, nurturance, and resistance in the slave community.

Although slave women's labor will derived from the African ontological precepts that formed a part of the traditional beliefs in slave communities, its impetus turned on the labor-intensive cash crop commodity production that dictated the boundaries of their existence. As agriculturalists, female slaves were aware that their labor production produced striking dissimilarities in African and New World societies. In African societies, monies garnered from farming could be used to supplement family income, pay student fees, or serve as a gateway for economic independence. As Claire Robertson states, "It is widely recognized that there are African societies where matrilinearity, female economic independence, or both gave (and give) African women more autonomy and precolonial political power."[30]

However, in the transplantation of agricultural expertise to the New World, the same labor-intensive agricultural production in America was designed to ensure the economic impoverishment and political powerlessness of slave women, despite the fact that they constituted a major element in the plantation economy. On some plantations, even their voluntary labor in the slave community was based on the production demands of the master. Liza McGhee, an ex-slave, recounted that the slave laborers on her plantation had limited down time because every minute was determined by the needs of the master. "We had no time to make a garden of our own. We had to make cotton and corn for Marster Jim."[31]

The labor will of slave women developed in the context of their material oppression and was intensified by the exploitation of their labor power. Slave women understood their collective oppression in the context of their female work collectives, African traditions that kept freedom a living memory, and their own longing for freedom. Ironically, it was the marked contrast between conventional female labor practices in African societies and their exploitation as women on Southern plantations that precipitated slave women's resistance. Their labor will activated a climate of collective and intergenerational resistance; the politicalization of the slave community on the issues of existing inequalities and the continuous exploitation of labor; and gender as a mode of social organization on the plantation, where female work collectives created the space for discourse and resistance to emerge.

SLAVE WOMEN ACTIVATING THEIR LABOR WILL

In exercising their labor will, female slaves were motivated by forces antithetical to the slave community's interest. In general, female slaves' resistance was triggered by a hostile environment that posed a threat to the well-being, survival, and freedom of the slave community. It is not difficult to see that the material conditions of the slave community were constant factors in shaping dramatic rebellions, confrontations with authority, and daily resistance. As slave women exercised their labor will, creating a climate for various modes of resistance to be effective, they were also planting the seeds of intergenerational resistance. Doug McAdam, in commenting on contemporary black insurgency, notes that group insurgency, a collective process that depends on a combination of environmental opportunities, cohesive infrastructure, and leadership, takes time.[32] Hence, a culture of resistance drew on the daily dialectical dynamic of oppression and the desire for freedom by replenishing the community's survival tenets. For the slaves, Webber notes, slave communities served as a buffer against white oppression, and a prevailing theme "suggest[ed] strongly that an aversion to whites was an attitude quite consciously held by quarter people and openly expressed among themselves."[33]

One of the central survival tenets that facilitated a climate of collective resistance was the kinship network of family, "fictive kin," and other community members. Because slave-community members enforced the obligation of family among themselves, this obligation solidified the community's internal cohesion. Familial obligation and the material conditions of oppression fostered a "we" feeling of community. Because the slave community was a racially structured community and a component of a caste system, the "they" represented the white slaveholding class. Tilly argues that defensive mobilization group solidarity concerning specific issues develops in communities where members perceive a common enemy. The slave community was besieged daily by a common enemy that circumscribed the lives of its members. For slave women, the common enemy was the slaveholding class that dominated and controlled their lives. While female slaves engaged in such resistance strategies as poison, arson, and murder, they created a climate of resistance where individual and collective actions were sanctioned.[34]

Slave women were politicized through recognizing the existing inequalities on the plantation between slaves and their masters, as well as through more traumatic experiences, which included enslavement; being bought and sold on the auction block; and separation from children, family members, and loved ones in the community. Ex-slave Harriet Miller recalled the existing inequalities of plantation life: "Dey neber hed much ter eat. De white folks got de good grub end de slaves got common grub."[35] Often, these inequalities caused slaves to comment on the hypocrisy of slaveholders attempting to enforce values of integrity and honesty. Ex-slave Josephine Howard stated, "Dey allus done tell us it am wrong to lie and steal but why did de white folks steal my mammy and her mammy? . . . Dey de sinfulles' stealin' dey is."[36]

Slave women who quickly mobilized their resources and made a dash for freedom usually had engaged in a great deal of reflection about their children being enslaved or the immediate threat of being sold. Mary Ennis, alias Licia Hemmin, escaped from Delaware in the winter of 1854 with her two children. Ennis stated that although she had constantly thought of freedom, not until "she was convinced that her children were to be sold" could she "muster courage to set out on the journey." Harriet Shephard, who did not want her children growing up as slaves, organized an escape party consisting of her five children and five other slaves, commandeered her master's two carriages and four horses, and escaped from Chestertown, Maryland. In Wilmington, Delaware, they were rescued and transported by abolitionists, first to Philadelphia and then to Canada.[37]

Most frequently, however, the difficulties that slave women escaping with children faced proved to be insurmountable, and many of these women "with freedom on their minds" demonstrated their resistance by planting seeds of resistance among their children and grandchildren. One ex-slave remembered the important lesson of resistance that mothers would teach their children in the slave community: "My mother used to teach me how to listen and hear and keep my mouth shut."[38]

Slave women would also organize "resistance sessions" in their quarters with other slaves from neighboring plantations. One former slave recalled the "sessions" that his mother would have: "Sometimes she would have a little meeting and some of the slaves from neighboring farms would come over. We children had better get out or at least make like we were not listening to what was being said and done. She used to call me to her and say, 'Now don't you tell anybody that so and so was here, or that you saw me do so and so.' She would caution me because she knew the white folks would be trying to pick some things out of me."[39]

Mothers had to encourage independence and resolve among their children and a readiness to create and take advantage of opportunities to escape. "It was easier for slaves to escape alone; consequently, some parents encouraged their children to literally break the chains of slavery."[40] Harriet Jacobs, who lived in her grandmother's attic for seven years until she could effect plans for her escape, depended on her grandmother, ex-slave Molly Horniblow, to provide her with food, information, contacts and care for her children.[41] Lucy Delaney recalled that her mother had planted such strong seeds of resistance in her two daughters that, by the time Delaney was twelve years old, she was "forever on the alert for a chance to escape." "Lucy was not hesitant about leaving her mother, who had prepared her for running away." When Lucy's sister, Nancy, ran away, Lucy witnessed the joy in her mother, which further strengthened her resolve. "Upon hearing that Nancy Delaney had succeeded in running away, her mother danced, sang, and clapped and waved her hands with ecstasy."[42]

One of the means by which slave women fortified their resistance was through their participation in female work collectives. Female work collectives were fertile grounds for evolving consciousness by affording their members opportunities to experience a deeper understanding of the complex lives and oppression of female slaves. Because such work units were formed along intergenerational lines, they fostered bonding among their members, sharing of task assignments, mutual support for pregnant and sick members, and sharing of life experiences.[43] Here, from the reconstructed memories of the older women, female slaves provided the stark contrast between their lives in Africa and their lives as slaves in a foreign land and a still more alien environment. As Nancy A. Naples notes in her examination of contemporary women's activism, "This interaction between the everyday life experiences of injustice, inequality, and abuse and processes of reflection occurring within localized networks with specific gender, race, and class dynamics opens spaces for 'oppositional consciousness' and activism."[44]

Slave women reconstituted their "workplace" to address the needs of its members, distribute the workload more effectively, and engender female solidarity. The combination of material oppression, a closely knit labor structure, and female solidarity created a cohesive unit that politicized its female members. The daily participation by the women created an environment for oppositional consciousness against the patriarchal structure of plantation life to emerge and spread throughout the slave community.

THE ACTIVE AGENCY OF RESISTANCE

Resistance was not a singular force of episodic dramatic occurrences in which rebellions, mayhem, death, and destruction determined the measure, worth, courage, and anger of the challengers: rather, it was an active agency of African American slaves engaged in a struggle against the hegemonic slavocracy. Acting solely or collectively, black slaves lodged a persistent intractable challenge, their rebellions varying in frequency and duration but creating disruption of the slave system while seeking ultimately to undermine the slave economy's viability. Resistance was a laborious process in which the resentment of slaves against their material conditions at decisive points intersected the danger of confrontation and subversion, with the cumulative rage serving as the catalyst for overt and covert acts against the system.

Slave insurgents, continually acting to create and manipulate conditions and circumstances, sometimes made erratic strikes at the vulnerability of slavery for the express purpose of garnering some measure of dignity and self-worth. Other slaves legitimized their resentment against their enslavement with episodic collective acts such as labor strikes, protest, and violence, as well as with covert forms of resistance. Still other slave insurgents engaged in organized rebellions in pursuit of the goal of liberation. Slaves who frequently practiced covert resistance by destroying farm equipment were often emboldened at later points to participate in more active aggression. A combination of methods utilized by slaves over a period of time was not uncommon, because oppression triggered many complex psychological factors that gained currency among the oppressed in their freedom-seeking efforts.

Within the plantation system, slaves' insurgency, whether real or perceived, assumed myriad forms and guises that frequently drew on the planter's resources and undermined slavery's institutional potency. As James Oakes notes, "So much of the slaveholders' energies were directed to thwarting real or supposed rebellions that the slaves commonly resorted to more indirect forms of resistence."[45] On one level, seemingly innocuous acts—for example, individual slaves striking back at the system by the method of covert disobedience—constituted a resistance level where slaves created a psychic shelter for themselves and harbored a measure of dignity through these surreptitious activities. Covert disobedience provided a safe vantage point from which slaves could mount twin challenges—one against their material oppression and the other against the institution.

Another level of resistance, that of more protracted struggle, was the utilization by slaves of both clandestine and confrontational methods in defying the system. The clandestine activities were a direct engagement with the system and constituted both protest and resistance. As already mentioned, female slaves employed the covertness of poison and arson as methods of protest and resistance.[46] Whereas one could not always gauge whether slaves were actually clumsy or ill, poisoning a master over a prolonged period of time or setting fire to a barn were acts of open defiance against the slave system, even when performed covertly. Some slaves, both male and female, opted for more confrontational strategies to release their pent-up aggression and defiance. Webber comments that "some slaves stood up to whites and openly defied white power and authority."[47] Rebellious slaves maintained a measure of dignity and self-esteem despite their enslavement and garnered the respect of even the most submissive slaves in the slave community. These slaves, sometimes recognized as "bad or crazy niggers," were those who would not bend to the whims and will of the masters and overseers, could not be broken by the harshness of conditions, and refused to be whipped.[48]

One female ex-slave commented on her mother's resistance to white authority on the slave plantation: "My mother certainly had her fault as a slave. She was very different in nature from Aunt Caroline. Ma fussed, fought, and kicked all the time. I tell you, she was a demon. She said that she wouldn't be whipped, and when she fussed, all Eden must have known it."[49]

The most dramatic form of resistance, Vincent Harding notes, was "the fear of widespread black rebellion [which] was akin to an occupational disease among Southern white officials." Dramatic rebellions were meticulously planned, organized armed struggles of an aggregation of rebels that dislodged the temporary complacency of slaveholders and produced social tremors that could be felt throughout the South. Subsequent to these slave uprisings, Southern officials usually passed a rash of restrictive legislation further circumscribing the lives of black slaves and refining their behavior in the existing superordinate-subordinate racial relations between slaves and the white community. The increased fear and vulnerability of slaveholders after slave uprisings, as well as the seeming loss of authority over the slave community, increased the brutality and punishment of both innocent and guilty slaves. Over time, the harsher physical reprisals that were the common fare of the system, the material conditions of enslavement, and the desire for liberation were continually "punctuated by periodic and often sustained acts of resistance."[50] Invariably, slave resistance was continuous throughout the history of slavery, sometimes undertaken by individual rebels and at other times by an aggregation of resisters that, combined, placed cumulative pressure on the institution from within while simultaneously nurturing an environment in which resistance was legitimized and operationalized among slave-community members.

The culture of resistance does not suggest that all slave-community members subscribed to it but rather that the community created space for resistance to be fostered and sustained. Common experiences under oppression invariably created varied responses. As Patricia Hill Collin states, "Being Black and female may expose African-American women to certain common experiences, which in turn may predispose us to a distinctive group consciousness, but it in no way guarantees that such a consciousness will develop among all women."[51] Group consciousness was sometimes tacit in the slave community; this prevailing consensus encouraged major, minor, and supporting players in the strategies and tactics determining resistance. Despite the fact that key slaves receded from leadership positions over time as courtship, marriage, family, and age became contributing factors affecting stability, other slaves emerged to replace the existing cadre. Social factors such as the breakup of nuclear family units or the lack of familiarity with the "etiquette" of new plantations and surrounding terrain on the part of newly purchased African slaves may have thwarted some organized rebellions, but slave-community members were still socialized into this culture of clandestine resistance.

Slave-community members employed collective clandestine resistance to aid individual freedom attempts and surreptitiously undermine the system's control over their lives. Webber notes that "if a quarter slave decided to attempt to escape from slavery altogether, it was usually with the blessing and often with the assistance of his community."[52] Andrew Jackson, in his slave narrative, recounted that the slave community came together when a slave was ready "to take the long walk." The affirmation of freedom permeated the entire slave community. Slaves often saw a validation of their own humanity in assisting other slaves who were challenging the system. A former Georgia slave, Leah Garret, recalled that a slave couple with three children survived for seven years in a nearby cave because "diffunt folks helped keep 'em in food."[53] Covert activities bonded slaves to each other, reinforcing a sense of solidarity and community. Within this community, many slaves challenged the institutional control and domination of the slave system, operating individually and informally, often spontaneously, which afforded some measure of control as well as some degree of success.

The root of much of slave resistance was the exploitation of slaves' labor power, and resistance was intensified by the excessive physical brutality used to ensure discipline, placing slave communities, in various stages of cohesion and defiance, against the ruling white patriarchy. Webber observes that slave communities afforded their members a degree of mutual protection. "Most quarter communities occasionally acted in concert in order to protect individual members and the community as a whole from overwork and white abuse."[54] Slave laborers were aware of their abilities to transform the land into a fully productive unit, and runaways, malingerers, and saboteurs hampered both the plantation management and the economy while supporting the culture of resistance. Even though they used physical abuse to enforce discipline and to reinforce psychological manipulation, planters were heavily dependent on slave laborers for their livelihood. Skilled workers or leaders in slave production units could subtly extract demands from planters and create space for some recognized and hidden resistance activities.

The slave quarters, where slaves practiced and passed down African cultural traditions, nurtured slave resistance. Oakes states that African cultural traditions empowered slave resistance. "It mattered to both master and slave that large numbers of bondsmen openly and persistently resisted, that the slave community—with its powerful religious traditions, its rich folk culture, its adoptive family structure—sustained and encouraged that resistance."[55] This community protection fostered a buffer against the common daily oppression and was often intertwined with inspirational freedom and a wellspring of hope for all of its members. Austen Steward stated that within the slave community, the more that they "knew of freedom the more we desired it, and the less willing were we to remain in bondage."[56] Resistance as an ongoing struggle on disparate terrain in the plantation South placed black women at the center of struggle in the slave community. To deny or ignore the role of black women in this liberation quest is to notice the bloom on the flowers without acknowledging that at some point seeds had been planted.

Slave women were at the vortex of oppression and the rituals of control, domination, and slave commodity production. Despite the racial, class, and gender subordination intertwined with the logistics of the plantation economy, slave women created an environment of survival and resistance in the slave community. Circumscribed by material oppression, slave women utilized their singular resource, their labor will, in employing strategies of resistance. By any measure, slave women engaged in a protracted struggle, given that the linkage between Southern planters and Northern financiers dominated the entire antebellum era and the rise of nascent capitalism. Both of these market economies were inextricably tied to the exploitation of slaves. Hence, slavery, resistance, the plantation economy, and nascent industrial capitalism were organically linked to one another.

CHAPTER 2

Troubled Waters

Invisible Boundaries of Resistance

> Always, under the surface of slavery, the river of black struggle
> flowed with, and was created by, a black community that moved
> actively in search of freedom.
>
> VINCENT HARDING, *There Is a River*

UNDERLYING THE ECONOMIC RELATIONSHIP BETWEEN NORTH-
ern capital and Southern slavery was a slave community created by
African male and female laborers' disparate African traditions, New
World cultural influences, the modes of production, the exigencies of
slavery, and the yearning for dignity and freedom. In this creative process,
slaves drew upon their historical memories of an African homeland, an
emerging class consciousness, and a racial solidarity born out of the
Southern caste system that circumscribed their lives. Chaney Mack, an
ex-slave from Mississippi who was interviewed by the Federal Writers
Project in 1937, recalled the oral tradition that was passed down in her
family. "My father wuz a full-blooded African. He wuz about eighteen
years old when dey brought him over. He came from near Liberia. He
said his mother's name wuz Chaney, and dat's whar I gits my name."[1]

Forging kinship and fictive kin ties that enabled them to withstand a
common oppression, slaves from disparate tribes and areas of the African
continent became a people. Eugene Genovese has argued persuasively
that the social bifurcations in society generated by slavery made these
blacks victims of class exploitation. Both class and race were major components shaping the forces of slavery; it was the inevitability of blackness
that made these laborers slaves and, correspondingly, an active racism on
the part of white society in their domination of all blacks that made slavery a racial caste system. Paul D. Escott observes the racial and class
construction of Southern society: "Southern society was organized first

along racial, then along class, lines. Without exception whites dominated blacks, which is the essence of a caste system. Even among the whites, racism served as a fundamental support for the social system."[2]

Black female slaves played a pivotal role in the creation and sustenance of slave culture. As culture bearers, they passed the oral history on from generation to generation: "it was frequently the role of mother to transmit the stories of Africa," giving the historical past continuity.[3] Memories of Africa were also cast in a deeply spiritual context: "Being on good terms with the ancestral spirits was an overarching conceptual concern for Africans everywhere in slavery," with many slaves believing that the ancestors would protect the community and mitigate the harshness of servitude.[4] Coupled with their role as culture bearers, female slaves also occupied the political role of nexus women, utilizing the culture to continuously transform the environment into a climate of resistance. Female slaves' influence upon the slave community was primarily due to their lack of interplantation mobility, gendered and nongendered labor assignments, and collective female work coalitions.[5] Their resistance ethos and the varied uses of their labor power on behalf of the slave community, combined with the spirituality that permeated the quarters, empowered female slaves and the entire community in nurturing an active personal and collective agency of resistance.

As a direct antithesis to plantation hierarchy, a vibrant slave culture fortified slaves in their resistance to slavery. In affirming the human dignity of enslaved people, slave culture provided strong bonds of community life in the midst of chaos and enabled slaves to deal with the vicissitudes of bondage. Slave culture and its ability to thrive as an integral part of plantation life sent a signal to planters that their domination and control, despite varied methods of plantation management, were tenuous and fraught with difficulty. As White notes: "Blacks knew that they were a despised race, oppressed for their skin color, and they dealt with the world on those terms, thus underlining the gap between master and slave."[6]

Solomon Northup, a free black who was captured in the North, enslaved for twelve years in the South, and subsequently freed through his wife's diligent efforts, reflected in his narrative on the resistance ethos that permeated the slave quarters. "They are deceived who flatter themselves that the ignorant and debased slave has no conception of the magnitude of his wrongs . . . A day may come—it will come, if his prayer is heard—a terrible day of vengeance, when the master in his turn will cry in vain for mercy."[7] In keeping with this community ethos, Ellen Cragin, an ex-slave, vividly described her mother's act of resistance when her young master tried to beat her:

> My mother she didn't work in the field. She worked at a loom. She worked so long and so often that once she went to sleep at the loom. Her master's boy saw her and told his mother. His mother told him to take a whip and wear her out. He took a stick and went out to beat her awake. He beat my mother till she woke up. When she woke up, she took a pole out of the loom and beat him nearly to death with it. He hollered, "Don't beat me no more, and I won't let 'em whip you." She said, "I'm goin' to kill you. These black titties sucked you and then you come out here to beat me." And when she left him, he wasn't able to walk. And tat was the last time I seen of her until after Freedom. She went put and got an old cow she used to milk—Dolly, she called it. She rode away from the plantation, because she knew they would kill her, if she stayed.[8]

According to Lulu Wilson, another ex-slave, her mother combined religion, prayer, and resistance on Wash Hodges's plantation in the Deep South. "My maw was cookin' in the house . . . She could cuss and she warn't 'fraid. Wash Hodges tried to whop her with a cowhide, and she'd knock him down and bloody him up . . . But she was a 'ligious woman and 'lieved time was comin' when niggers wouldn't be slaves. She told me to pray for it."[9]

In the slave community, those African cultural traditions that survived—music, dance, folktales, funeral rituals, religion, and conjure—were employed by slaves as psychological mechanisms of survival and endurance as well as an ongoing wellspring of hope and resistance. In some instances, certain folktales and the practices of religion and conjuring were clandestine activities performed away from the scrutiny of whites. The more slaves could fortify the linkages to their African past, the more they could strengthen themselves in collective slave resistance. Historian V. P. Franklin comments on slavery, religion, and resistance: "Faith in God not only helped to sustain His children in the land of bondage, but also supported their attempts to resist the brutality and injustice of the slave regime."[10]

Several scholars have engaged in a lively discourse on the study of African cultural traditions, attempting to determine the extent and nature of African retentions surviving in the diaspora.[11] What is most compelling, however, is that disparate African cultural traditions survived the enslavement process and, over time, were infused with American and Native American influences, emerging in new forms and expressions in slave communities as slaves fashioned a transatlantic culture. Demographic variables such as the location of the plantation; a majority black population in the state; the number of slaves who were from Africa or the Caribbean or were native-born Americans; absentee land ownership; and the insularity of the plantation were all contributing factors in the retention of African cultural traditions in plantation life.

For slaves, the centuries of struggle on the African continent mired in the slave trade and the abduction and resistance of the captives were all part of the collective memories of Africa that were passed down to the next generation. Former slave John Brown recalled that his mother frequently repeated the story of his grandmother's capture in Africa.

> One day, a big ship stopped off the shore and the natives hid in the brush along the beach. Grandmother was there. The shipmen sent a little boat to the shore and scattered bright things and trinkets on the beach. The natives were curious . . . the next day some of them walked up the gangplank . . . Two-three hundred natives on the ship when they feel it move . . . Grandmother was one of them who got fooled . . . The boat men came up from below where they had been hiding and drive the slaves down in the bottom and keep them quiet with whips and clubs. The slaves was landed at Charleston.[12]

In addition to the historical memories of Africa and the slave trade that became embedded in slave culture, older slaves also passed on other features of African cultural traditions, such as the complexities of the African musical tradition. "A number of instruments used by the slaves were clearly African in origin."[13] Instruments, hand clapping, and intricate foot stomping, all to the tune of replicated African musical sounds, accompanied the sacred and secular singing and dancing in the slave quarters. In many ways, "slave music reflects the unity of West African culture through syncopation, antiphony, group singing, improvisation, and instruments used, and through its organic tie to dance," leading several scholars to note its significance in laying the foundation of the African American musical tradition in the New World.[14]

Music and dance gave meaning to the daily experiences of slaves, offered a brief respite from the tedium of agricultural labors, and marked the transmission of social values. Similar to the stories and folktales that permeated the quarters, music could also be heavily laden with emotional content about Africa and the perils of enslavement. Chaney Mack recalled that her father's memories of Africa were very poignant and that he often used music as a release of those emotions. "I'd be settin' on my daddy's lap and he'd tell me all 'bout when he lived in Africa. He usta play de fiddle and sing 'bout 'Africa—Dat Good Ole Land'—and den he would cry, when he thought of his mother back dere." Mack also shared ways that African music and dance were passed on to her generation. "He made him self a fiddle outa pine bark and usta play fer us to dance. He taught me to dance when I wuz little like dey did in Africa."[15]

Folktales were used in the transmission of social values to members of the slave community. Folktales that employed animals such as lions, elephants, tortoises, spiders, and rabbits were commonly recognized as African tales. "While many of these tales were brought over to the South, the African element appears most clearly in the animal tales."[16] Since these animal tales frequently strategized the ways in which slaves, in their daily engagement with the plantation hierarchy, could use their wits in gaining small advantages, these tales were never told in the presence of whites. For example, in recounting these animal tales, smaller animals such as Anansi, the spider, and Brer Rabbit often symbolized the slaves and their employment of wit, intelligence, and agility in outwitting the more powerful and aggressive bear or fox, animals that symbolized the slaveholder and other white members of the slave structure. Annie Reed, an ex-slave, recounted that Brer Rabbit often outwitted Brer Fox by begging Brer Fox not to throw him in the briar patch. "So dey tuk him and th'owed him in de brierpatch. And Br'er Rabbit . . . laugh and say, 'Thank you, Br'er Fox. I was bred and born in a brierpatch.'"[17] For slaves, the smaller animals utilized strategies of covert resistance, "puttin' on ol' massa," strategies that were part of the slaves' arsenal of daily survival tactics.

Just as many animal folktales performed the function of the slave community's covert resistance to slavery and in every sense were a healing balm for the community's woes, other folktales employed heroic figures, or tricksters, who used their mystical abilities as transcendental figures to manipulate the social environment and outwit the more powerful forces on the plantation. The trickster High John the Conqueror, noted Theophus H. Smith, who made the journey with the slaves from Africa to the New World, was "a kind of spiritual material emanation that emerged from an enslaved people in the extremity of their suffering and their need for a champion." In some folktales, High John the Conqueror brought the healing balm of laughter as a survival mechanism, and "that laughter-in-the-midst-of-suffering appears here as the very emblem of a people's transcendence and will-to-survive."[18] In other tales, High John the Conqueror overtly challenged slavery, demonstrating the underlying anger, resentment, and resistance of slaves to their oppression. He openly declared his hatred for the institution and made bold strikes against the system whenever possible, with the intent to liberate all slaves from their burden. High John the Conqueror was also imbued with ancient wisdom, and long before the Civil War, slaves believed, he informed them of the inevitability of freedom. In these tales, High John the Conqueror symbolized the "bad or crazy nigger," whose resistance to slavery garnered the respect of even the most timid of slaves.[19]

The role of conjuring, which paralleled the rise of evangelical Protestantism in the slave community, was another way in which slaves merged the temporal and transcendental planes in the quarters in combating the injustices in their daily lives. Through the practice of "magical shamanism," slaves sought to temper the psychological and physical abuses of the system.[20] Since "magical shamanism" could be used for good or malevolent purposes, slaves sought out the conjurer to intervene in their daily lives. Illness, love, a healthy child, or the protection of loved ones against beatings or sale frequently involved the use of shamanism. Countersorcery was employed if one believed that a "spell" had been placed on them. Under the exigencies of slavery, it may be assumed that the sorcerer's "spells" on masters received diligent attention.

Marrinda Jane Singleton, an ex-slave born in Hartford, North Carolina, and raised in Norfolk, Virginia, noted that slaves practiced conjure derived from Africa and the diaspora. "The practice of conjuration was carried on by quite a few. The Negroes who were from the Indies and other Islands were greatly responsible for these teachings. Although much of it was handed down from the wilds of Africa."[21] Slaves believed that those born with veils over their faces had special powers. Sarah Hatley, an ex-slave, stated that her sister had these gifts. "I know my sister could see ghos'es. an' I tell you she could scare me to death."[22] "Ma" Stevens, an ex-slave, recalled how she had been conjured by a neighbor when she invited her in for a cup of coffee. "I had duh coffee, an' I stay an' talk. Atta a time, I came back home. All ob a sudden, I feel sick. My head wuz dizzy, an' I hab tuh sit down on a chair. Right away, I knowed dat woman hab conjuh me."[23]

But conjuring was far more compelling than magical potions, and as Smith indicates, "conjure is not only sorcery or witchcraft but also a tradition of healing and harming that transforms reality through performances and processes involving a mimetic use of medicinal and toxic substances."[24] Some of the more powerful members of the slave community were the priests and priestesses who practiced shamanism and, according to Joyner, had considerable influence among the African Christian slaves.[25] Conjuring became an essential healing force in the slave community, and African priests and priestesses who were enslaved in America had the daunting task of being "the healer of the sick, the interpreter of the unknown, the comforter of the sorrowing, the supernatural avenger of wrong" for the rest of the slaves.[26] The invocation of transplanted African deities in the New World mitigated the psychological dislocation of enslavement. African cultural traditions, albeit in an attenuated form, undergirded the slave community's collective strategies of survival, and intrinsic to that survival was a climate of resistance as an integral feature of their lives.

THE SACRED COSMOS
AND THE SLAVE COMMUNITY

Despite the disparate African religions that appeared in the slave community, those that conceptualized humans and the gods in an ongoing struggle or those that emphasized humanist consciousness found reinforcement in the slave communities of the New World. Undoubtedly, slaves, seeking their own connection to the Supreme Deity, found succor in those African deities and New World religions that forged a harmonious relationship with the human spirit and the Creator. Over the centuries, many Africans had developed a cosmic worldview that was reflective of natural phenomena, "where humankind was the centerpiece of the spiritual linkages between the spiritual and material worlds."[27] In these societies, African ontological moorings rested upon the embodiment of the spiritual world and the world of objective reality as a creative source representative of continuous divine power. The interconnectedness of these two worlds in the African community meant that all life and energy forces were mutually supportive, each drawing spiritual energy and nourishment from the other. This view of the cosmic world, notes Gayraud Wilmore, fueled "the release of the human spirit, the sacred vessel in which the vital forces of the universe coalesce," creating freedom in this infinite view of life.[28]

This African belief system was premised on the interrelationship of the cosmos with God, the Creator, the spirits, the ancestors, and the human race, connecting all entities in the universe. At the center of the universe was the divine creation of the human race, forming mutually supportive roles for supernatural and natural forces, inanimate and animate objects, all viewed as complementary forces that served to continuously reenergize and propel the continuity of life. As life evolved, the sacred "force, power or energy permeating the whole universe," emanating from the Creator, spiritually endowed people such as conjurers, spirit mediums, priests, and priestesses, who used this energy source for both beneficial and malevolent deeds.[29] Africans perceived a world order where all supernatural and natural forces coexisted "in one comprehensive, invisible system that has its own laws which sustain the visible world and ordinary life for the good of all."[30] The sacred order of the cosmos defined Africans in harmony with the universe.

The African community represented humankind with divine attributes, evincing a connection to the deity, the spirits, and the moral and cultural barometers, the ancestors.[31] In the African pantheon of lesser gods or spirits, these male and female deities shaped and guided the community's spiritual connectedness to the Creator and the universe. Rituals, ceremonies, and prayers were frequently offered to the deities in the hopes of appeasement. Ancestrology, where the ancestors were attributed spiritual and supernatural abilities, proved to be another spiritual dimension. Once the ancestors were cleansed after death, they were imbued with spiritual powers by the community and occupied the spiritual realm as communicants with the pantheon of spirits, the Creator, and the community that they served. For Africans, "the ancestors are the custodians of the morality of the tribe or community" and reinforced the social cohesiveness of the group.[32] The spiritual connections of Africans to the sacred cosmos were severed in the transplantation to the New World, creating a psychological fragmentation of the soul and spirit and the religious essence of life that reflected the African universe.

The social dislocation and psychological trauma incurred by the transplantation process made African slaves cling more strongly to their African religious belief systems and cultural traditions in an effort to reintegrate the inner spirit to confront an external hostile world. Through African slaves' early encounters with Christianity, "the juggernaut of evangelicalism," they could reconnect themselves to the Supreme Deity and other divine forces. "It was from within an African religious framework," comments Paul Radin, "that the slaves made adjustments to Christianity after hearing the gospel." In this gradual fusing of African religions with Christianity, "the antebellum Negro was not converted to God. He converted God to himself." The amalgamation of both religious traditions over time produced an African Christianity that offered slaves succor and measured release from the harsh exploitation that defined their material existence while simultaneously encouraging resistance against domination and oppression. "The liberation of the whole person—body, mind, and spirit—from every internal and external constraint not deliberately and purposely elected was the first requirement for one who would be possessed by the Spirit."[33]

EVANGELICALISM IN THE SLAVE COMMUNITY

Many slaves never came in contact with evangelical missionaries, and of those who did, some favored the retention of their African forms of worship and sought spiritual comfort in a fragmented world with the wisdom that had bonded their people for centuries. Even with those who took on the trappings of the new religion, it was still a gradual, uneven process, as Africans, in seeking spiritual integration, found the African parallels of God in Christianity. Charles Joyner correctly notes that "to underestimate the Africanity of African-American Christianity is to rob the slaves of their heritage."[34] Slaves found particularly appealing Christianity's priestly function, which validates the status quo and simultaneously assesses society's morality, and saw a redemptive path to both sacred and secular freedom.[35] African-Christianity and African religious worship, both coexisting in slave quarters, provided stabilizing influences in the slave community, affording slaves an evaluative system of justice and redemption as well as transcendental visions that, in allowing respite from their earthly woes, became wellsprings of hope.

As the institutionalization of the slave system became coeval with the rise of evangelical Protestantism, formerly resistive antebellum planters gradually perceived the interlocking variables of Christianity and plantation slavery as vehicles to fostering tractability and compliance in their slaves. But slaves found in Christianity's emphasis on moral rectitude—contained in the priestly function—assertiveness, self-esteem, protest, and freedom, their own views of oppression.[36] In the dichotomization of the soul and the spirit, slaves created a visionary inner sacred self that was separate from the material world that defined their condition. This visionary self was not always otherworldly, for it also contained the optimistic expectations of the oppressed—that harsh material conditions could be alleviated and that worldly dreams, particularly of freedom, were possible.

Often their spiritual strength, induced by the religious conversion experiences, emboldened slaves to question the primacy of being owned by anyone but the Supreme Being. Fannie Moore, an ex-slave from Moore, South Carolina, described the freedom and empowerment that her mother felt following her religious conversion, which allowed her to challenge her mistress and in effect transformed her life of powerlessness under servitude to one of hope and resistance:

> My mammy just grin all over her black wrinkled face and say: "I'se saved. De Lord done tell me I'se saved. Now I know de Lord will show me de way. I ain't gwine to grieve no more. No matter how much you all done beat me and my chillen de Lord will show me de way. And some day we never be slaves." Old Granny Moore grab de cowhide and slash Mammy cross de back but Mammy never yell. She just go back to de field a singin'.[37]

The religious doctrine, principally packaged for slave obedience by planters, was juxtaposed to the redemptive qualities of African-Christianity sustained in the slave community. Understanding the religious ploy of their masters, slaves instead were also empowered by their new-found God, who, possessing the qualities of generosity, hope, and divine retribution, would soon save them from their oppressors. Slave women, providing "healing spaces" in the community as buffers against oppression, were not solely healing the physical self but also the resulting psychological fragmentation that had occurred among slaves. The nurturance provided by slave women, in addition to the practices of the African traditional religious systems or the eventual amalgamation of African traditional religion and evangelical Christianity, did forge a psychological and emotional reconnectiveness to spirituality for African Americans, fortifying them for resistance. For scholar Lawrence W. Levine, "The slave's religion principles were colored by his own longing for freedom."[38]

LABOR WILL AND NASCENT
BLACK POLITICAL CULTURE

While religion and spirituality were the primary catalysts in mobilizing slaves into a community, this mobilizing activity was intrinsic to the multidimensional aspects of cultural development. Female slaves influenced both labor production and the development of a nascent black political culture that employed covert and overt resistance as strategies of survival, protest, escape, and eventual eradication of the slave institution. Black women's labor will stemmed from their intertwining sacred and secular roles as religious leaders and nexus women in the slave community. Derived from an African-influenced cultural apparatus, black women's labor will became one of the major sources of the slave community's empowerment and resistance. Despite cross-gender sacred and secular leadership roles and a prevailing white patriarchy, religion and agricultural production in slave communities were female-centered, creating space for female leadership to emerge and evolve within an African-based community.[39]

As Patricia Hill Collins states, "Afro-American women drew on an Afrocentric worldview to cope with racial oppression . . . In societies that denigrate African ideas and peoples, the process of valuing an Afrocentric worldview is the result of self-conscious struggle."[40] Female religious leaders or secular leaders such as nexus women, although often both were intertwined, rose to a valued position in the slave community as a "result of self-conscious struggle." As religious leaders, female slaves strove to utilize the transcendental power of the cosmos as a spiritual force in transforming the material realities of oppression. Cheryl Townsend Gilkes contends that "African women's response to New World slavery was influenced not only by the distinctive nature of cult service and the religious foundation of their everyday life, but also by their tradition of collective politics."[41] Enhancing the spirituality of the slave community were black female evangelists like Zilpha Elaw, who, when masters permitted, spread evangelical Protestantism to the slaves and simultaneously protested against slavery.[42] As nexus women, female secular leaders connected the slave community to their heritage, revisited the African connections through the culture, and created a real or imagined dichotomy between freedom in Africa and slavery in America. Female leadership, in general, provided a bridge either to the past, the future, or the cosmos, all angles of vision establishing a contextual framework for the dialectical opposites of oppression and resistance.

The transformation of black women's labor will for the slave collective was to undermine the slave system. By activating their labor power to foster an environment of individual and collective resistance, female work collectives, field gangs, and nurturance of families and other slaves were all opportunities for female slaves to plant seeds of resistance. White notes that female slaves also saw medical needs as opportunities for covert resistance. "Female cooperation in the realm of medical care helped foster bonding that led to collaboration in the area of resistance."[43] Brown and Walford argue that slaves functioned with a sense of personal obligation toward other community members, "grounded in an African-American prophetic tradition," believing that only through collective activism can change occur in society's institutional arangements.[44] In this instance, blacks strove to alter the institutional arrangements in society that would release them from bondage. In this political culture of resistance, female slaves produced a configurative effect: in seeking to transform the environment that pivoted upon the powerlessness of slaves, female slaves transformed themselves as well.

The inequalities on the plantation resulting from the intertwining of the gender division of labor and white male patriarchal control and domination were stark. Female slaves, who performed the majority of the arduous agricultural labor on the plantation, were acutely aware of the pseudogender dichotomies between male and female slaves. Rose Williams, an ex-slave from Bell County, Texas, described the intensive field labor on William Black's plantation. "Massa Black am awful cruel, and he whip de cullud folks and works dem hard and feed dem poorly . . . We-uns have to work in de field every day from daylight till dark, and on Sunday we-uns do us washin'."[45] Caroline Hunter, an ex-slave born near Suffolk, Virginia, evinced a poignant reminder of her days as a field hand. "Lord, I done been thew somepin'. When I'se five years old I had to wuk. I had a job cleanin' silver an' settin' de table. A few years after dat I was put out in de fiel's to wuk all day. Sometimes I wished I could run away."[46] For ex-slave Nancy Boudry of Georgia, labor and corporal punishment were intertwined. "Master was a hard taskmaster . . . I had to work hard, plow and go and splitwood jus' like a man. Sometimes they whup me. Dey whup me bad, pull de cloes off down to de wais'."[47]

The experiences endured by many female slaves lingered long after freedom. For Anna Harris, a former Virginia slave who witnessed the sale of her sister, the loss was tied to her hatred of white people: "No white man even been in my house. Don't 'low it. Dey sole my sister Kate. I saw it wid dese here eyes. Sole her in 1860, and I ain't seed nor heard of her since. Folks say white folks is all right dese days. Maybe dey is, maybe dey isn't. But I can't stand to see 'em. Not on my place."[48]

Former slaves were well aware of the obvious class distinctions between whites in addition to the racial and class distinctions between slaves and masters. For Rosa Starks, a former slave, "Dere was just two classes to de white folks—buckra slave owners and poor white folks dat didn't own no slaves."[49] Harriet Miller, a former slave from Pike County, Mississippi, saw clear distinctions between masters and slaves. "De white folks got de good grub en de slaves got common grub. No slave eber got a biskit, en dey niver got any cakes or pies."[50] One of the corn songs that field hands use to sing was also indicative of class, racial, and gender exploitation:

Missus in de big house,
Mammy in de yard.
Missus holdin her white hands
Mammy workin hard.
Missus holdin her white hands
Mammy workin hard.[51]

Slaveholders departed from prevailing white patriarchal middle- and upper-class gender standards when it came to female slaves, employing their labor in all areas and phases of household sufficiency production as well as cash crop commodity production. Yet black women were undervalued as workers, commodities of exchange, and women. Ironically, in a slave system that maximized the exploitation of black women's reproductive capacities and their labor power, female slaves were able to construct cultural identities empowering themselves as laborers so that they could influence labor production at the flashpoint of their oppression.

FEMALE SLAVES AND THE SEEDS OF RESISTANCE

Some scholars examining resistance have focused on the dramatic rebellions or covert operations of black male slaves in their valiant struggle for liberation. While some acknowledge black women as vital participants in slave uprisings and rebellions, black women are not considered actual leaders of slave revolts or resistance.[52] Recently, however, other scholars have noted both the multidimensional forms as well as the gender-specific ways of slave women's resistance.[53] Darlene Clark Hine and Kate Wittenstein, for example, argue that gender-specific forms of resistance by slave women dovetailed with their explicit economic and sexual oppression. Such initiatives as sexual abstinence, abortions, and infanticides were slave women's conscious methods of resistance to undermine the slavocracy as well as to provide a challenge to their sexual exploitation.

"The slave woman's resistance to sexual, and therefore to economic exploitation, posed a potentially severe threat to paternalism itself, for implicit in such action was the slave woman's refusal to accept her designated responsibilities within the slave system as legitimate."[54]

Other scholars, largely historians, have explored the vast terrain of slave women's resistance by centering their pattern of defiance in the amalgam of African traditions and New World material oppression. Gerda Lerner, for example, argues that slave women employed a broad range of forms of resistance to the system. However, while "slave women took part in all aspects of resistance, from slave rebellions to sabotage and passive resistance," the most significant form of resistance was survival.[55] As female slaves fought for slave survival, they forged skills reinforcing courage, tenacity, and endurance. Elizabeth Fox-Genovese posits that slave women's pattern of resistance was shaped as much by their material conditions as by "the African legacy . . . [that] made a central contribution to slave women's self-perceptions."[56] This centrality of Africa, Rosalyn Terborg-Penn maintains, formed the core of a common pattern of resistance of both continental and diasporan African women that "reflect[s] the heritage and world view of traditional African women, . . . and the adaptive behavior of African women transplanted to New World communities."[57] Politically, their African-centeredness and contemporary material conditions, that is, the "economic and political subordination, created the conditions for Black women's resistance."[58] Common to both groups was the ideological concept of self-reliance and determination as black women forged bonds, created female collectives, and shared spiritual endeavors that strengthened their solidarity.

Primarily, it was in the daily resistance struggle, where the tools of oppression were transformed into weapons of empowerment and resistance, that slave women assumed primacy of place. It was in this culture of community that slave women fostered the power of the idea of defiance, instilling hope of survival and a life that allowed slaves to transcend their material conditions. Despite massive setbacks and futile attempts at freedom magnified in the slave community by their oppressors, this environment of resistance was legitimized and sanctioned by the slave community. Feeding hope were the poisoning of planters, the mysterious arson, runaways, outliers, truants, abortionists, confrontational slaves, and dramatic rebellions continuously threatening the system's economic and social viability. Vincent Harding argues that this resistance, whether individual or collective, fed the larger struggle—"a river"—that characterized the movement of black resistance in American society "undermining the foundations of slavery."[59]

FEMALE SLAVES AND POLITICAL RESISTANCE

Slave women's broad political functions were in providing a nexus between African self-reliance and resistance, establishing intergenerational network linkages, nurturing the tenets of survival and freedom within the slave community as a right of the oppressed, and maintaining consistent pressure on the slave system.[60] Politically, slave women, by centering themselves in their African traditions, created adaptive responses to their oppressive condition by utilizing their labor will and labor power to activate a culture of resistance; activating an environment of resistance that served as a healing center while simultaneously nurturing an environment for varying forms of resistance activities to take place; creating a female identity and embryonic consciousness among female members of the slave community that undergirded and defined patterns of resistance; and engaging in individual acts of courage, subversion, sabotage, and, ultimately, insurgency as methods of undermining the slave system.

Ironically, female slaves' lack of mobility within the plantation system, where "the division of labor on most plantations conferred greater mobility on male than on female slaves," reinforced gender-specific space and roles that slaves practiced in the community's traditional structure.[61] By sustaining the social network of communal life, slave women provided succor to slave members while simultaneously creating political space that legitimized individual acts of courage, subversive outrage against the system, collective forms of protest, escape, and insurgency as rights of the exploited. One ex-female slave recalled her mother's challenge to slave plantation authority:

> One day my mother's temper ran wild. For some reason Mistress Jennings struck her with a stick. Ma struck back and a fight followed. Mr. Jennings was not at home and the children became frightened and ran upstairs. For half hour they wrestled in the kitchen. Mistress, seeing that she could not get the better of ma, ran out in the road, with ma right on her heels. In the road, my mother flew into her again. The thought seemed to race across my mother's mind to tear mistress' clothing off her body. She suddenly began to

tear Mistress Jennings' clothes off. She caught hold, pulled, ripped and tore. Poor mistress was nearly naked when the storekeeper got to them and pulled ma off.[62]

Female slaves exercised their labor power in their performance of more gender-specific tasks and in their female identity, a reflection of their African traditional roles. Although comparable field workers to black male slaves, the traditional female tasks—washing, spinning, weaving, cooking, cleaning, making soap and candles, preparing foods, and gardening—in the slave community enabled female slaves to center themselves and the slave community by preserving some of the gender roles that dignified African family structures.[63] "Though dimmed by time and necessity, the outlines of African work patterns endured among the slaves." Undoubtedly, slave women found a great deal of therapeutic value and satisfaction in determining how they could "freely" utilize their labor.[64] Their labor will was evinced in the arduous extension of slave women's twelve-to-fourteen-hour day in the fields, was demonstrated by their commitment to their own sense of being and wholeness, and was reflected in their dreams of freedom and the creative use of their energy. These gender-specific tasks were actively encouraged by planters, who believed that a slave familial structure was securing their commodities against escape as well as ensuring slave complacency.[65] Ex-slave James Curry recalled the arduous labor that his mother endured as she maintained the "triple" roles of her oppression:

She would not get through to go to her log cabin until nine or ten o'clock at night. She would then be so tired, that she could scarcely stand; but she would find one boy with his knee out, and another with his elbow out, a patch wanting here, and a stitch there, and she would sit down by her lightwood fire, and sew and sleep alternately, often till the light began to streak in the east; and then lying down, she would catch a nap, and hasten to the toil of the day. Among the slave children, were three little orphans, whose mothers, at their death, committed them to the care of my mother. One of them was a babe. She took them and treated them as her own.[66]

Slave women forged intergenerational social networks of female cohesion and solidarity by utilizing common labor activity as female collectives. Much of their own sustenance was gained from the reciprocity that nurturance provided as well as in the existing female subcommunities, where female slaves spent major portions of their day on common labor tasks. "This work system forged the women of all ages into a tight network."[67] Female slave collectives engendered female cohesiveness, socialization, and communication within the group structure. Female solidarity was a common feature of "trash gangs," a female work collective comprised of pregnant women, lactating women, youngsters, and older women who were assigned the field work of "raking stubble, pulling weeds, or doing light hoeing."[68] As part of the socialization process that occurred through this labor activity, young girls entered this preexisting circle of women where, via the group process of socialization, methods of endurance, camaraderie, and resistance were passed to the next generation.

Deborah Gray White states that mutual support was central to the bonding in these female collectives by workloads being shared in times of stress and illness or when members were experiencing childbearing difficulties.[69] Michelle D. Wright observes that "this separate work group was instrumental in forging a coalition of African American women that worked for a common goal." She terms this female solidarity process "community coalition" and argues that its unifying elements among slave women laid the foundation for female collectives following emancipation.[70]

In allocating their labor power for the collective, slave women drew upon their African ontological framework for spiritual guidance and determination to inform and sustain their resistance and to empower the slave community. "Many older women practiced the healing arts in their combined role of midwife, root doctor, healer, and conjurer."[71] By employing a variety of tactics and strategies derived from their daily labor activities on the plantation, slave women fostered an environment of resistance that all members of the slave community drew upon at various points in their lives.

Often, a substantial portion of black women's ongoing struggle was the resistance preparation in slave communities, including promoting the ideas of survival and freedom as legitimate rights of every member of the slave community. One mode of discourse was to place their right to freedom in the context of their African past. "I had always heard it talked among the slaves, that we ought not to be held as slaves; that our forefathers and mothers were stolen from Africa, where they were free men and free women."[72] Another aspect of the discourse was to tie the essence of freedom to the covert activities in the community, simultaneously legitimizing the idea and the expression. "Of course, the slaves don't tell folks what's passing in their minds about freedom," one ex-slave sagaciously commented, "for they know what'll come of it, if they do." As freedom discourse circulated among the slaves in the community, there was a corresponding growing critique by some of the more outspoken slaves of the institution of slavery itself. "The fact is, slavery's the father of lies. The slave knows he ought to have his freedom, and his master knows it, jest as well as he does; but they both say they don't; and they tell me some folks this way believe 'em."[73]

Freedom signified many things to the slave community and was inextricably tied to mastering the skills of reading and writing. For slaves, these skills represented the realities of the liberation process, and they saw not only their enlightenment but also the more pragmatic uses of literacy such as forging passes for themselves and others. Despite the antipathy to slave instruction and the stringent laws prohibiting teaching slaves to read and write, slaves continued the subversive practice of attempting to secure an education. "It seemed to me now, that, if I could learn to read and write, this learning might . . . point out to me the way to freedom."[74] Viewed as educational resources in the community, slaves who acquired the skill taught other slaves to read and write and gathered and disseminated information to the members of the slave community that impacted their lives. Slaves were involved, for example, in the distribution of David Walker's *Appeal to the Colored Citizens of the World,* one of the more strident antislavery materials of its time. When caught, however, slaves refused to reveal the sources of the distribution network.[75] Despite the rash of stringent laws prohibiting instruction for slaves, which were applied more severely immediately following insurrections or the distribution of "incendiary material," slaves continually pursued dangerous attempts to master the skill.

Even children were socialized early in subversion against the system and a reaffirmation of self through the process of education. Susie King Taylor reports in her memoirs that she and her brother, as slaves, attended a school run by a free black woman in Georgia. "We went every day with our books wrapped in paper to prevent the police or white persons from seeing them."[76] Some female slaves viewed the education of others as their mission of resistance. Milla Granson was a slave woman in Louisiana who ran a midnight school on a plantation until she had educated several hundred slaves.[77] Several of Granson's scholars forged passes, escaped from plantations, and headed for Canada.

Sabotage and subversion were other methods of daily resistance, with slave women proving themselves adept at poison and arson either by "putting jimsonweed seeds in the coffeepot or torching the barn."[78]

This type of resistance damaged the slaveholder's property, the most valued commodity in slavery. Utilization of both methods depended upon female location and labor assignments. House slaves, particularly cooks and kitchen helpers, could avail themselves more easily of poison, and field workers, closer to the master's property, could utilize arson as a vehicle of protest. Poisoning the master over a prolonged period of time with minute dosages, house slaves hoped to escape culpability as well as rid themselves of an abusive master. On the other hand, arson provided field slaves with an opportunity to destroy the master's property, create distance between themselves and the incident, and escape detection. Undoubtedly, women chose these methods of resistance because they indirectly confronted the system and offered opportunities to escape. The satisfaction of saboteurs was inherent in the success of the deed and the inner knowledge that one had struck out against injustice.

Slave women also saw escapes and truancy from plantations as viable strategies of resistance. In some cases, the details of the plan as well as its ingenuity contributed to its success. One slave, Lear Green, using a sailor's chest, had herself shipped to freedom in Philadelphia. Others, conscious that slave women away from plantations would arouse suspicions of whites or invite sexual abuse, disguised themselves as men. Maria Weems, disguised as a boy, ran away to freedom. In 1848, Ellen Craft donned a disguise as a white Southern man and with her husband, William, posing as her manservant, escaped by steamship and train to Philadelphia. Eventually, fear of apprehension after the passage of the Fugitive Slave Law of 1850 drove the couple to seek sanctuary in England.[79] Many other slaves escaped using the informational networks in the slave community for meeting places and times that would take them on the first leg of their journey. Informational systems were also instrumental in the famous rescue efforts of Harriet Tubman, the legendary conductor of the Underground Railroad. Undoubtedly, as word was passed of her impending arrival and departure dates and times, all who knew of her presence in the area did not make the journey but knew of the option. Through these viable strategies, the ideas of resistance were given life and passed on to others in the community.

Through their labor power, slave women created an amalgam of resistance patterns that localized their struggle to the slave community and regionalized the mode of challenge against the slave condition. Employing a broad range of strategies to facilitate resistance, they drew inspiration from their faith, African traditional roles, the means and mode of slave commodity production, and their desire to shape their own destiny. The conversion and transformation of labor and the labor will into practical tactics and strategies depended upon a host of variables, including mobility, labor location, knowledge of the terrain, informational networks, possible disguises and forgery, familial and kinship ties, and assorted paraphernalia to carry out a successful mission. Inevitably, whatever methods were employed, slave women were challenging their political and economic oppression and disrupting the normal flow of the slavery system. If one looks at the larger environment in which resistance was negotiated and carried out, one notes the courage and determination with which slave women resisted their oppressors. Simultaneously, slavery created two oppositional discourses—one most certainly of oppression and the other a culture of resistance—that slaves incorporated into their daily lives.

As slave women created the infrastructure of resistance into the fabric of the slave community, they were transforming their labor activities to challenge the slave hierarchy. The significance of black women's labor will was the symbolic and substantive representation of the cultural retentiveness of an African heritage and the resolve of slave women to transcend the powers of enslavement. Just as enslavement and the Southern economy shaped the political and social role of female slaves, industrialization and urbanization in the "freedom cities" of Boston, New York City, and Philadelphia would transform antebellum free black women's social and political activism. Amid the industrializing process and their marginalization in the marketplace, black women would contour an agenda of urban resistance.

PART 2

Defining Moments
of Freedom

CHAPTER 3

Weaving the Colors of Oppression

Black Women's Urban Resistance,
the Market Economy, and the Cult
of Domesticity

> Throughout the long years of history, woman has been the weathervane, the indicator, showing in which direction the wind of destiny blows. Her status and development have augured now calm and stability, now swift currents of progress. What then is to be said of the Negro woman today?
>
> ELISE JOHNSON McDOUGALD, 1925

THE MIGRATION OF BLACK WOMEN INTO NORTHEASTERN INDUSTRIAL cities in the 1830s was the catalyst for their social, economic, and political transformation. Industrialization and urbanization would not merely transform black women's lives but also would permanently relegate black women to the bottommost tier of the socioeconomic ladder. In migrating to urban centers, these black female workers were experiencing the semirural "push" from Southern slavery or Northern indentured servitude while simultaneously responding to the "pull" of urban centers, where there was the promise of free wage labor as well as the added advantage of participating in the sacred and secular activities of free black communities. On a psychological plane, black women could now own themselves, their time, space, dignity, reproductive capacity, and labor arrangements.[1] Just as important, black women desired stable family and community lives, where the psychological pain of loss due to the sale of family, friends, and community members did not constitute life's daily experiences.

"Freedom cities" like Boston, Philadelphia, and New York were urban centers that attracted the largest free black female populations, whether they were migrants from the Upper South, fugitives seeking freedom and anonymity, or urban black women who were making the transition from the abolition of slavery to the quasi-freedom status of free blacks. Many escaping fugitives saw these freedom centers as respite points, but the fear of re-enslavement propelled them on to Canada. Other black women, understanding the tangential limitations of these cities but having found domestic jobs working for affluent whites, chose to remain in the city. Once they found lodging, usually with a black family, black female boarders depended on their hosts to provide access to the sacred and social activities that fostered the social cohesion of black community life.

Many black female laborers had worked and lived in urban centers. Although some black female workers had been urban slaves in northeastern cities, other female laborers had been industrial slaves working as "hired hands" in antebellum tobacco factories, flour and iron mills, and railroads in domestic service, particularly in Southern manufacturing cities such as Richmond, Virginia.[2] A number of black female workers had gained industrial labor experience from working in Southern cotton mills. Morris W. Preyer states that by the start of the antebellum era, black labor was intrinsic to Southern cotton mill production. "In the eighteen-thirties cotton mills employing Negro labor exclusively were to be found in Virginia, Tennessee, North Carolina, South Carolina, Alabama, and Mississippi."[3] Despite prior work experiences in factory production, black female workers were relegated to the household labor that poor white women shunned. Nevertheless, for some of these Northern and Southern female migrants who headed for northeastern cities, urban life, while harsh, was somewhat mitigated by prior city experiences.

Black women constituted the majority of these black urban laborers, and alongside black male workers, they soon discovered that Northern racial attitudes were the bane of their existence. Despite freedom's promise, the racial climate in Northern cities that undermined the tenuous emancipation of African Americans characterized much of the prevailing sentiments of white citizens. Emancipation for blacks in most Northern states came encumbered with legal restrictions and, amid the racial customs, laws, and social proscriptions already embedded in the body politic, placed blacks in a political and legal quagmire. Such factors as the gradual abolition of slavery in Northern states, the escalating volume of kidnapping of urban dwellers from the 1830s to the Civil War, the persistence of Southern slavery, and the illicit slave trade in Philadelphia and New York City constituted part of the core of the daily oppression that determined black people's lives and increased their vulnerability.[4]

By 1837, the increased kidnapping activities in the cities caused the *Emancipator,* the weekly newspaper of the American Anti-Slavery Society, to warn the black community of imminent danger. "Look out for Kidnappers. We are informed that the notorious NASH has returned from the South, and is prowling about the city for more victims. Colored people should be on their guard."[5] In Philadelphia, whites' consternation in the 1820s and 1830s of black in-migration following the rebellions of Denmark Vesey and Nat Turner was tightly interlaced with the desire to supplant blacks' freedom status with legal and social controls. In the wake of Southern rebellions, "white Pennsylvanians predicted that free blacks, forced to leave the states of the Upper South, would move North and relocate in Pennsylvania," and they felt justified in restricting the freedom of black Pennsylvanians.[6]

Northern and Southern slaveholders, legislators, financiers, city officials, and public sentiment acted in concert, if not in total accord, to deny blacks their rights as citizens. Although black men and women fought for suffrage in New York City until the Civil War, flooding the state legislatures with numerous petitions, they could not garner the support of white citizens. George E. Walker comments, "This drafting of petition after petition was the avowed object of the New York Association for the Political Improvement of the People of Color."[7] Couched in legitimacy, the legal apparatus established the political context of oppression, fortified by state referenda at periods where there were high tides of black protests and demands, so that the potentiality of freedom was severely circumscribed. Daily discriminatory practices, ranging from blacks being excluded from public accommodations and conveyances, to black women being taunted on the streets, to antiblack race riots were also characteristic of this circle of oppression, and a powerful alignment of interlocking forces—legal, political, and social—reinforced racial subordination.

The underlying climate of antipathy toward all blacks reinforced white supremacy, partly contributed to by Northern economic linkages to the Southern slave system, with disparate classes of whites as willing participants in creating blacks as a subordinate caste. Even foreigners noted the intense racial discrimination embedded in Northern social conventions. In journeying through the United States in 1831, Alexis de Tocqueville claimed that it "appears to be stronger in the states that have abolished slavery than in those where it still exists."[8] Free antebellum African Americans were also cognizant of the intractable racial environment in Northern cities. Frederick Douglass argued that black servitude and whites' perception of black inferiority relegated blacks to contemporary servility. "We are then a persecuted people; not because we are colored, but simply because that color has for a series of years been coupled in the public mind with the degradation of slavery and servitude."[9]

The ubiquitous forces of Southern slavery and Northern indentured servitude cast a long shadow over the lives of black urbanites. The preparatory stage of gradual abolition set the stage for blacks to be reabsorbed into the indentured or wage labor force in a quasi-servitude status that contributed to the notion of black inferiority and racial discrimination in the marketplace. The influx of white immigrants to northeastern cities as wage laborers supplanted the need for slaves and, over time, displaced the indentured labor system as well. "The rapid growth of a class of white workers made the support of slaves unnecessary."[10] The failure of Northern states to provide long-term education and economic initiatives for newly freed persons left blacks to fend for themselves against the forces of racial and economic discrimination in urban areas.

Since industrialization was predicated upon a large supply of unskilled laborers, this quasi-permanent reserve pool of black laborers soon found themselves competing with the reserve pool of white laborers for menial jobs. While blacks in the urban areas of Pennsylvania and New York had made the transition from indentured servitude to wage labor, the competition between them and Irish menial workers for the same jobs eventually marginalized their existence in the marketplace. Black women, for example, as domestic workers were in competition with Irish women for these jobs and by the 1850s were being replaced by Irish female workers. In antebellum New York City, "as late as 1855, some 87 per cent of the gainfully employed Negroes of New York City worked in menial or unskilled jobs, and this appears to represent their economic conditions in other northern cities."[11] In a sense, the gradual abolition of slavery in the North, which was an extension of servile labor for blacks, created space for them as free laborers at the bottom of the socioeconomic ladder. This foreshadowed the quasi-servitude status that free blacks would hold in the industrializing process.

By midcentury, the tenuous political, economic, and legal status of black Americans made the creation of black communities vital to black self-preservation. In opposition to the oppression and out of a desire for self-determination, African Americans created communities with a supporting institutional infrastructure, as well as societies and associations to inveigh against disenfranchisement, and in the process mobilized the collective for social change. Black women were laborers and activists in all phases of the community's development and utilized economic and political participation as a springboard to their political and social agenda.

Karl Deutsch views this massive social change as social mobilization: "It denotes a concept which brackets together a number of more specific process of change, such as changes of residence, of occupation, of social setting, of face-to-face associates, of institutions, roles, and ways of acting, of experiences and expectations, and finally of personal memories, habits and needs, including the need for new patterns of group affiliation and new images of personal identity."[12] Black nationalism, an ideology and movement that focused on blacks pursuing a common social and political agenda based on shared oppression and a common destiny, was the impetus behind African Americans creating an alternative social structure.[13]

One of the earliest forms of collective black urban protest and separatist expression was the founding of the black church in Philadelphia in 1797. William Gamson informs us that "mobilization is a process of increasing the readiness to act collectively by building the loyalty of a constituency to an organization or a group of leaders."[14] These mobilization efforts, as well as discrimination in white churches, resulted in the black church's phenomenal growth in northeastern cities by the antebellum era.

Gayraud Wilmore notes that at the helm of black community life, the black church "was the beginning of the black revolution in American history—the first stirring of rebellion in an organized, mass-based way, and on a national scale."[15] Gaining thousands of adherents, the black church served the dual role of providing for the sacred and secular needs of the black community. By the 1830s, with its supporting institutional infrastructure of mutual benefit societies and the emerging black press, it represented the political voice of the black masses.

Black women fought for inclusion in male-dominated ecclesiastical affairs, and there were clearly early leadership tension and efforts. For example, Zion Baptist Church, a predominantly female body, was an offshoot from Abyssinian Baptist Church in New York City and by the next decade had a membership of 450 parishioners. Another congregation that emerged from Abyssinian was Concord Baptist Church of Christ in Brooklyn, whose members met at the home of one of their organizers, Maria Hampton, before the church became a reality.[16] For the most part, however, black women's evangelicalism, prayer groups, church societies, and participation in the daily operation of the church provided critical leadership to the black community.

As black women struggled to stabilize a community that reflected their political consciousness and identity, goals of spiritual redemption, economic survival, and political participation in the body politic, they manifested the black self-determination inherent in black nationalist expression. Challenging the society on their own terms placed them in direct opposition to the existing white hegemony. "Black freedom" rapidly became a system of collective constraints, legally and politically proscribed, supported by the existing culture of white privilege to racialize all blacks into conditions of social death and economic marginalization. The building of community, identity, and "consciousness of kind" by black women allowed them to transcend their proscribed freedom trajectory and in the process create self-determination and racial solidarity. The cathartic race consciousness, the instrument utilized for political mobilization, embodied for black women not only a pragmatic collective agenda for early sustainable institutional formation but also visions for self-discovery and collective redemption.

Facilitating the community's thrust for self-reliance, as well as black women's desire for community leadership and economic survival, was the development of mutual benevolent societies. Black urbanites, who had few social outlets, responded to the new wave of social reform permeating cities in the 1820s and 1830s with a host of benevolent societies, self-improvement associations, literary societies, lyceums, and fraternal orders. Voluntary associations facilitated the transition to urban life and strengthened the coping mechanisms needed to navigate the daily labyrinth of racial discrimination and social ostracism. These societies provided for those crises in members' lives, such as sickness, death, and economic distress. Members could take comfort in the fact that their societies constituted an economic support system mitigating some of the harshness of their lives. Members also responded to the camaraderie, the sharing of resources, the debates on prominent issues that impacted upon their lives, and the establishing of enduring social ties—all of which, in many instances, reflected the extended kinship network system typical of many African and slave communities. Watkins argues that black voluntary associations were critical in providing a stabilizing influence in black communities undergoing the socioeconomic shifts in society. Frequently, these associations had overlapping functions, emphasizing self-help and an array of community projects, with members belonging to several simultaneously. While several associations were short-lived, there were an estimated 106 in Philadelphia by 1848 and approximately 50 in New York City by 1850.[17]

Mutual benefit societies countered Northern racial attitudes, emphasized black pride, and were intertwined with the abolitionist movement that was gaining currency in Northern cities. While some societies focused on the economic needs of its members, others concentrated on community outreach projects, and still others had more direct ties to the antislavery movement. The African Clarkson Association in New York City, incorporated in 1829, was founded as a "charitable society of African descent to afford mutual means of education to the members thereof and relief to their families in case of sickness and death."[18] A similar type of association, the Daughters of Africa, was founded in Philadelphia in 1821 by "nearly 200 working-class women who banded together to help themselves."[19] Other societies, like the African Dorcas Society, a prominent female organization in several Northern cities, concentrated on a variety of community projects. "The Philadelphia group distributed groceries, clothing and small sums of money," while the society's program in New York City provided clothing for schoolchildren.[20] In Boston, the Female Benevolent Firm, founded in 1850, was similar to the Dorcas Society in its method of community outreach.[21]

Other groups, male and female organizations, sought more direct linkages to the abolitionist movement. As Benjamin Quarles comments, "An evidence of this close bond between abolitionism and Negro self-improvement was furnished by the American Moral Reform Society which, at its first meeting, pledged itself to make 'one common cause' with the American Anti-Slavery Society." The Phoenix Society of New York, the Philadelphia Library Company, and the Adelphic Union Association of Boston either had officers of the club who were abolitionists or frequently invited antislavery lecturers and politicians to their meetings.[22] Similarly, black female societies, such as the Female Literary Association of Philadelphia, the Afric-American Female Intelligence Society in Boston, the Minerva Literary Society, and the Edgeworth Society, the latter two in Philadelphia, held frequent antislavery lectures that were cited in antislavery newspapers.

Members of the Ladies Literary Society of New York expressed their political commitment by their fund-raising efforts for the black newspaper the *Colored American* and for the New York Committee of Vigilance to aid in the committee's vigorous efforts of rescuing fugitives. Founded in 1835 under the fiery abolitionist David Ruggles, the Committee of Vigilance, comprised of male and female members, could boast of handling over 1,373 cases in a seven-year period.[23] "During its first three years, the committee was involved in over five hundred fugitive slave cases."[24] A predominantly black women's committee, the Female Vigilant Association of Philadelphia, founded in 1838, worked as an auxiliary to the all-male group, the Vigilant Association of Philadelphia, to stem the tide of kidnapping activities.[25] On the one hand, these societies sought to dispel the myths of black inferiority by advocating self-reliance; on the other, their ties to the larger resistance efforts heightened and refined their political consciousness.

The black press became the mobilizing agent, employing political discourse in the struggle for equality and uniting disparate black communities under the umbrella of "the first attempt at national race-solidarity."[26] The *Rights of All,* a newspaper edited by Samuel Cornish in 1829, had agents in the United States, Haiti, Canada, and England.[27] Closely aligned with the abolitionist movement, the black press still espoused the tenets of black nationalism, which focused on the collective elevation of all blacks. It was not only critical that blacks took up the gauntlet for their own liberation but also that they effectively laid the groundwork for a national discourse on slavery and racism. "We wish to plead our own cause. Too long have others spoken for us." Pledging a commitment to abolitionism, the black press vowed to fight for "our brethren who are still in the iron fetters of bondage."[28] Equally, the black press mobilized the black community around the external forces that shaped their social and political repression. "Our paper is devoted, as well as to our social, moral and religious improvement, also to our civil and political rights."[29]

To promote a national political consciousness among African Americans, the black press adopted a political strategy of strident criticism of the internal contradictions in American society that afforded whites both privilege and complacency. This approach led to a reinterpretation of the Constitution and Bill of Rights, which many abolitionists had perceived to be a proslavery document, and laid the groundwork for their claim to their inalienable rights and to their rights of political discourse and resistance. "Their rights to citizenship of the United States is based upon a firmer foundation than legislative precedents, or judicial decisions, it is based upon the very meaning and definition of the term citizen."[30] This transformative analysis, which Mari Matsuda cites as "dual conception," became the crux of some of the ideological schisms in the black community in the 1850s and led Frederick Douglass to change his position regarding the nature of the Constitution: "We are Americans, and as Americans, we would speak to Americans."[31] With this new interpretation of the Constitution, blacks were demanding access to American political life.

Once blacks had validated their right of resistance, the *Colored American* placed their oppression in its proper political context by declaring, "The colored people of these United States are the involuntary subjects of a social and political despotism, alike unrighteous and cruel."[32] The black press, such as *Frederick Douglass' Paper*, strove to illuminate for Northerners that slavery could not be "christianized" and thereby made an acceptable societal institution. "I hope, therefore, that you will take the ground that this slavery . . . is of a lawless character, and cannot be christianized nor legalized."[33] While the black press galvanized sentiments for the emancipation of the slaves, most Northern whites were fierce advocates of the racial subordination of blacks.

The black press politicized black communities on the common thread of racial oppression throughout the diaspora. Much of the impetus for the diasporic connection came from the victorious struggles of the Haitian Revolution of 1804, where slaves led an uprising resulting in their independence.[34] Black emigrationists also saw Haiti, a black government in the Western Hemisphere, as a continuous source of inspiration to the self-determination and resistance efforts in black communities in the United States. All blacks, however, chafed at the lukewarm acknowledgment that the United States had given the Haitian Revolution, and this lack of support only served to forge stronger racial bonds. The black abolitionist Maria Stewart commented on the inconsistencies in America's foreign policy regarding the new sovereign nation: "We know that you are raising contributions to aid the gallant Poles; we know that you have befriended Greece and Ireland; and you have rejoiced with France, for her heroic deeds of valor. You have acknowledged all of the nations of the earth, except Hayti."[35]

Despite the fragmented and episodic growth of the black press, it politicized black communities regarding the praxis of struggle. Thus the struggles for the emancipation of the slaves, the eradication of racial discrimination toward free blacks, and the elimination of racial oppression throughout the diaspora were intertwined in the black press and remained a steadfast commitment. The sheer numbers of oppressed people sharing this common bond lifted the veil of isolation from this group of free blacks, allowing them to redouble their efforts of resistance. Frederick Douglass sought to capture the immediacy of the moment by urging collective mobilization: "If there ever was a time that calls for united action, it is now."[36]

Free black women shared a common vision with black men of racial and spiritual redemption and formed a critical mass initiating community institutional development.[37] The building of the community's institutional infrastructure was designed to stabilize community life and create a political and social platform to advocate for the emancipation of the slaves and civil equality for free blacks. Yet the protracted development also reflected the conventional gender tensions within the larger society and in the black community, as many blacks sought parallels with the norms and mores of middle-class American society. For black women, freedom represented a shifting in the broad-based roles that slave women played to the more restrictive gender roles that were in sanction with male domination. Most noticeably, the developing black church shifted its religious authority from the more widespread influence of male and female spiritual leaders of the slave community to a formalized male hierarchy of authority, attempting to alienate the influence of black women in ecclesiastical affairs.[38]

But black women forged their own path of urban resistance. As black women moved into the marketplace, primarily as household workers, they became critical to the family's survival and to the economic viability of black communities. In fact, their economic support of families, amid the high unemployment of black men, enhanced the quality of life in black communities and placed them in pivotal economic positions, which ultimately became a springboard for their community activism. In similar fashion, their labor will, which had been used to foster slave community resistance, was refined under industrialization to include broad-based strategies of community activism. Expressing their sacred and secular commitment through the vehicle of economic initiatives, church and community organizations, societies, and associations, black women transformed their political and social commitment. In a most profound sense, black women's economic and political activities were determined by the urbanization process; racial, gender, and class discrimination; and aspiring capitalism.

INDUSTRIALIZATION AND URBANIZATION

Although the emergence of nascent industrial capitalism was predicated upon such factors as innovative technology, the expansion of domestic and international markets, the mass production of consumer goods, wage labor, and the consolidation of wealth among merchants, much of the wealth that determined those fortunes came from the involvement of Northern merchants in the slave trade and slave commodity production. Karl Marx posited that "the turning of Africa into a warren for the commercial hunting of black-skins, signalized the rosy dawn of the era of capitalist production."[39] By 1807, England outlawed the slave trade, as did the United States, although the illicit slave trade continued to flourish. W. E. B. DuBois states that while England had abandoned the slave trade in favor of the more profitable colonial imperialism, the United States continued the illegal slave trade until the 1850s.[40] Charles H. Haswell, a New Yorker who lived through much of the nineteenth century, indicates in his memoirs, *Reminiscences of an Octogenarian,* that "it is historical that Eastern merchants purchased Baltimore clippers, a class of vessels (foretopsail schooners) designed for speed, to be used for transporting fruit or oysters, and especially for slaves." Haswell also commented on the duplicity of Northern merchants in circumventing the 1807 law barring the importation of slaves. According to Haswell, Northern merchants, while purportedly using their vessels for the purchase of "bone and ivory," had instead outfitted them for transporting slaves and were engaged in the lucrative illicit slave trade off the coast of Africa. "These same men fitted these vessels for the coast of Africa, for the alleged purpose of procuring 'bone and ivory,' . . . while, if captured after leaving the Coast, the 'bone and ivory' were in the form of negro men and women."[41]

Northern financiers, in addition to winking at the 1807 law banning the importation of slaves, benefited from slave commodity production. While Boston and Philadelphia competed with New York City for the vibrant trade in slave products, New York City dominated the trade, most particularly the cotton trade to Great Britain, until the Civil War. Following Whitney's 1793 invention of the cotton gin, "Britain's cotton imports rose from eleven million pounds in 1784 to 283 million in 1832," of which the United States supplied three-quarters in the 1830s.[42] At the triangular center of the cotton trade, New York City forged economic linkages between the Southern market economy, Northern capitalism and its manufacturing base, and port cities in Europe. Lankevich and Furer detail the triangular pattern of production. "Many New York—owned ships sailed directly to Europe from the South filled with cotton, and returned via New York laden with textiles, manufactured goods and immigrants; they then refilled their holds and coasted southward to begin the triangle once more."[43]

Although profits were derived from the ownership of these ships by Northern merchants, additional profits were gained from such ancillary merchant services as insurance for the cargo, cash advances for Southern planters for their crops, and credit lines for merchandise purchased in Northern cities. Southerners contended, at times somewhat peevishly, that 40 percent of all monies from the cotton trade went to New York City businessmen. Although many believed Stephen Colwell's 1859 figures to be conservative, he cites that New York City merchants alone amassed $200 million annually, solely on the transactions of the cotton trade.[44] James D. B. DeBow, a slave apologist, boasted that New York City carried on such a volume of business in regards to the slave trade that it was "almost as dependent upon Southern slavery as Charleston itself."[45] Yet this economic relationship, which also hinged upon international trading commitments and investment capital, could have grave repercussions that were often felt worldwide. "So crucial was this exchange," note Carroll and Noble, "that shifts in cotton production affected financial commitments throughout the world, an economic phenomenon responsible for such banking crises as the panic of 1837."[46] New York City merchants did such brisk business in the illegal slave trade from the city's ports that they were dubbed "the greatest slave-trading mart in the world."[47]

Many shipping companies, to increase their volume of business in the slave trade, located either their headquarters or branch offices in New York City, with other offices placed strategically in large, Southern port cities. Savannah, Mobile, Galveston, Richmond, Norfolk, New Orleans, and Charleston were viable trading port cities, and business could be transacted from any or all of these trading venues. Shipping companies, like J. P. Marshal and Company and Phelps-Dodge, maintained either branch offices or companies in Southern cities. Southern companies, like Edward Matthews and Company, Hewitt Lees and Company, and John Frazer and Company, who maintained large offices in New York City, were regarded as Northern companies. Northern companies, seeking to increase their revenues in slave commodity production, sought an even more extensive connection to Southern slavery. According to Joseph A. Scoville in *The Old Merchants of New York,* the large merchant company of Daniel Parish and Company maintained five Southern branch offices in five different Southern cities, centering a large part of their business on strengthening their Southern-based operations as well as their Southern-European trading connections.[48]

Southern planters were consistently encouraged to come to New York City. Northern capitalists evinced few compunctions about the moral or ethical questions of slavery but instead saw the vibrant ecosystem of slavery and slave commodity production as an opportunity to increase monies for both expansion and profits. They may have been more in concert with the Southern newspaper the *Richmond Enquirer,* which touted in 1856 that "freedom is not possible without slavery," than they realized.[49] One businessman, in conversation with Samuel J. May, the influential abolitionist, candidly remarked on Northern interests in Southern slavery:

> Mr. May, we are not such fools as not to know that slavery is a great evil, a great wrong. But a great portion of the property of the Southerners is invested under its sanction; and the business of the North, as well as the South, has become adjusted to it. There are millions upon millions of dollars due from Southerners to the merchants and mechanics alone, the payment of which would be jeopardized by any rupture between the North and the South. We cannot afford, sir, to let you and your associates endeavor to overthrow slavery. It is not a matter of principles with us. It is a matter of business necessity . . . We mean, sir, to put you abolitionists down by fair means if we can, by foul means if we must.[50]

Cotton profits—and to a lesser extent, the profits from those slave products of wheat, rice, tobacco, and corn—were subsequently reinvested as loan capital in manufacturing initiatives in Northern cities. Monies from the vast slave trading network, notes historian David Brion Davis, also stimulated industrial expansion and increased the division of labor. "As a stimulus to shipbuilding, insurance, investment, and banking, the slave trade expanded employment in a diversity of occupations and encouraged the growth of seaports on both sides of the Atlantic."[51] Profits from the cash crop economy were also used by entrepreneurs as venture capital stimulating the expansion of artisan workshops; the building of small and medium-sized shoe, straw, garment, and textile factories; and the shipment of the Northern products of hardware, shoes, boots, men's and women's garments, and perishable food items to the South, Midwest, and Europe.[52] As economist Douglass C. North observes, "The cotton trade was the immediate impetus for this regional specialization."[53] This continuous reinvestment of capital, derived from the profits of slave labor, allowed Northern cities to specialize in certain industries and increase the division of labor as they developed into primary manufacturing centers for national and international commodity distribution.

The dialectical relationship between household sufficiency production and factory production was clearly evident by the 1840s as manufactured goods quickly increased in volume, producing a corresponding decline in domestic production. The expansion of manufactured goods and the production process of transforming raw cotton into a coarse cloth depended on cheap labor sources; "cotton from Lowell" depended on the raw cotton being produced and ginned by slaves in the Deep South, and "boots and shoes from Lynn" depended on the hides from California, where Mexicans provided the source for cheap labor. The cotton mills spun off other specialized industries—machine tools, metal production, tool engineering, locomotives—spearheading greater capitalization and industrial expansion.[54] By the 1850s, the appearance of the sewing machine in mass production revolutionized the industry, fostering a greater consumer demand for the finished items of cotton apparel, shoes, and boots.

Douglass C. North calls subsidiary industries that are spawned as a result of industry specialization and increased division of labor "backward linkages." He contends that it was the "backward linkages into the textile machinery which had the most important consequences for the growth of manufacturing."[55] Moreover, these subsidiary industries created similar expansions in complementary industries. The textile machinery industry stimulated a greater demand for iron castings, leading to an increase in overall iron production. Railroads and iron forgings were produced, as was the kitchen stove, the consumer product that reorganized antebellum women's household labor.[56] Other industries evinced a similar path of technological development, most particularly the woolen industry, creating mass production for a national market.

At the helm of industrialization and urbanization, New York City and other northeastern cities, with their magnetic pull of jobs, urbanity, and economic prosperity, drew succeeding waves of immigrant groups, particularly the English, Irish, and Germans emigrating to the United States prior to the Civil War, ultimately quadrupling in size.[57] European immigrants saw America as a land of economic mobility. For most of the Irish immigrants, who were in the majority, the confluences of the enclosure movement and a series of potato crop failures led to their mass exodus to the United States. By the 1860s, the Irish emigration of more than two million unskilled, rural peasantry had settled primarily in New York City and Boston, securing both factory and menial jobs and becoming part of the new laboring class critical to emerging industrialization. Numbering approximately 22,185 in Philadelphia, 12,274 in New York

City, and 2,261 in Boston, blacks comprised a varied group of those who were recently freed from urban slavery, fugitives seeking anonymity in large cities, and newly arrived migrants, all of whom were seeking a sense of freedom, job opportunities, and education.[58]

The flavor of these cities was soon characterized by many languages and speech patterns reflecting the manner and customs of their diverse group of inhabitants and the density of their populations. The emerging ethnic enclaves that featured dilapidated housing and slum dwellings for the workers were juxtaposed to the fine Georgian townhouses for the affluent.[59] Alongside the immigrants, Southern and Northern black migrants, and other poor folk who flooded every city, the early captains of industry emerged with industrialization and the capitalization of commodity production.

Fueled by "unfettered capitalism," the construction, design, and constant reshaping of the city's internal structure were primarily aimed at increasing capital and developing the technology of mass production to expand the city's manufacturing base. "As they built their 'America by design,'" Ronald Takaki notes, "they were employing technology as a mode of production as well as an instrument for the domination and reinforcement of social relations in a capitalist society."[60] Indeed, the significant focus of New York City's construction in the 1830s, before the panic of 1837 created anxiety among financiers, was the monies used for the expansion of its harbors and waterways to increase the volume of foreign trade; the construction and design of the Wall Street area, dubbed the "golden toe" of Manhattan, to consolidate commercial transactions; and the development of the City Hall area with hotels, entertainment centers, and retail shops that catered to wealthy clientele on nearby Broadway.

Slaves carrying packages and walking deferentially behind their masters on shopping trips to the most exclusive shops on Broadway became a part of the urban landscape. Too, the robustness of the slave trade intertwined with capitalist growth could be seen in the coffles of slaves in daily transit through the cities, being bought and sold at dockside and then transported to Southern auction houses, farms, and plantations. European travelers, Southern planters, and Northern upper classes commingled at Broadway shopping centers, the counting houses on Lower Broadway, and frequently on the docks to negotiate the wealthy cotton trade of the Lower South, the lucrative tobacco shipments from the upcountry, and numerous slave production products.[61] Ordinarily, planters stayed at the finer hotels, dined at the best restaurants, and at night were often seen engaging in discourse at some of the city's "tipplin'" houses.

Thus their influential social standing and comfort level clearly reflected the fact that Southern planters and Northern businessmen benefited from the commercial enterprise of slavery and slave commodity production.

SLAVERY, RACE, AND CASTE

Slavery, race, and caste were inculcated into nascent capitalism, fostering a national phenomenon of consciousness of race and racism. Although regional variants were decidedly different, slavery, race, and caste were integral to society's social, political, and economic institutions, fully circumscribing the lives of African Americans. The oppression of African Americans played a functional economic and social role in the market economies of the North and South. George Fredrickson comments that planters "had very strong economic and social incentives to create a caste of hereditary bondsmen."[62] According to political scientist Milton D. Morris, it was the system's inherent racial bias, underpinned by slaveholders' unabashed economic greed and their ability to construct laws, enforce slave codes, define prevailing custom, and determine social policy, that institutionalized racial subordination. "Black subordination through the institution of slavery was legitimized by a complex array of laws and customs designed to ensure the dehumanization of all blacks or at least establish their inferiority to whites."[63]

The complexities of Northern racial discrimination drew upon a number of interrelated factors, including the ideology of white supremacy, the vestiges of slavery and prevailing racial attitudes, the economic collusion and social relations between planters and financiers, a reserved labor force critical to industrial expansion, and foreign capital in slave cotton production. All of these factors, in addition to the interweaving of the two market systems, blurred the distinctions between the exploitation of slave labor and the status and treatment of free black labor. Free Northern blacks' political, economic, and social quagmire was reflective of their freedom status with none of the rights and privileges of citizenship. "Legal and extralegal discrimination restricted Northern Negroes in virtually every phase of existence," notes Leon F. Litwack. "Where laws were lacking or ineffectual, public opinion provided its own remedies."[64] While slavery was viewed as the primary catalyst shaping racial discrimination and the oppression of Northern blacks, customs and attitudes also severely hampered how blacks could earn a living.

Slavery, race, and caste served the underlying economic intent of maintaining racial and class cleavages in society so that capitalism could prosper. The economic significance of slavery to Northern industrialism meant that all blacks, enslaved or free, were reinvented as slaves, both symbolically and economically, in the mind and imagination of whites at each stage of technological development. Not merely intrinsic to capitalist expansion, as slavery, race, and caste were embedded in nascent capitalism, they served to mitigate the psychological displacement felt by white workers in flux in the industrialization process. Under the tensions created by the new economic order, there was a growing "need to define the norms for white society," which "had a specific relation to the age of Market Revolution and capitalist class needs in an expanding wage-labor structure of social relations."[65] Operating as interactive and multidimensional components, slavery, race, and caste formed a racial construction of superordinate-subordinate relations of whites vis-à-vis blacks.

In this ideology of white supremacy, whites were perceived as powerful, superior by having the advantage of white skin color, and in control of society; in juxtaposition, blacks were viewed as powerless, degraded by virtue of black skin color, and thereby inferior. Takaki argues that the interaction between "the social, political, and economic racial oppression" of Northern blacks and the "cluster of negative images of blacks" resulted in the "patterns of discrimination, segregation, and mass violence" that urban blacks confronted daily.[66] David Potter, in recognizing the biregional oppression of blacks, argues that "the dominant forces in both sections spurned and oppressed the Negro."[67] Frederickson concurs with Joel Kovel that the biregional oppression of blacks had distinguishing or "crucial differences in the salience of the racial attitudes that predominated."[68] Northern racial attitudes were more evident in Northerners' "aversion" or exclusionary racial practices that denied blacks societal access. This racial patterning that defined black-white relations in city life centered society's normative behavior on a cohesive "American" identity and an ideology of racial supremacy, while placing blacks as "outsiders" to the body politic.

Black powerlessness, inferiority, and social and economic degradation served as a catalyst for white group cohesiveness in Northern centers. Amid the chaotic upheaval often associated with massive economic change, whites needed coalescing agents to aid in their adaptation to the industrialization process. The social degradation of blacks gave white urban dwellers a sense of order in the chaos, a lessening of anxiety and tension, a relative purpose associated with commodity production, and a distorted view of themselves as superior beings. Their false sense of superiority induced a widespread sense of complacency to obfuscate capitalism's erratic trajectory. This "white supremacy production," by removing blacks to what Kai Erikson calls the "outer edges of group life, give[s] the inner structure its special character and thus supplies the framework within which the people of the group develop an orderly sense of their own cultural identity."[69] As white society nurtured its in-group identity, its "we-ness," blacks were placed on the periphery of every aspect of social life.

As industrialization progressed by the 1840s, white urban dwellers found that despite the prevalent racial and caste mechanisms that alienated blacks from mainstream society, their personal anxieties were further exacerbated by the developing class structure based on material wealth that quickly positioned all societal classes. As affluent neighborhoods were carved out in urban areas that were mainly off limits to all but the wealthy, they became symbolic of the increasing class distinctions in urban life. Irving Lewis Allen has commented on these class cleavages that were becoming more pronounced in city life. "By the 1840s the great American market cities of free-flowing capital had produced a disturbing new social order of rich and poor and amazing new ways of life."[70] A racial hierarchy of whiteness developed as a unifying force of disparate white classes and as a component of the larger doctrine of white supremacy buttressing those poor whites who could not be absorbed into the differentiated class structure of the market economy.

While the upper classes clearly exploited free and enslaved black labor and profited immensely from the vast ecosystem of slavery, the ideological racial construct effectively hid their class biases, creating a racial differentiated labor pool and subverting the class and caste flaws in capitalist expansion. Thus a poor white male worker could take refuge in his whiteness and small tokens of derived superiority and feel justified as he advocated the exclusion of blacks from menial wage labor that barely provided sustenance for his own family's survival. Racial constructions, by being integral to the industrializing process, were dependent upon the pervasive psychology of whiteness to ease industrial transitions for disparate white workers. All whites, in fact, were shaped by slavery, race, and caste and, depending on the vagaries of class, benefited from the slave economy and nascent industrialization.

One may argue convincingly, as Kovel does, that the creation of blackness in American society facilitated material success by whites.[71] By locating themselves in whiteness and the doctrine of white supremacy, whites held the psychological and economic tools of economic competitiveness. With blacks at the bottom of the economic hierarchy, a lack of material success in no way detracted from whites' self-esteem, as blacks provided an outlet for negative aggressive impulses stemming from failure and resentment. Indeed, this highly charged outlet could detract attention away from the early failures of capitalist expansion and its inability to absorb new workers into the system. As Allen notes, "The new industrialization and unfettered capitalism, while generally raising levels of living for the masses in the long run, in the short run created a huge urban proletariat that cyclically fell on hard times."[72] If blacks had never been slaves, their necessary presence in the symbolic and substantive interpretations of the market system would have relegated them to the same social and economic position in order to sustain and buttress the American psyche primed for economic activity. The safety valve that blacks provided also cushioned the white reality and evaluation of capitalism and its impact upon their lives. The presence of blacks gave whites a unilateral view of the market revolution. Slavery and race, then, depended on this pervasive psychology of whiteness and combined with industrial development to ease industrial transitions for many white workers. Simultaneously, the operationalization of slavery and race during the early stages of industrial development excluded free blacks from all but the most menial jobs in the marketplace as well as from all forms of social and political participation.

BLACK WOMEN'S URBAN RESISTANCE

The urban resistance of black women laid the groundwork for their independent economic initiatives, shifting family roles, community activism, and insurgency as black abolitionists. The social and political conditions that blacks confronted in Northern cities and the perennial question of slavery, as well as black communities challenging the exclusionary practices in American society while fortifying the group's racial consciousness, provided the context for black female resistance. Whether it was independent economic initiatives, allocation of family resources from monies that black women earned, community-based activism, or the larger abolitionist movement, black women's transformative role in these ventures fostered their active political and social resistance. By the antebellum era, black women had a long history of resistance in the New World and indeed had emerged from their historical experiences as slave women in commodity production with an ethos of resistance. Based upon their shared oppression and collective experiences, they began redefining their gender and political roles in industrializing cities. The meshing of slave and free experiences of black women, replenished continuously by escaping fugitives and female migration in Northern cities, augured a cross-fertilization of resistance. Subsequent development of female collective coalitions were effective, for the most part, because of America's formal and informal policies of containment of African Americans. Despite the massive efforts of blacks to engage in political and social participation, this social isolationism relegated blacks to an outsider status "creat[ing] all conditions conducive to mobilization for systematic change."[73]

Black female workers utilized their skills and their labor will, honed initially in slavery and then developed in the market economy, as tools of self-empowerment. Consistently, black women fortified their individual psyches by negotiating a hostile environment confronted daily, most particularly the mistress-servant power relationships intrinsic to their role as domestic workers in white households in urban areas. In their efforts to eradicate the crippling effects of racism, black women employed those same skills—household management, task-orientation, decision-making processes, and goal-setting behavior—to create female collectives that focused on group-centered leadership. One collective, the Female Literary Association of Philadelphia, proclaimed, "As daughters of a despised race, . . . it becomes a duty . . . to cultivate the talents . . . that by so doing, we may break down the strong barrier of prejudice."[74] While the institutional infrastructure in black communities operated on male-centered leadership with high visibility to coordinate group efforts, as Ella Baker, the modern civil rights leader, contends, group-centered collectives often provided more independence.[75] Creating a subcommunity of urban resistance, black women were able to effect individual and collective uplift in tandem with black communities' efforts.

The crucible of black female urban resistance was forged out of the evolving synthesis of the oppression of black workers, black communities as centers of struggle, determination, activism, and the coexisting modes of commodity production in the larger society. For black women coming into urban areas and constituting the black majority in those cities, their relationship to other workers, their pivotal role in black communities, and their labor participation in the industrializing process were the factors that formed the constituent elements of their reality. The transformations in their lives as they moved into the market economy, sought stable families, and pursued sacred and secular activities were all politicizing forces in their lives. As Gary Nash contends, through the black church, the dominant institutional anchor of black communities and "the primary instrument for the forging of black consciousness," black men and women had "the protective space whereby each could contend with the other about common concerns" in their evolving spirituality and consciousness.[76]

Black churches that advocated radical abolitionism—that is, the immediate emancipation of the slaves—depended on their parishioners for participation in the Underground Railroad, ancillary church organizations, and community-based abolitionist activities. Black women needed little encouragement for their involvement in emancipation efforts, for the continuum of slavery, fugitive slave laws, kidnappers, and the vast governmental apparatus that supported slavery were the bane of every black person's existence in Northern cities. Its direct antithesis, grounded in the emancipation of the slaves, the liberation of oppressed peoples, escaping fugitives, the black underground, vigilance committees, and the larger abolitionist movement, was catalytic in shaping black female resistance. Improving the quality of family and community life also placed black women in the realm of social activism. In addition to participating in all facets of resistance efforts, black women's collectives initiated fund-raisers, concerts, lectures, mutual benefit societies, and antislavery organizations in their efforts to generate revenues for a financially strapped movement, while raising the community's consciousness regarding the thought and praxis of struggle. Benjamin Quarles notes the political activism of black women in New York City: "In New York the Negro women held annual fairs at the Broadway Tabernacle for the benefit of the Vigilance Committee." Similarly, Quarles observes, black women in a Philadelphia female collective demonstrated their shared purpose of resistance: "Over a four-year span the colored Women's Association made donations for fugitive slave work, giving $50 in 1851."[77] Black women who came in from rural areas, migrants from Southern towns and cities, or those who had been urban slaves and were already a part of the cities' mélange constituted in the antebellum years a broad-based critical mass of resistance. Free black women's collectives, resembling the female slave coalitions and networking systems that were evident throughout the antebellum era, contributed to free black women's consciousness.[78]

Critical to black women's urban resistance was their economic relationship to the industrial market economy. The market economy that expanded the affluent classes and their concomitant needs for domestic servants also limited the steady work for black men, placing black women, as breadwinners, in contraconventional gender roles. "Often, when men could find no jobs or only seasonal or erratic employment, their wives' more continuous income was critical to the maintenance of the household."[79] Black female workers' peripheral participation in the labor market stymied their industrial potential, and whether they were unskilled, semiskilled, or skilled workers, they were usually forced to labor as domestics, for a prolonged period of time, in white households. This labor exploitation, long hours of backbreaking work, numerous duties that were impossible to complete in a day, and little pay were a continuous source of rancor to black women, serving "as a tangible reminder of the days of bondage."[80] The conundrum of race, class, and gender inherent in the exploitation and marginalization of black female workers in the industrializing process varied little, forming a continuity of their oppression from slavery to freedom. Economist Julianne Malveaux locates the contemporary economic oppression of black women in slavery. "Though the occupational position of black women has its roots in slavery, black women have continued to be segregated occupationally and in different ways than are white women."[81]

As I have noted elsewhere, "black women's earning power proved to be a transformative component in the psychological and social benefits they derived from being economically viable members of black families and communities."[82] Just as female slaves' engagement in commodity production engendered the slaves' culture of resistance, the "pattern of employment" of free black female domestic workers "made women an extremely important part of the financial life of the black community."[83] Encouraged, black female workers established their own economic initiatives and became a measured political and social influence in black communities. Their work as household workers in white homes enabled white upper-class women, who now had leisure time, to become politically and socially active. Similarly, as Horton and Horton maintain, "the expanded role of working women also freed middle-class nonworking black women to be socially and politically active."[84] As laborers, black women undergirded much of the political and social activism of women and black communities, as these groups mobilized to challenge the existing white male hegemony.

As a supportive apparatus for the development of group consciousness, black women's organizations and collectives fostered group cohesion while initiating pragmatic programs of self-improvement and community activism. Because black women were denied access to factory jobs in Northern cities, they did not form factory collectives as did white women. Black women, did, however, organize working-class community collectives and mutual benefit societies, which were reflective of all groups in black communities. Although a tiny elite had emerged in black communities during the antebellum era, Emma Jones Lapsansky indicates that in the profile of the African American elite in Philadelphia belonging to the Committee to Recruit Colored Troops (for the Civil War), the wives were equally active in social organizations, and "almost all had some dwellers who were not part of the nuclear family." Lapsansky also compares class differentiation and labor among black and white women: "Whereas in the white community employment for women was the lot of the lower classes, more than half of the wives of committee members combined motherhood, income-producing labor (e.g. as seamstresses, boarding house keepers) public service, and perhaps even lectures or publications."[85] This interactive involvement in church and secular activities by disparate classes of black women was also a contributing factor in the developing group consciousness among black women.

Despite black women's singular efforts to negotiate the travails of working both inside and outside of the home, their double burden was a source of tension in many families and communities. Many black men, subscribing to the middle-class cult of domesticity regarding gender roles, received additional reinforcement from the black church and the black press, both touting conventional gender roles for black women. Female subordination, while popularly expressed by the black male-dominated institutional infrastructure that formed the cadre of visible leadership in the community, proved less than pragmatic and remained conflictual, at best, in black communities. Realistically, the black family or the black communities' infrastructure could not be supported by the seasonal employment of black men. Black women's labor and monies were needed to augment the families' incomes, and their collective financial contributions and their political activism were critical to emancipation efforts and overall black progress.

By 1837, the black newspaper the *Weekly Advocate* was encouraging black women's political activism, and "many black women were recruited by men to become antislavery speakers."[86] Black male leaders, ironically, also worked on many political committees with black women, particularly vigilance committees and antislavery societies, where women were active participants and recognized leaders. The steady economic activity and the subsequent political and social activism of black women were not only a source of pride but tension as well as many black men harbored more traditional values. Clearly, as James Oliver Horton contends, the "black woman was then trapped by pressures from her community, from the wider society, and from the economic reality of her times," as well as from her abilities to be productive outside of the home.[87] For black women, however, their increasing self-esteem, which, paradoxically, was shaped by labor that was undervalued in society but recognized as a valued commodity in black communities, enabled them to define their own unique course of urban resistance. Black women, as individuals and working in collectives, adopted a two-pronged approach to challenging the sexism in black communities as well as the racial, class, and sexual oppression that circumscribed their lives in the larger society.

THE BLACK FEMALE MAJORITY IN NORTHERN CITIES

The preponderance of black females in industrial cities, contributed to in part by such social indicators as manumission, emancipation, and natural increase, was also heavily influenced by the economic expansion that created a corresponding need for private household workers for the affluent classes. Other social indicators responsible for black population growth by the late 1820s in port cities like Philadelphia, New York, and Boston were in-migration, fugitives, and the influx of Haitian émigrés, a large group coming primarily to Philadelphia in the aftermath of the Haitian Revolution of 1804. The 1820 U.S. Census indicates that there was a majority of black females, in comparison to black males, in each of these cities, and that majority remained for several decades. For example, Philadelphia had the largest free black population, 11,891, with 6,671 (56 percent) being black females. The second largest black population was in New York City, with 10,368 black residents and black females numbering 6,174 (59.7 percent) of the free black community. Boston's black population, which was relatively small compared to the others, had approximately 1,726 blacks, with a black female majority of 952 (55 percent) of the total group. In these three cities, black women were still finding ways to earn a living, largely as domestic workers, and in-migration and stability were factors in their increasing numbers.

For black men and women, the ability to earn a living in the new marketplace determined the quality of their lives and the fullness of their lives as well. A decided shift in the job market for black men in the early

1840s brought more of them into the cities, where they were still facing occupational segregation but found more available menial jobs. Despite the market's growth and the intense capitalization of the wearing apparel, commercial, shipping, and manufacturing industries, black men were relegated to such occupations as waiters, coachmen, stewards, caulkers, chimney sweeps, porters, peddlers, dockworkers, seaman, bootblacks, common laborers, and household servants.[88] In Boston, Horton and Horton report, "the job of porter was most desirable because most black laborers were employed on the docks where the work was more sporadic and seasonal than that available in the downtown commercial areas for black porters."[89]

For black women, "whose labor . . . was equally important to the survival of black households," the market's growth did not spell entry into marginal factory jobs where a number of white female workers were located but instead into the household labor force desired by the rising affluent classes.[90] Black female workers, whose occupational structure was more restrictive, worked primarily as domestic workers, laboring in sharp contrast to many poor white female workers before the 1840s, who benefited from the new factories and the expansion of the apparel and textile industries. In retrospect, poor white women, who were exploited by business owners, received mixed benefits at best from their factory jobs.[91] The location of black men and women in menial jobs underscored the market expansion of the 1840s and the continuous need of the affluent classes for service labor while simultaneously excluding black workers from the developing mainstream industries. Despite the market's growth and expansion during the antebellum era, albeit several economic contractions as well, the occupational structure for black men and women in menial jobs remained relatively permanent.

Philadelphia, for example, saw an increase of black males from 5,220 in the 1820s to 8,316 in the 1840s, with a larger proportional increase among black females from 6,671 in the 1820s to 11,515 by the 1840s.[92] The black female ratio in 1840 was 1,387 to 1,000 males, a slight increase over the earlier ratio of 1,383 females to 1,000 males in the 1820s, which may be related to a natural increase but more likely included a vibrant black in-migration to the city. The opportunities for black women in domestic services in Boston also contributed to a black female majority in that city. Boston's 1850 census, which appears more reliable than its 1840 census, evinces a slight black population increase, with black females still holding a majority. Since the Irish immigration to Boston "increased from 443 in 1836 to a high of 65,556 in 1846," black migrants in that time period, in competition with these immigrants for the same menial jobs, would generally migrate to other port cities seeking work.[93]

By the 1840s in Philadelphia, on the other hand, the increase in black females to males, "sixteen to every five in the city," was more indicative of the industrial expansion of that city and the corresponding needs of the upper classes for female household servants. By the 1840s–1850s, the same industrial growth and need for household labor that brought black women to the cities had trickled down to black men in the Philadelphia black community, causing a slight increase of black males in the city as more menial jobs became available. In the middle years of the 1840s, the potato rot in Ireland brought a flood of Irish immigrants to New York City, resulting in a sharp decline of 2,500 in New York City's black population and indicating a competitive shift in job prospects for both black males and females.[94] The decline of job prospects for black males and females in New York City was very similar to the job competition between the Irish immigrants and blacks in Boston during the same time period, where the black labor force, chiefly menial laborers, was supplanted by the influx of Irish laborers.

Despite the fact that the black population was never more than a fraction of these cities' populations—8.85 percent of Philadelphia's; 2.68 percent of New York City's; and 1.46 percent of Boston's—by the 1850s Irish immigrants, desperately seeking menial labor, had eroded the need for black laborers, making it difficult for blacks to find work.[95] Arguably, these cities had such small black populations that blacks could not possibly have been a competitive labor force for any white laboring class and could have readily been absorbed into the market economy. Yet this labor competition, real or perceived, most certainly fueled by racial discrimination and antiblack riots, kept many blacks either unemployed for lengthy periods of time or experiencing episodic employment or seasonal work or migrating to different port cities in search of work. In 1853, Frederick Douglass commented on the trends in the labor market that exacerbated blacks' economic plight: "White men are becoming house-servants, cooks and stewards on vessels—at hotels.—They are becoming porters, stevedores, wood-sawyers, hod-carriers, brick-makers, white-washers and barbers, so that the blacks can scarcely find the means of subsistence—a few years ago, a white barber would have been a curiosity—now their poles stand on every street."[96]

Scholars have argued that the influx of white male immigrants seeking menial jobs, combined with occupational segregation and racial prejudice, seriously reduced the job availability for black males.[97] Equally important was the labor displacement that occurred among black female domestic workers by Irish female immigrants who were also seeking menial jobs. Many black female domestics, particularly those who had "live-in" situations providing room and board or steady work with one employer, found these jobs now going to white female workers. This left many black domestics seeking a combination of "day's work" with a variety of employers or other combinations of labor arrangements, such as self-employed laundresses working at home part of the week and providing "day's work" on other weekdays to provide a steady income. Additional strain was placed on the family budget and on marriages, as the tenuous employment of black men forced many of them to migrate to other port cities seeking work or to upstate New York farms for seasonal farming or contractual monthly farming, leaving black women as the sole providers for the families for a substantial portion of the year.[98]

Despite the fluctuating financial picture, a black population in these port cities still remained, struggling to secure an economic foothold. While black populations suffered a decline in the 1850s in Boston and New York City and witnessed a miniscule increase in Philadelphia, blacks, buoyed by hope and a taste of freedom, still responded to the pull of these cities for their livelihood. At the same time, blacks saw refuge in black communities' cohesiveness, which provided a bulwark against racial prejudice.

BLACK WOMEN AND SHIFTING IDEOLOGIES

Black women's labor activity in industrial centers was thwarted by the shifting ideologies of the epoch, the pervasive tenets of the cult of domesticity, and the fluctuating market strategies of commodity production. By the 1820s, the surge of the market economy and its need for workers had resulted in an appropriation of the republican ideology of patriotism. Single white women, lured by their patriotic duty as well as by a desire to escape farm life or families strapped for funds, moved into the low-paying factory jobs in industrial centers.[99] By the 1830s, the expansion of the cotton trade, coupled with the cotton planters' land acquisitions in the Lower South, caused a tremendous surge in economic activity. "Between 1831 and 1836 the value of cotton exports almost trebled, rising from $25 million to $71 million."[100] Although the process was uneven, the disparate regional expansions led to greater centralization of commodity production and specialization, eventually throwing the economy into the successive crises of 1834, the panic of 1837, and the depression of 1839.[101]

In the aftermath of the panic of 1837, when thousands of workers lost their jobs, the ideology of the cult of domesticity took on a new intensity. Black female workers were faced with the conundrum of shifting ideologies that were concomitant with the varying market strategies. While the republican ideology drew upon patriotism as its centerpiece, pulling women as wage earners into the new factories, the economic crises of the 1830s required a new ideological perch. In that sense, the cult of domesticity that presaged the displacement of women from industrial centers to their homes was integral to the capitalist fluctuations of the 1830s and expanded the space in which female workers, by then poor white and poor black women, could be exploited.

As poor white and black women—a more exploitative source of labor that would serve as part of the market's corrective measures—entered the labor force, they replaced the prior white farming class.[102] Gerda Lerner, pointing out this class rotation in the marketplace, posits that the domestic ideology "took on a certain aggressiveness and shrillness precisely at the time when increasing numbers of poorer women left their homes to become factory workers."[103] Class and race rotation, however, did not occur in the marketplace. As poor white female workers moved into the workforce, they encountered the middle-class ideology of the cult of domesticity. Forced to work, these female workers daily confronted the class cleavages in society.[104] Black female workers, unable to find jobs in the marketplace and forced to work for daily survival, became household workers as a means to an end. Since poor white female workers looked down upon domestic work and opted instead for the put-out or outwork systems essential to industrial expansion, they created the labor space for black female domestic workers. Too, many affluent employers, before the influx of Irish female domestic workers, saw the employment of black domestic workers as a measure of their status and influence. The cult of domesticity, which exacerbated the conflicts of all female workers, reinforced the race, class, and gender quagmire already existing for black female workers.

Black female workers were not only confounded by the cult of domesticity's compatibility with industrial capitalism but also with its moral lens, which associated homemakers with piety and working-class women with immoral conduct. Black women, already facing this morality question inherited as one of the by-products of the slave legacy, now

confronted the issue of virtue, albeit reshaped, in this early period of freedom. The "Jezebel" myth perpetuated under slavery, which purported
that black women were lascivious, was now reenergized under the cult
of domesticity.[105] Both economic systems—slave and market—positioned black women in the labor force, one involuntarily and the other
by necessity, and used compatible ideologies to rigidify their position
while simultaneously impugning their virtue. In giving affluent white
women the normative space within the home, and thereby legitimacy, all
working women, particularly black women, were made perverse, leaving
them vulnerable and voiceless in industrial cities. Facing antebellum freedom, black women had to combat the "Jezebel" myth, the myth of
African inferiority, gender marginalization, and their working-class status. Imprisoned by their gender, race, and class, black women, of necessity, confronted urban industrialization with nothing but their labor
power and the determination to meet the basic material necessities of life
for themselves and their families.

Black female workers confronted the burgeoning industrial moder-
nity, with its technological innovations of commodity production in the
new ready-to-wear apparel industries. As these new industries stream-
lined the production process with the specialization of tasks, they
absorbed, on a fluctuating employment basis, most of the white immigrants and migrants into the moderate- and low-paying menial jobs. Put-
out or outwork systems, which drew poor white unskilled and
semiskilled white women into commodity production and thereby into
marginalized arenas of the market system (for example, hat making,
spinning wool into yarn, weaving cloth for clothing items, shoe binding,
and sewing raw material cutouts of pants, shirts, and gloves into finished
products), rarely included black women.[106] Malveaux's comments,
though speaking of a more contemporary period, are applicable here as
well: "Though the occupational position of black women has its roots in
slavery, black women have continued to be segregated occupationally
and in different ways than are white women."[107]

By 1847, a Northern study concluded that "there was not a single
trade in which Negroes were allowed to work beside white people."[108]
Despite the divergent class differences in the industrial wage-force, all
whites, by practicing informal policies of exclusion, were able to capitalize on and benefit from racial discrimination. "Racial prejudices excluded
black women from competing in the same labor markets as whites."[109]
While black women could gain employment sometimes as chambermaids
in downtown hotels but most often as domestics in affluent households,

other services that were spawned as a result of urban expansion, such as in restaurants, schools, museums, shops, libraries, and hospitals, rarely employed them. In fact, societal proscriptions excluded African Americans from entering and utilizing these public accommodations. Despite the upheavals and flux of the new industrial workforce and the employment of thousands of workers in urban centers, race, class, and gender components underpinned black female workers' labor activity, entrenching their position in the economic structure as a permanent caste of menial workers.

Black women's labor activity in northeastern industrial centers closely paralleled their work experiences under urban and industrial slavery but provided a marked contrast in the type of jobs available to them. In the Southern labor system, the planter and urban-industrialist aristocracy controlled all labor arrangements for both poor whites and blacks. Although largely domestic workers in the rural towns or urban areas, slave men, women, and children worked in Southern tobacco factories, iron and flour mills, construction trades, and seaports under the hiring-out system. "Not infrequently, black women worked in the mine banks, and some labored in the furnace and forge."[110] Both the planter-industrialist aristocracy and Southern white urban workers were ambivalent about slave labor in industry. This "integration" of black slaves into Southern industry daunted planters, who saw an erosion of their domination and control over the slaves as well as their way of life. Equally apprehensive were white workers who perceived slave labor as a source of competition for their jobs as well as a loss of psychological superiority that white-skinned privileges afforded. In their quest to maintain hegemony over the total labor market, the planter-industrialist aristocracy, who received their most strident protest from white workers when blacks were trained at skilled jobs, made labor concessions to preserve the social order.

Despite the tremendous labor market that fueled capitalism, the entry of free black female workers into the industrial centers was tangential, fragmented, and episodic. Working primarily as domestic workers in white households or as self-employed domestic laborers, the nature and type of black women's labor activity and the limited spheres of labor centers stagnated black women's industrial development. "Excluded by their sex from skilled jobs, and harassed because of their race by even the newest immigrants, free black women normally found themselves confined to the most onerous jobs."[111] As peripheral laborers, however, black women were not only intrinsic to the means of economic production, particularly as domestic workers for the affluent, but also were defined and bound, as were all workers, by the growth, spurt, and changes of the production process. In fact, there was a definite correlation between the market's contractions and expansions and black women's labor activity, with market fluctuations directly impacting their lives. Contractions and crises in the market system forced affluent classes to conserve their expenditures, reducing full-time domestic workers to part-time service, thus leaving black women seeking additional "day's work" to supplement the loss of wages. The typical $2.50 to $4.00 weekly wages, now reduced to $1.00 to $2.00, made it necessary for these women to seek other sources of income. Being located on the periphery of industrial expansion and being at the intersection of the pernicious forces of race, class, gender, and work discrimination, black women were at the vortex of oppression.

The irony of black women's location in the marketplace was that it was in stark contrast to the inherent long-term flexibility of capitalism for white male workers. As the stratification of society was being destabilized for white males entering the market system, it was simultaneously being rigidified for black women. The marketplace for black women, largely reflective of society's caste, class, and racial culture, was inflexible. Because black women were members of groups whose value was predetermined in the colonial era and expanded under industrialization, their worth was not only eclipsed in the marketplace, but the combination of racial stigmas, class, gender, and work discrimination rendered them invisible in antebellum society. Representing the obverse side of the tremendous technological progress that enlarged the possibility of wealth for all white males, black women were instead a critical component of the racial, gender, and class cleavages that transcended preindustrial development, becoming an integral feature of urban industrialization and the proletarianization of the labor force.[112] In contrast to the expanding urban regionalism taking place, these social conflicts were integrated in the new market system, diminishing the earning capacities of women, blacks, and the poor and relegating black women to the bottom of the labor structure. Ironically, their poor wages, onerous work conditions, and menial jobs subtly served as the bellwether for the exploitation of all poor female workers.

Black women's labor activity under urban industrialization was pregnant with the promise of jobs, stable familial ties, and community structures, expectations brought on by the major shifts in the societal economic structure. Their steady trek to northeastern port cities held dreams larger than their definitive places in society. They dreamed lives of freedom, with families and a vibrant social and secular life that defined a place in society for all African Americans. Instead, free and enslaved African American women were caught up in the economic maelstrom of the antebellum era, including the expanding cotton trade, the new market economy, and urban industrialization. In the Lower South, female slaves' labor activity and reproductive capacity bolstered the cotton trade and industrial expansion and the meteoric rise in cotton prices in the 1830s, which stimulated more land acquisition and slave production by cotton planters. The Northern articulation of the collusion between planters and industrialists resulted in a racial and gender oppression that marginalized black women's labor activity in industrial centers. Free black female laborers combated the consequences of their slave legacy, their perceived immoral character, and the contemporary social stigmas associated with working women in the free market system, as ideologies shifted to meet the capitalist ethos.

GENDER, LABOR, AND BLACK WOMEN IN CITIES

Although the initial stages of capitalist expansion broadened the economic potential and social class status of white males, creating almost unlimited opportunities for material success, it simultaneously exacerbated the racial and gender constructions of the colonial era. During this transitional phase, from colonial household sufficiency production to capitalist commodity production, the marginalization of women in the workplace paralleled the racial and gender subordination of women in the larger society. Prior to capitalist development, colonists engaged in household sufficiency production, producing the necessities for their extended family unit and limited consumer products for local, regional, and national markets as well.[113] Within this household production system, white women and colonial slaves were essential labor units operating under the supervision of the dominant male of the household. This class-stratified society, which offered colonists with limited means few options for financial success, was transformed with the advent of the market system. Under the market system and its newly constituted industrial workforce, the colonial structure of household sufficiency was transferred to manufacturing centers of mass production, offering white men who engaged in factory commodity production an opportunity to accumulate wealth and power.[114] "The development of capitalism established equality of rights between all white men, extending to all the freedom to self-advancement."[115] While capitalism made episodic progress in the early stages, disparate classes of white men, no longer constrained by a class-stratified society, could now participate equally in the industrial labor force.

Capitalism dichotomized the lives of men and women into separate spheres of influence, men to focus on economic competitiveness and accumulation and women to supervise and maintain the domicile.[116] While the new labor system offered white men almost endless economic opportunities in their quest for wealth—"Everywhere Americans seemed enmeshed in an obsessive pursuit of wealth"—it routinely diminished and marginalized women's economic value and their position in the labor system.[117] By capitalism encouraging white men in a ruthless competitiveness and endless jockeying to obtain power, position, and influence, the labor system proved limiting in only offering this specific labor segment its benefits. Those white men who were successful competitors were deluded into thinking that they had meritoriously arrived at the pinnacle of success rather than acknowledging that the market restricted everyone else's participation. The economic shift from household production to factory labor meant that the home production process, particularly of textiles, which had previously been under the domain of women, left women estranged from the factories or workplaces.[118] The "genderizing" of labor during the transitional stages led not only to the subsequent marginalization of women's work but also to the exploitative sexual division of labor in the new marketplace for those women who were forced to labor outside of their homes.

The market shifts of labor power and economic production, locating women in now marginal household workplaces and placing white men in pivotal centers of production, appreciably diminished women's utilitarian value as laborers. With industrial prosperity and the rise of affluent classes, urban middle-class women became increasingly absorbed into the domestic sphere.[119] While the relegation of women to the home certainly predated capitalism in American society (although women were formerly connected to the labor market by their commercial production), this new emphasis on female domesticity took on the trappings of a cult under capitalist expansion, particularly with the removal of men from the home to public spheres of economic influence. "The result of the emergence of the family as a social sphere," observes Julie A. Matthaei, "was not only the constitution of homemaking as an important social vocation, but also as a social vocation reserved exclusively for women."[120] The subsequent emergence of this cult of domesticity placed middle-class women well within the boundaries of gender conventions and away from the white male—dominated economic sanctuary of commodity production. To subscribe to the cult of domesticity, however, with its manifold trappings of family and home management and its very real estrangement of women from possible economic independence and a sense of their self-worth, women had to be either a part of the urban middle class or, most certainly, upwardly mobile middle-class aspirants.

Philanthropic causes, which centered on regenerative missions among the city's poor in the 1800s, could be attributed, in large measure, to middle-class women seeking gendered social outlets and a validation of their own worthiness away from the centers of production. The reinforcement of middle-class cultural values as the proscribed norm in social causes, while it led to conflict between the middle class and the poor, sanctioned the self-validation of middle-class women in a shifting economic structure. Poor people were placed in the dubious position of needing social services yet having their private lives discussed and scrutinized as if they were invisible. In their zeal to justify their own shaky status in a vacillating capitalist system, urban middle-class women failed to take stock of the fact that poor white working women contended with a lifetime of seasonal paychecks, malnourished children, substandard housing, and poor health care, as well as the worry and stress frequently associated with women working outside of the home. Inevitably, class resentment and distinctions between the poor and the uptown "swells" intensified, creating ideological and gender divisions among white women and frustrating poor white women's survival efforts. In the marketplace, where male economic activity was dominant, poor white working women did not have the support of middle-class women, reinforcing a gendered division of labor supporting the marginalization of women in commodity production.[121]

Poor white female workers, who had greater access to the market system than did black women, still faced the crippling effects of a "genderized" market. Most of these laborers moved into the market system either as marginal factory workers or outworkers, completing items of clothing or other goods for a manufacturer for a fixed rate at home. Within the factories, job categories and occupations were now being reclassified. Jobs such as spinning and weaving, for example, which had been female preserves in colonial households, were now shared equally by men and women in factories.[122] In New England cities and towns, where textile and shoe-binding factories were developed, these job sites "created work for a predominantly female labor force" averaging $3.50 per week.[123] There were rare instances when black women could get these jobs. While her husband, the abolitionist Frederick Douglass, was away on extended lecture tours, Anna Douglass maintained the family by working as a shoe binder in a New England factory. More than likely, it was her antislavery connections and influence that made her an exception to the prevailing rule. Although these factory jobs offered low pay, tedium, and long hours, such work did provide social contacts, bonding, and, for migrant single women, communal living arrangements among other female workers.[124]

Outworkers, on the other hand, were largely married women who could care for children and home and at the same time complete their factory assignments. While many of these women did sewing at home, a study of white female workers from New York City's Five Points—considered by many to be the city's worse district—indicated that some "braided hats, made buttons, or rolled cigars" as outworkers to supplement family income.[125] Businessmen employed thousands of outworkers, enabling manufacturers to lower production and labor costs and increase the profit margin, although their significance in capitalist expansion may have been vastly underrated. "By 1860, the renowned Brooks Brothers, for instance, employed 70 workers inside and 2,000 to 3,000 on the outside."[126] Outworkers, often at the mercy and whim of the manufacturers, would receive little or no pay when returning assigned work if the job did not meet the employers' work specifications or if employers thought that they could get away with the exploitation of these female workers. In both instances, women performed tedious tasks for substandard wages.

The struggle that characterized poor white female workers was far more daunting in the lives of black male and female workers who were not only racialized in the marketplace but, because of their limited options, were always bordering on the brink of impoverishment. Black women and men shared a common oppression that severely limited their job possibilities. "Segregation, employment discrimination, disfranchisement, and restrictions on personal freedom circumscribed their lives."[127] Studies on the job prospects of Northern blacks revealed the pervasiveness of racial discrimination. "There was not a single trade in which Negroes were allowed to work beside white people. They were banished to the galleries of menial labor."[128] New York City officials refused to grant licenses to black men to become cartmen and draymen, claiming that they wished to protect them from the abuse of white men. The discrimination against black cartmen was not just prevalent in New York

City, however, but was widespread throughout the North, excluding black men from this line of business. The discrimination was still pervasive in 1851 when the *African Repository* reported that "rarely is he allowed to drive a cart or public conveyance. White men will not work with him."[129]

The majority of black female workers were employed in "domestic service in the homes of an increasingly affluent urban middle class."[130] These household workers contributed a vital part of the family's income, in many instances the only income for much of the year, as the family struggled to get by. "Black women returning from domestic jobs in the homes of the wealthy provided crucial sources of income for many households."[131] Some black female workers worked in a variety of white households on a per diem basis. "By 1847," Sharon Harley notes, "the majority of black Philadelphia women were washerwomen and domestic servants, numbering 2,085 of a total female population of 4,249." Additionally, black women, while experiencing gender discrimination in common with white female workers, found that they were excluded from factory jobs and outwork partly because of the racial attitudes of white women.[132] Undoubtedly, employers fostered this division as one method of lowering all workers' wages, while white women discriminated against black women by threatening owners with reprisals if black women were employed. Collectively, these white factory workers and their employers collaborated in sustaining the existing racial and gender divisions that constrained black women's labor activity.

The marginalization of black women with respect to the industrial labor centers dealt a severe blow to their labor potential in urban cities. The tenuous collusion of white employers and employees, across gender lines, characterized much of the racial discrimination of the era and operated to exclude black women from the main centers of industrial activity. However, two developments emerged as a result of these exclusionary labor practices. First, free black women's labor actually undergirded the industrialization upon which the social and political activities and ultimately the economic activity of affluent white women rested. Second, by black women becoming the primary source of household labor in white households, affluent white women's development and enlargement of the domestic sphere to include philanthropic causes and political activism became possible. It was capitalist expansion, which slave women's labor power had figured in significantly, that created the burgeoning upper classes that required domestic services.

Christine Stansell notes the gender and class shifts as middle- and upper-class white women hired domestic workers. "The disengagement of mistresses from household labor gave them a great deal of leisure for shopping, entertaining, making calls and working for evangelical and charity associations."[133] These affluent women benefited directly from black women's slave labor, which fueled industrialization, and from free black women's labor, which allowed for the development and maintenance of white women's domestic sphere. While affluent white women's lives of privilege depended upon black women's labor and poor white immigrant domestic workers by the 1840s, it is equally true that the affluent classes in general were able to flourish because of the urban proletariat, slavery, the slave trade, and the marginalization of poor white women in the industrial sectors. When one peers across the chasm of antebellum racial and gender relations, racial and class boundaries were necessary ideological constructs that maintained the existing social order.

Black women were politicized by their labor activity via slavery and the new market economy. In large measure, black women's labor, which defined their social and economic place in society, became the essential aspect of their womanhood. In this way, they became interpreters of their own material reality.[134] Black women's detachment from mainstream industrial activity shaped their perception of middle-class conventional norms not only by the pervasive ideology but also by their observations of the intimate superordinate-subordinate familial relationships and realities of middle-class life. As with their slave experiences, black women were able to perceive the tenuous circumstances circumscribing white women's privilege. "Forced to labor outside of the home, black women's reality was contrary to conventional ideals of the era that emphasized women's domesticity. These standards automatically pitted black women against the norm that characterized and shaped white women's lives."[135] While there were many middle-class aspirants in black communities, to be sure, material realities placed black women in opposition to all of the ideological precepts that formulated the cult of domesticity. Undoubtedly causing stress and conflict as black women questioned their own womanhood, these contradictions also allowed black women to create their own values of the worth and dignity of women's labor and reconstituted the social and political actualization and context for a self-defining womanhood. Black women's tangible benefits from slavery and industrialization were meager, but these interlocking systems of labor served as the linchpins for their economic, social, and political agenda.

CHAPTER 4

As Quiet as It's Kept

Black Women's Urban Economic Activity and Empowerment

> If, then, women were to answer the challenge of the new economy and place themselves again among the producers of the world, they must change their status from that of home makers to that of industrial workers and change their activities from valueless home duties to those that resulted in the production of goods that have a price-value.
>
> SADIE TANNER MOSSELL ALEXANDER, 1930

MUCH OF BLACK WOMEN'S ECONOMIC STRUGGLES, INITIATIVES, and enterprises provided the impetus for black community development. In that sense, black women's economic empowering process captured the realities, dreams, and imaginations of black city dwellers. Influenced by the collective struggle for daily survival, the hope of an improved quality of life for their children, the education and uplift of the community, or the success of owning their own business, black women sought economic survival, autonomy, and a measure of independence that would allow them to mitigate their adverse circumstances. Black women's economic empowerment hinged as much on the material realities that shaped the collective struggles of black people in urban areas as it did on their colonial and contemporary economic relationships to the market system. In the midst of societal transitions, black migration, and the marginalization of blacks and women was economic life. Economic life—whether it was the vacillating job market, overcrowded and substandard housing, or shopping for provisions with a steady eye kept on an increasingly shrinking budget—was harsh for poor city dwellers. But it was almost insurmountable for black urbanites who were consistently threatened with the far-reaching tentacles of slavery and the intransigence of

Northern racism. In his study of the economic status of New York City blacks, Robert Ernst indicates that their "wages failed to keep pace with rising rents and the prices of provisions, while in depression years, as in 1857, unemployment swelled the relief rolls."[1] Ironically, some scholars contend, blacks were not better off economically in the North. Despite the northern migration of blacks for jobs and freedom from oppression, Leonard P. Curry's perusal of city directories between 1800 and 1850 led him to conclude that "employment opportunities for blacks were clearly superior in the Lower South cities, worst in those of New England, and better in the urban centers of the Upper South than in New York and the Lower South."[2]

Despite the collection of forces that combined to stultify black economic development and marginalize free black workers' participation in the market system, a number of black entrepreneurs created "pockets of grace," thereby broadening opportunities for their singular financial success while securing black communities' economic foundation. "Tailors, shoemakers, carpenters, sawyers, tinsmiths, coopers, cabinetmakers and upholsterers, nurses, cigar makers, and jewelers accounted for . . . 107 Negro working people of varying degrees of skill."[3] As blacks attempted to forge footholds in urban centers, black economic development evinced measured gains during the antebellum years. For many black communities, these economic enterprises symbolized black pride, an emerging group consciousness, self-reliance, and the desire on the part of these entrepreneurs to participate in the economic life of the nation.

The earliest records of black female entrepreneurship were of Sara Noblitt, who in 1771 applied for a license to operate a public house.[4] Although Noblitt was refused the license, the application does indicate that free black Northern women saw themselves as entrepreneurs and contributing economic members of black communities. Elleanor Eldridge of Rhode Island "transformed a variety of gender-based domestic and manufacturing activities into profit-making enterprises." Eldridge ran her whitewashing and soap-manufacturing enterprises while she simultaneously held such occupations as a nurse, mattress maker, and domestic worker.[5] Invariably, working as common laborers as well as independent economic entrepreneurs proved catalytic for black women by the 1830s, creating pathways for their political activism.

Black entrepreneurship dated back to the early 1700s, and, in large measure, antebellum black entrepreneurs benefited from the black artisan labor force of the late 1700s and early 1800s, where some free blacks, but mostly slaves, labored as unskilled workers and skilled artisans in northeastern cities, towns, and surrounding rural areas.[6] By practicing a diversity of occupations in this period, some black artisans and their descendents were able to establish their own business enterprises. "Two black New Yorkers converted employment opportunities available to chimney sweepers into a successful business venture with the establishment of the partnership of Jackson and Smith in 1825, an enterprise that operated a century later under the name George Smith and Son."[7] Black artisans were employed in such occupations as tanners, maritime laborers, ironworkers, blacksmiths, stonecutters, carpenters, printers, caterers, seamstresses, goldsmiths, grocers, silversmiths, and shoemakers.[8]

Leonard Stavinsky contends that the skills of many black artisans originated in Africa, particularly those skilled in working with ivory, bone, iron, wood, and gold. Many of the skills displayed by black women were also honed in Africa. "Many were spinners and seamstresses; others made soap and starch and dyed clothing."[9] In some instances, blacks who were engaged in skilled occupations were already self-employed. "There were fifteen free blacks listed as following the shoemaking trade in Philadelphia in 1819; seven shoemakers and eight cordwainers."[10] Free blacks were also able to become shoemakers in New York City. In the same year, 1819, free Philadelphia blacks were practicing the blacksmithing craft. Some black entrepreneurs did not engage in only a single enterprise. For example, Richard Allen, the first bishop of the African Methodist Episcopal (AME) Church, combined several business enterprises, undoubtedly initially to make ends meet, but several eventually prospered. Allen, who owned his blacksmith shop where the Free African Society first met, was copartnered with Absalom Jones, one of the cofounders of the Free African Society and the founding pastor of St. Thomas's Methodist Episcopal Church in 1794, in a nail factory business. "He, moreover, owned a chimney sweep business, a livery stable, and had rental property throughout Philadelphia."[11]

Even with the persistence of racial discrimination and slavery in the pre-Revolutionary and post-Revolutionary periods, Whittington B. Johnson contends that the early national years, 1750–1830, were the "promising years" for blacks, creating opportunities for employment in the skilled trades and business enterprises.[12] The significant industrial expansion in that period, which created opportunities for the domestic production of manufactured goods through household sufficiency production on farms or plantations, artisan production, early factory conversions into mass-producing mills, or iron works, stimulated an increased demand for black laborers in unskilled, semiskilled, and skilled jobs.

The movement of black workers into nonagricultural industries correlated with their availability as a cheap labor supply for white entrepreneurs. Many white entrepreneurs purchased slaves who served as apprentices in their business, and a system that Butler calls "intrapreneurship" developed, when skilled slaves operated and managed businesses for their owners.[13] Urban slaves who were hired out by their masters for a fixed period frequently worked in the nonagricultural sector of the economy. When slaves accumulated monies from the utilization of their hired time or from side deals negotiated with owners or employers as incentives, Walker observes that these monies became a source of venture capital to purchase freedom for family members and themselves.[14] Free black workers, working alongside slaves, were often placed in competition with hired-out slaves and a tiny pool of white workers and forced to work for low wages, causing "blacks to monopolize many occupations because of the complementary interests of black laborers and white entrepreneurs." Black women who were hired out by their masters to work in cotton factories and who were noted as exceptional workers would find that, as free antebellum women, these same factory jobs would be unavailable. "In July 1827, Ivy Cotton Works in Baltimore County, Maryland, presented a black female employee 'a beautiful dress' and two others received handsome shawls for their exceptional productivity."[15]

Just as important as the needs and demands associated with developing businesses and free market growth in the early national period, blacks' monopoly of some occupations could be directly attributed to the small numbers of whites who were in competition with slaves and free blacks for skilled, semiskilled, and unskilled jobs of arduous labor. Ironically, before the successive waves of white immigrants seeking jobs in northeastern cities in the 1840s and 1850s, there were laws in some states restricting whites from their engagement in certain forms of menial labor.[16] The lack of white competition for these jobs, coupled with the fact that whites were self-employed artisans, journeymen, or farmers or shunned work perceived as "servile labor," thereby maintaining their superior status, provided blacks with more than limited access to the diversity of jobs and enterprises.

Northern manumission laws and postabolition apprenticeships for newly freed slaves in many cases allowed black workers to continue the same trades mastered in Africa or during slavery and were also contributing factors to a diversification of black male laborers in skilled and unskilled employment. After slavery and varied forms of indentured servitude, free Northern blacks were able to develop business enterprises, particularly in the areas of personal service, including catering, barbering, midwifery, and domestic service, as those whites seeking work in the industrial sector would view these occupations to be beneath them. All of these personal service occupations, however, placed blacks as the "invisible ear" to the negotiations of business, politics, and personal affairs of the white establishment and thus vital sources of information to black communities.[17] Abram Harris noted that "in personal service enterprises, the free Negroes had practically no competition . . . And the fact that white persons tended to avoid enterprises of this character because of their servile status gave free Negroes an advantage in this sphere."[18]

If Johnson's thesis is correct, that the early national period provided more economic opportunities for blacks than at any other time in the nineteenth and early twentieth centuries, it points us in the direction of the shifting economic spectrum for blacks by the time of the antebellum era.[19] The economic picture had changed appreciably regarding blacks' access to jobs and business activities by the 1830s and 1840s. The increasing industrial expansionism in the cities and the concomitant reconstitution of the labor force, as white workers left farms and rural areas in the United States and Europe to resettle as wage laborers in Northern cities and factory towns, forced the marginalization of black workers in the marketplace. Circumscribed by social and economic proscriptions, black economic life was severely curtailed. Even with this intense marginalization process, however, such business enterprises as hairdressers, millers, seamstresses, tailors, bakers, and caterers remained an established economic niche for black entrepreneurs.

"Throughout the North, Afro-Americans engaged in food service businesses, but in no city were they as successful as in Philadelphia where they gained a wide reputation for their excellent confectionaries, restaurants, and catering services."[20] Renowned for her excellent cooking, Rachel Lyon of Philadelphia operated her restaurant from 1808 until midcentury. Cornelia Gomez, owned and operated a catering business for wealthy whites in New York City. Katie Ferguson, noted for her work among poor children in the city, took over Gomez's enterprise, garnered a broad-based clientele from her reputation as a pastry chef, and maintained the business operation until the 1850s.[21] Black female entrepreneurs were also successful in other economic initiatives. Grace Bustill Douglass, another Philadelphia entrepreneur, following in the independent footsteps of her father, Cyrus Bustill, who owned and operated a bakery, "learned a trade and operated a millinery store from her Arch Street home."[22] Douglass was able to combine her business enterprise and abolitionist activities from her home. Sarah Eddy, the daughter of Richard Allen, combined a dressmaking and millinery business. Similarly, Henrietta Bowers of Philadelphia, the wife of one of Philadelphia's better-known tailors, was a dressmaker. A female entrepreneur in Boston, Chloe Spear utilized her skills as a laundress and boardinghouse keeper to accumulate enough capital to purchase her own home.[23]

Nancy Gardner Prince's journey of self-discovery and spiritual redemption illuminates the economic plight and enterprising potential of black women who were born in post-Revolutionary America and lived to be influenced by the urbanization, industrialization, and reformist ethos permeating the antebellum era. In 1824, when she was a twenty-five-year-old domestic worker, she married Nero Prince, a widower. "Prince was a man of standing in black New England, a grand master of the Prince Hall Masonic Lodge and a sailor who had spent a dozen years as a footman at the court of the Russian czar."[24] The couple emigrated to St. Petersburg, where Prince experienced freedom from oppression for the first time in her life: "there was no prejudice against color; there were there all casts, and the people of all nations, each in their place." Conversant in the Russian language after six months, she owned and operated a profitable business selling children's garments and enjoyed the patronage of Russian nobility.[25]

Prince was forced to return to the United States because she could no longer endure the harsh Russian winters, and her life became strikingly similar to those of other urban black women. With the death of her husband in Russia before he could rejoin her in the States, Prince's life began its downward economic spiral. Despite her autobiography's concentration on her life in Russia and her evangelical missionary work in the West Indies, she was barely able to make ends meet in Boston until she found work with antislavery advocates.[26] In 1853, Prince, financially destitute, followed in the tradition of other black female evangelists and wrote a narrative of her life. For Prince, racial oppression in a capitalist society shaped her financial fortunes in the United States just as much as the freedom from that oppression in Russia allowed her to capitalize on her talents.

By the 1830s, the limited economic access blacks had to business activities and the entrenched racism in northeastern cities, particularly as the black population was increasing, created an alternative economic and class structure within black communities, grouping a tiny elite of skilled laborers, professionals, and entrepreneurs at one end of the economic spectrum and the masses, the majority of black unskilled workers, at the other end. Still, black entrepreneurship persisted and developed. An 1838 Philadelphia analysis of the census data indicated that there was diversity among black female occupations. The most common included 1,071 washers, 309 service providers, 581 domestics, 150 dressmakers, 67 seamstresses, and 30 shopkeepers. Black women were also included among the hucksters, hairdressers, cooks. Additionally, black women were also listed as boardinghouse proprietors, biscuit makers, nurses, milliners, and midwives. "A Register of Trades of Colored People in the City of Philadelphia and Districts" listed 57 occupations that black Philadelphians held that year. Black female Philadelphians owned and operated a number of businesses, including 81 dressmakers and seamstresses, 4 dyers and scourers, 2 fullers, and 2 papermakers.[27]

Within the spectrum of diversity among black entrepreneurs, some occupations were commonplace. Referring to antebellum black entrepreneurship in Boston, Horton and Horton observe that "to be a hairdresser, a barber, a blacksmith, or a used-clothing dealer, the most common skilled or entrepreneurial occupation among blacks, was to be a person of relatively high standing in the community." Hairdressers like Edward Bannister before he became a renowned artist, or grocers like John Henry, or clothing-shop owners like Thomas Smith or Lewis Hayden were all part of Boston's rising black elite.[28] David Walker, who penned the *Appeal to the Coloured Citizens of the World,* a treatise advocating the right of violence and, more specifically, slave rebellions, was a successful clothing dealer and an integral part of Boston's respected black community. By placing the incendiary pamphlet "in the ample pockets of the jackets and trousers he sold to sailors bound for Southern ports," Walker was able to use his business to disseminate this militant material to Southern antislavery activists and slaves.[29]

Black entrepreneurs like Stephen Smith and Joseph Cassey of Philadelphia and Peter Van Dyke of New York City, who were moneylenders extending money and credit to finance other business enterprises in black communities, were a critical resource for black economic development. These moneylenders operated in support of the numerous mutual aid societies, which also made small loans to developing entrepreneurs, and collectively fostered the black community's economic development and expansion. Actually, moneylenders and budding entrepreneurs shared common interests and needs. Since budding entrepreneurs had limited options that they could explore for capital, these revenue sources in the community proved vital in establishing business linkages, networking, and the ultimate success of their enterprise. On the other hand, successful black entrepreneurs had few options for the investment of their surplus capital, as racism prohibited their participation in the stock market or in the banking system.[30] "It is related that a mulatto who attempted to deal on the New York Stock Exchange was denied the privilege."[31]

Having established successful enterprises and seeking to invest the revenues from those businesses, this small black elite was constantly reminded of the difficulties of fledging entrepreneurs. These financial difficulties became the paramount concern of the 1851 black convention meeting in New York. A banking proposal was introduced for a black mutual savings bank that would extend blacks credit for mortgages and business development. Integral to this banking initiative was the conventioneers' eyes on the $60,000 that blacks had in New York banks that they hoped would underwrite the new bank's dealings in real estate, mortgages, financial loans, and bonds. Although the 1855 convention, again meeting in New York, highlighted the same issue and a similar plan was evolving in Philadelphia, the proposal never went beyond the preliminary stages. The lack of development of a broad-based financial institution to underwrite community enterprises meant that black moneylenders played an increasingly critical role in the community's economic development. But their monies could not facilitate or stimulate the vital growth that was necessary to stabilize segregated enclaves on the periphery of economic expansion.

While black entrepreneurship was powered by individual and collective determination as well as by the desire to achieve economic prosperity, the gains for the group, despite all of the plans, tedious work, and effort, were measured at best. Blacks had to overcome racism; limited access to capital, credit, and networking systems; frequent antiblack riots that always destroyed property in black communities; and fierce labor competition between black and white laborers, which proved to be strong and persistent factors thwarting black economic development. As Jean Matthews notes, "Their exclusion from participating fully in this culture, the disabilities that prevented them from achieving in its terms, was felt acutely and personally as deprivation of freedom and as humiliation."[32] While individual entrepreneurs were to be commended for their tenacity and determination, they also reflected the disillusionment and frustrations, along with the impetus and inspirations, of the total community. Still, the majority of black workers had few opportunities and had to be singularly concerned with living from day to day. Mutual aid associations, with their strong emphasis on financial assistance, for most African Americans became the economic support system that allowed them to endure. Juliet E. K. Walker comments on black business initiatives during the antebellum era: "The existence of black entrepreneurship, both slave and free, provides an example of an economic arrangement in this nation's . . . free enterprise system that was fundamentally capitalist . . . Afro-Americans, were not fundamentally free."[33]

Despite the quasi-citizenship status, the immediacy of earning a living confronted black urban dwellers. For black women, single or married, jobs to augment the family's income were of dire necessity. The problem confronting black women, who were viewed as a cheap, unskilled labor supply primarily of household workers, was how to transform their skills and their marginal places in the urban marketplace into economic initiatives that would ensure them survival and some measure of independence. As black women sought some dignity as laborers, they were largely utilizing the Northern racial proscriptions as their stepping stones.

BLACK WOMEN'S ECONOMIC EMPOWERMENT

At the same time that northeastern market expansion and industrialization excluded black female laborers from mainstream industrial centers, black female workers were creating alternative economic initiatives for survival, independence, and autonomy. As peripheral workers to the industrializing process, black female workers were forced to utilize their own creativity and initiatives to ensure the economic survival of their families. Whether they labored as skilled, semiskilled, or unskilled workers, black female workers broadened their workspace, creating a measure of autonomy where they could operationalize their labor will as an integral component of the community's urban resistance. Ironically, the alienation from industry proved catalytic for black female workers who, confined to more flexible labor spaces than contemporary factory wage laborers, were able to reconstitute workspaces for self-empowerment.

Industrialization, then, provided an impetus for black women's economic development. By relocating the sphere of black women's labor activities to homes of the wealthy and to their own homes and communities, black women had sufficient autonomous space to enable them to impose their labor will over the spheres of their work activities. In some sense, because the nature and type of labor activity were not altered substantially from their labor will activities in slave communities, black women transformed the venue of their labor will to their work centers, there to become self-empowerment tools while simultaneously meeting the critical income needs of their families. The extension of their labor universe constituted the initial stages of black women's self-empowerment in urban areas. As they launched these economic initiatives that appeared menial from society's vantage point, black women empowered themselves with a measure of independence and lent meaning and dignity to their lives and the lives of those around them.

Whether they were laboring as domestic workers, plying their economic acumen in the black community, using the urban streets as their "market system," or combining various economic enterprises, black women were able to become valuable economic contributors to their families. In a time and place when most black men were employed in sporadic menial jobs, the wages of married black women augmented a shrinking family income. Employing various methods of "survival economics," black female workers embraced a full range of occupations that included domestic workers, street peddlers, hucksters, cooks, laundresses, food vendors, seamstresses, milliners, hairdressers, and boardinghouse keepers. Those who were particularly hard-pressed with no other means of a livelihood attempted to eke out a living as ragpickers.[34] Even single black women, who comprised the majority of the black inmigration flow to urban areas, were able to earn subsistence monies in the urban marketplace and have a few shinplasters (privately issued paper money) to spare. A few black women even managed to prosper. Lodging with black families in their dwellings, homes, or boardinghouses that were usually managed by women, single women's rental charges supplemented families' incomes while providing a measure of economic independence for the women themselves. Although black female workers' incomes were, by and large, meager and families were constantly chasing the wolves away from the door, the pooling of household economic resources often made the critical difference between impoverishment and getting by.

Black and white women were moving into community spaces at the same time, and both were seeking self-validation. But white middle-class women were seeking a validation of their identity from the larger society, whereas black women's influence in black communities emanated from their labor productivity. "Wages that were crucial to the family's survival altered conventional decision-making patterns within the family structure . . . This additional power and influence gained in the decision-making process resulted in increased visibility of black women in community life."[35] Using their economic activity as a springboard for community activism, black women used both informal and formal social networks to create a base for their overlapping economic, political, and social activism. This developing political consciousness, derived from the material realities of their lives, was a well-honed "tradition of resistance" which "suggests that a distinctive collective black women's consciousness exist[ed]."[36] Their social activism led black females into entrepreneurial activity, frequently combining both economic and political activities. Despite the economic barriers that they confronted on a daily basis, black female entrepreneurs "skillfully deflected these psychological attacks on their personhood, their adulthood, their dignity, these attempts to lure them into accepting employers' definition of them as inferior."[37]

HOUSEHOLD WORKERS

Ironically, the peripheral space created for black women's labor activity depended upon several contributing factors, including industrial expansion, the corresponding rise of the upper classes and their perennial search for "good help," and the shunning of domestic work by poor white women. By the mid-1840s, black women's monopoly of domestic work was threatened by the flood of Irish female immigrants seeking live-in domestic service in urban areas. Yet even with this strong competition, 49 percent of the black women in Philadelphia were still employed as washerwomen and domestic servants in 1847. But Irish female workers did make a significant penetration into full-time domestic service, and by the end of the 1840s they had captured approximately 25 percent of the available live-in jobs. By 1855, in New York City, however, where there was a strong Irish working-class population, 50 percent of black women still worked as domestics.[38]

Black women's participation in domestic service was mired in the complexities of confronting their own social and psychological dislocation anxieties resulting from urbanization, the critical economic needs of family life, and the imperious demands of white mistresses in affluent households. Largely a fluid labor arrangement, these workers were often at the mercy of their employers, and frequently the interplay between mistress and domestic servants mirrored the superordinate-subordinate racial relationships in society. Domestic servants found that their duties were often ambiguous and turned upon such factors as the existing number of household servants, the size and quality of the home, whether the employer had recently arrived—nouveau riche—or inherited money, and the capriciousness, self-esteem, and security of the mistress. Domestics in homes with several servants generally had the advantage of doing specific, assigned tasks. In these instances, black women who were cooks were responsible for preparing all of the family meals, which included shopping for provisions on a daily, biweekly, or weekly basis; doing the time-consuming food preparation; making numerous trips to the fire hydrant in the street for water, as all homes still did not have indoor plumbing; and waiting upon the family while serving the daily meals.[39] Most often, the family's entertainment schedule placed an additional burden on the cook, who supervised the additional kitchen staff. Cooks frequently used the family's entertainment schedule as a means of bringing in friends, relatives, or friends of friends who were seeking work.

Black female domestics found that their duties could become more burdensome and tedious if they were the sole household worker. While they searched "for the coveted 'day work,'" where workers went home at the end of the day and had a respite from the around-the-clock demands of live-in domestics, black women took whatever they could find.[40] Live-in domestics, averaging $1.00–$1.50 per week in addition to room and board, soon found that, despite the initial interviews and the somewhat pretentious description of expectations and responsibilities, they were "maids for all seasons" and greatly exploited as workers. As Elizabeth Clark-Lewis notes in her study of black domestic workers, "Each woman remembered being taken to the employer, who then lectured her on the definition of a 'good servant' . . . The introduction unfailingly emphasized the employer's lofty status, unparalleled standards, grand moral obligations, and unbounded benevolence."[41]

Whether they were day workers or live-in domestics, the general domestic duties included washing and ironing; shopping for provisions; preparing, cooking, and serving the meals; making all of the beds; polishing all of the silver; dusting, sweeping, and cleaning all of the rooms; drawing water from the hydrants on the street; building and banking of fires; and endless "fetch and carry" errands for the mistress of the household. For day workers, quitting time and salaries often varied, and, particularly around quitting time, they were frequently subjected to numerous duties that were improvised on the spot by the mistress, seeking to exact as much work as possible from her employee. In contrast to the frequent complaint of affluent white women to anyone within hearing range that "good help is hard to find," domestic workers were consistently exploited. Frequent medical complaints of domestic workers—swelling of hands, ankles, and feet; aching joints; and persistent lower back pain—can be attributed to their backbreaking labor under the critical eye of the mistress.[42]

In sharp contrast to the drudgery of domestic work, not very different from household labor in slavery, the intimacy of the workplace afforded black female domestic servants an embryonic class-gender analysis of white women's real and perceived power vis-à-vis black domestics and white males. "Live-in domestics, for their part, saw the white household as a weapon in the hands of the white woman. Many of the tyrannical indignities imposed on domestics by their mistresses came about because employers were cautioned against creating a kinder, more humane environment."[43] As survival tactics in this workspace, black female workers maintained an "inner consciousness," which Darlene Clark Hine perceives as "a culture of dissemblance, to protect the sanctity of inner aspects of their lives," affording psychological buffers or a cloak of invisibility for black women with which to assess and grapple with their material realities.[44] Affluent white women, who were largely protected from the exigencies of gender exploitation as long as they remained within the confines of the home, mirrored the superordinate-subordinate power relations between capitalists and workers, mistresses and slaves, blacks and whites, that pivoted upon economics, power, control, and domination. These household centers of labor activity, which turned upon the white mistress's perceptions of power, duty, and mission and her quest to control some aspect of her life, also characterized the ingrained superiority that white women brought to all relations with black women. Engaged in the white male patriarchal structure for the material rewards that were garnered by racial superiority and class privileges, the supercilious "mistress behavior" widened the racial and class schisms already developing between these two groups of women.

Some scholars, like Jeanne Boydston, have correctly argued that hiring domestics did not free aspiring white middle-class women from the drudgery of housework, and these mistresses often viewed domestics as an extra pair of hands in the sharing of household duties.[45] In the antebellum era, where the emerging professional middle classes were seeking an economic perch in society, those women and domestic servants jointly shared household labor. Those more solidly based in the middle class, however, held different perspectives of household duties and domestics, hiring help specifically to escape household chores, thereby facilitating the housework with supervision as opposed to labor. In these instances, labor relationships turned as much upon power, control, and establishing superiority as they did on the performance of household duties. Indeed, the household duties became the context in which middle-class mistresses could actualize their superior status, deriving smug satisfaction from being able to purchase someone else's labor power.

The hiring of black domestics, then, the most vulnerable of all workers, justified the mistress's own tenuous position in the affluent classes and obfuscated her own social and psychological dislocation in the industrialization process. The more affluent women could exercise control over their black domestics, the more they thought they had control over their own lives. "In the north, the home was the white mistress's stage. Task assignments and directions given to the staff were perceived as evidences of power."[46] Here, and only here, these white women could perceive that they, too, had power, as opposed to privilege, by virtue of tenuous social ties to the capitalist class.

In reality, while the home was seen as the affluent white women's preserve, the hierarchical power relationships between domestics and mistresses underwent significant alteration once the white male entered the home. White women, who were merely given the domestic space to exercise a tenuous control in the male's absence, were imperious with black domestics but deferential to white males. Black female domestics observed the domineering mistress do a complete about-face for the white male, employing a vast range of skills that included catering to male whims, cajoling him for household expenses, and providing vacuous notions of business or state affairs. All these ploys were consciously or unconsciously designed to buttress white male supremacy, and these power relationships proved instructive for black women. Undoubtedly, through such daily intimate contacts in affluent households, black women's analysis of class and gender roles in the context of power and domination among the "swells" appreciably enhanced their understanding of their material and social world.

Black domestic workers' labor activity was also integral to white women's domestic and political liberation. Upper-class women, who now possessed increased flexibility of time, were turning their attention to the public sphere. As these women entered the public sphere, they shifted the new emphasis on scientific management of factory production to homes and, by extension, to social missions that reflected their upper-class ideals.[47] The more these white upper-class women focused on scientific management of the home and their role in the public sphere, the more onerous the household duties became for black domestic workers. Later, as many middle-class women pursued the cause of women's rights, they also reflected a singular concern for their class, essentially missing the universal issue of gender oppression and, in that context, the racial, class, and gender plight of the women that they themselves exploited on a daily basis. This invisibility, which was maintained by the boundaries of race and class, thwarted cross-racial political and social alliances. Augmenting and undergirding the women's movement were black female workers and community activists who diligently labored in households as well as in churches, communities, and the abolitionist movement, as white women sought to free themselves from the constraints that effectively controlled their lives.

LAUNDRESSES AND COMMUNITY

Many black women sought empowerment through independent economic initiatives where their labor would serve their parental needs, provide some flexibility in time and activities, and begin to fulfill their desire for independence and autonomy. One of the more common occupations was that of laundress. "Black women often took on this lowly labor, one of the few paid employments they could obtain."[48] As self-employed laundresses working at home, for example, these black women could define economic relationships on their own terms as well as be meaningful participants in the community's culture. For many household workers, there was a clear distinction between a washerwomen and laundress. Laurlean Davis, a contemporary household worker, clarifies the difference: "a laundress . . . live-out, always, and, often they'd be able to serve in the houses of five or six families . . . a washwoman washing for money with no set people . . . A laundress had just her set people."[49] "In urban areas as many as eight out of ten women were day workers, most of them laundresses."[50]

Laundresses who had a thriving business usually had a weekly clientele of several households, working six days a week preparing clothes for delivery. Mondays were often spent securing work assignments, augmenting one's business, gathering work supplies, and setting up the general workloads based on expected days and times of delivery. Tuesdays and Wednesdays were designated as wash days, necessitating frequent trips to the fire hydrants, alternately boiling water while soaking clothes, washing and starching the clothes in steaming hot water, and then hanging them, using the clothesline across the courtyards and the makeshift ones strung diagonally across the kitchen, as well as vacated furniture that served multifunctional purposes. Thursdays and Fridays would be the days the clothes dried, and clothes were frequently rearranged to get the best exposure to the meager light coming into the apartment. Saturday was the day set aside for ironing, an all-day job, with women finishing late at night or early in the morning. "Saturday night! Dunk! goes the smoothing-iron, then a swift gliding sound as it passes smoothly over starched bosom and collar, and wristbands, of one of the many dozen shirts that hang around the room on horses, chairs, lines and every other thing capable of being hanged on."[51]

Yet while this was a demanding and onerous labor schedule, "her business sometimes keeping her up nearly all night," black women derived some measure of satisfaction from meshing business, family, and community activities.[52] Frequently, their business activities were sandwiched between their normal household duties of cooking, making beds, cleaning, washing, ironing, and scavenging the open-air markets for day-old provisions for their families, as well as the nurturing of their families. When family members were ill, laundresses integrated the care of the member into their already burdensome schedule. "Susannah's strategy of taking in washing permitted her to earn money while staying home, where she could care for her six children and nurse her husband."[53] Living space, already severely confined, served multifarious purposes and depended upon the creativity of the women. "The apartment is small, hot as an oven, the air in it thick and misty with the steam rising from the ironing table, in the corners, under the tables, and in all out-of-the way places, are stowed tubs of various sizes, some empty, some full of clothes soaking for next-week's labor."[54] Self-employed black laundresses, although generally receiving less monies for their labor than black women in full-time domestic service in affluent households, preferred this labor arrangement and the pride of being self-employed. Ironically, when employment patterns shifted for black female domestics in the 1840s, after Irish female workers garnered a large portion of domestic jobs by the 1850s, many full-time black live-in domestics became self-employed independent laundresses.

Part of the vibrancy of community culture for black working women were the formal associations and informal networks that they established as a part of the community culture. This vibrant community of laundresses still occupies an important niche for black female independent workers in black communities and has been cited by historian Elsa

Barkley Brown in her work on laundresses as entrepreneurs. Brown argues that these women utilized their skills and resources in creating businesses, as well as sustaining a viable culture among themselves.[55] In her study of contemporary household workers in Washington, D.C., *Living In, Living Out: African American Domestics and the Great Migration,* Elizabeth Clark-Lewis reports that household workers making the transition to more independent work could always rely on other laundresses to help them with "setting up" their business: "A lady that was just coming to they house to do laundry really helped me." These women also formed an association, the Twelfth Street Bible Club, with striking similarities to the antebellum mutual benefit societies. These women "have saved large sums of money together and assisted one another during hard times" and "support all activities and program honoring their members for church, 'court,' or community service."[56]

Similarly, in the antebellum era, black female entrepreneurs also maintained a community culture that served as a psychological buffer while creating economic resources. Founded in Philadelphia in 1821, "the Daughters of Africa" was an example of a group of working-class women who sustained community life while pursuing economic initiatives[57] These businesswomen could network with other laundresses, discussing rates for their labor and the expectations for their services, and may often have combined frequent deliveries to certain sections of the city. Undoubtedly, discussions also centered on demanding customers and on the problems of their enterprise—a sharing of personal, family, and community social problems, all exacerbated by the harshness of city life.

Black women often combined household duties with opportunities for socializing, such as shopping for provisions or scavenging in the open markets for marked-down perishables. For black female workers, visiting or having tea at one of the neighborhood shops to catch up on the local news had a special place in community life. There, black women, among friends, received healing and nurturance from each other. A consistent circle of visiting friends, usually around the kitchen table, provided sustenance for the next week's hard labor. Horton and Horton describe this form of social entertainment among black Bostonians: "Among poor people, visiting was often a chief form of entertainment. Black Bostonians frequently exchanged visits. Usually some food was served—Lydia Porter was apparently known for her coffee and pie. It was also customary to play cards, and much visiting went on around the table."[58]

MARKET WOMEN, VENDORS, AND STREET PEDDLERS

Largely due to the small amount of capital necessary for equipment and merchandise, some poor women launched into the occupation of tradeswomen, a portable enterprise. Black female street entrepreneurs negotiated space, purchases, and equipment for their products to sell in the open-air markets or on street corners of the cities. Courage, tenacity, and a hard dose of dire financial necessity sustained this economic activity. Street entrepreneurs quickly became urbanites, combining their knowledge of the city's terrain and their pluck and business acumen into a subsistence trade. This economic activity, developed by poor urban women in the early 1800s, by the 1830s saw black women, similar to their West African sisters, moving about the cities as street hawkers, vendors, and peddlers, selling fruits, vegetables, cakes, and domestic items from a bly positioned on their heads. Having no more than bare subsistence monies, women could start at primary entrepreneurial levels. Monies from sales were simply used to keep body and soul together if the women were single; if married, vendors used their earnings to supplement the existing family income while retaining a portion of the earnings to purchase the next day's sales items. Other tradeswomen who had more monies for an initial investment established a permanent stall in the public markets where they could sell previously prepared foodstuffs that would serve as a quick meal for workers and businesspersons near the downtown docks.[59]

In New York City, many black female vendors frequented public malls near the docks because of the lively commerce and informational sources in those locations. Similarly, in Philadelphia, open-air commerce and trade negotiations took place around Head House Square or at a permanent stall or a frequently traveled street, where many black female vendors sold hot or cold foodstuffs. Street entrepreneurs quickly became a part of the local landscape and used their mobility and contacts to gather news and information, network with other entrepreneurs, refer black newcomers to the city to boardinghouses, and dispense social information, all as they sold their merchandise. Although other vendors sold hot roasted corn, black women were known for the selling of hot corn, recognized as a delicacy both in New York City and Philadelphia, and the women could be heard singing a familiar tune that became associated with urban life:

Hot corn, hot corn, here's your lily white hot corn
Hot corn all hot, just come out of the boiling pot.[60]

In Philadelphia, the other delicacy was pepper pot, a hot stew prepared daily and sold by black women at marketplaces or on busy street
corners. Here, too, the vendors provided a tune to prospective customers:

Pepper-pot!
All hot! all hot!
Makee back strong!
Makee live long!
Come buy my Pepper pot![61]

In reshaping their labor activity, black female workers perceived the
urban marketplace as an economic and social network as well as a source
of daily sustenance for themselves and their families. Some women utilized the urban markets to dispose of goods and gain quick capital.
Nancy Ruffin, who migrated from Richmond, Virginia, to Boston with
her eight children, used the urban marketplace from time to time to sell
items that came into her family's possession. Ruffin's husband, a barber
in Virginia, sent monies as well as crates of fish and fruit, which she sold
in open-air markets to supplement the family's income.[62]

Despite all of the vitality and creative survival abilities of black
female vendors, street peddlers, and market women, they were barely
able to sustain themselves. Still, they moved beyond the boundaries of
black communities and created a defiant presence in port cities. Their
political and economic plight sensitized them to the realities of urban life.
Overall, while black women saw the urban marketplace as a source of
daily sustenance for themselves and their families, they also saw opportunity in these economic enterprises and constantly gained a renewed
sense of their own labor power.

SKILLED BLACK FEMALE WORKERS
AND ENTREPRENEURSHIP

Skilled black female workers, such as seamstresses, hairdressers, and
milliners, also sought empowerment through their labor activities and
used a combination of economic enterprises where they could mesh their
independent aspirations and community participation. These skilled

workers, comprising approximately 15 percent of black female entrepreneurs, like laundresses, also combined their need for independence, flexible time for parental and household duties, and need for community life with their occupation. There were those who had a thriving business working for several families at a time, sewing clothes and home furnishings for negotiable rates. Often, this type of work was contractual, and the seamstress could be employed in one household for several weeks at a time and then move on to another household for a similar amount of time where she would make clothes, draperies, curtains, and bedding. Contractual work was usually gained by references from previously satisfied customers. Most seamstresses, however, worked at home sewing specific items—piecework—for a prenegotiated price. But most often the hours were long, the work tedious, the jobs sporadic, and the agreed-upon pay for the job happenstance. Their wages, generally $1.00–$2.00 per week, were barely sustenance monies, and most single female seamstresses were boarders.[63] Frequently, seamstresses could augment their income sewing for transient boarders as well as for prosperous blacks in the community. When business was slack, seamstresses frequently relied upon laundresses to provide them with information regarding possible "day's work" to ensure a steady source of income.

Some black female entrepreneurs sought empowerment through creating community-based enterprises that catered to a largely black clientele. Although start-up capital was scarce, some female entrepreneurs received small business loans from mutual aid societies or from black entrepreneurs who engaged in money lending. "In order to generate capital, blacks organized for mutual assistance . . . in addition to mutual-aid societies, and because of the success of many Afro-Americans, there was a trade in money lending."[64] Black female entrepreneurs benefited from these sources of start-up capital and used them to establish or expand independently owned enterprises. By the time of the 1849 statistical inquiry undertaken by the Society of Friends, there was a tremendous growth in independently owned concerns by black women. Although approximately 47 percent of the women were listed as washerwomen, the occupations also included "216 dress-makers, 231 seamstresses, 19 tailoresses, 19 milliners, 33 keepers of boarding, eating and oyster houses, 13 school mistresses, 10 cake bakers, 60 white washers, 24 hucksters, 12 confectioners, 9 mat makers, 33 sewers of carpet rags, 35 shopkeepers."[65] Contrary to the gender conventions of the era, black women's labor activity was integral to their personal identities as women, and they possessed a sense of independence and the courage to operate in defiance of contemporary standards of womanhood.

Black women also played pivotal roles in family owned and operated enterprises. Once businesses were established, black women either worked in the shop, as domestics or vendors, or at other ancillary enterprises to supplement the family's income. Black women moved into positions of sole proprietorship, similar to white women, gaining these businesses upon the death of their spouses. "Widowhood was a common road to female proprietorship."[66] Elizabeth Hewlett Marshall became the sole proprietor of the family's bakery business following the death of her husband. Having previously worked as a domestic to augment the family's income, Hewlett Marshall took over the bakery in New York City and was soon able to support herself and her four children from the enterprise.[67] Similar to Hewlett Marshall's circumstances, Sarah Prosser of Philadelphia acquired her husband's oyster cellar business and ran it successfully until her death, when the business was passed on to her son.

BOARDINGHOUSE KEEPERS

One popular economic strategy that black women employed, as did white women needing to supplement the family income, involved creating an extension of their living quarters as a way to supplement family earnings. For most black families, "taking in boarders probably stemmed from both custom and economic and social necessity."[68] Boardinghouse lodgings could be informal, ranging from a small space on a family's floor to room accommodations with laundry services and meals included.[69] These arrangements obviously depended upon space availability, a select clientele, and home resources and often required considerable ingenuity on the part of the keeper. Women who attempted to create space in cramped tenements offered boarders floor space or a bed in the apartment for a small fee. Often, boarders could secure sleeping space at night in the living room when other household members went to bed. Other apartment dwellers with considerable space had several rooms to rent and offered laundry services and meals to their boarders for an additional weekly price.

Black women who had more formal accommodations as boardinghouse keepers provided rooms and lodging to boarders, drawing upon transient workers, sailors in port, recently arrived migrant workers, and permanent community residents. Single women were especially attracted to the family-type lodgings, and all workers seeking rooms found appealing not only the room space, with meals sometimes included, but also the home environment that was cultivated at such boardinghouses. Boarders seeking a home away from home or an entrée into the community found that the companionship and everyday camaraderie with other boarders, which might include discussions of news and events that impacted the black community, current community issues, local gossip, and job possibilities, were also appealing features of group living. For a fixed weekly price, workers could secure lodging and gain immediate entrée into the black community via the associational and residential ties of boardinghouse keepers. The more entrenched the boardinghouse keepers were in the community, the wider their reputation, and particularly their affiliation with the black church and several mutual benefit societies, the easier time their boarders had being accepted as a member of the community.

Black "elite" boardinghouse keepers could be found among the established proprietors who ran "respectable houses" and were regarded as pillars of the community. In contrast to white upper-class women, many black upper-class women worked at several occupations. Although the black elite were a relatively miniscule part of black communities, they generally enjoyed regional reputations as social activists and reformers, enabling them to draw upon a clientele that included a pool of community activists from other cities, students from well-known families who were in the city attending schools, and abolitionists on the lecture circuit. Invariably, these women combined these kinds of boarders with others who were permanent, such as laborers in the city recommended by other members of the community. Regardless of their economic status, "almost all [homes] had some dwellers who were not part of the nuclear family."[70]

Established boardinghouse proprietors often placed advertisements in the local black press indicating their desire for respectable clientele and at the same time taking pains to reinforce their own public reputation. Gracy Jones, located in Philadelphia near Lombard Street, where the Fortens, the well-known black abolitionist family, lived, advertised her boardinghouse business "for the accommodation of genteel persons of color." This respectability factor was important in distinguishing women who ran boardinghouses from those who ran "bawdy houses" where gambling, dancing, and music were the featured nightly entertainment. Some boardinghouse keepers stressed the positive environmental factors that enhanced their residence. Mary Jo Johnson advertised her boardinghouse in Harlem, emphasizing its genteel qualities as well as its primary location in one of the healthier areas of the city. Undoubtedly, Johnson was making a contrast with "Little Africa," located by Collect

Pond in downtown New York City, where the majority of blacks lived. In Philadelphia, Eliza Johnson employed the use of her home for several overlapping economic enterprises. While she was known for her boardinghouse accommodations, she also regularly sold light refreshments at her home for community residents.[71]

Community networking, entertainment, and economic enterprise were very often mingled. Some women used their homes as makeshift "shoppes" where pastries and candies were sold to children in the neighborhood. Some of these home "shoppes," if successful, were soon expanded to include household items that community female workers could purchase on their way home from work. Sometimes these homes provided light beverages and pastries, and female community residents stopped and gained a short respite during the day or early evening, catching up on community news and updated personal "sagas." Women who worked away from home frequently used this venue, as well as shopping for provisions and visiting, as a way of staying in touch with each other and as a reminder of upcoming community events and other social and religious activities. These "shoppes" were viewed as social centers by the community residents, and women visited often, relying on the shopkeepers and the "regulars" to be a treasure trove of information.

At the opposite end of the social-outlet spectrum were the "bawdy houses" run by black women that featured nightly entertainment, although they drew their biggest crowds on the weekends. The main attractions of these after-hours' joints were prepared meals sold at a fixed price, usually live musical entertainment, and continuous dancing. Oftentimes, illicit activities, such as gambling and prostitution, were the main staples of these houses, which thrived upon an interracial clientele. These business enterprises were operated on a strictly cash basis, although favorite customers and well-known shady characters were permitted to run a generous tab. Since these "bawdy houses" were in the community, they proved the bane of working community residents, who had to face long hours of backbreaking labor the next day. These houses proved to be a source of neighborhood conflict, and police were sometimes summoned to curtail the enthusiasm of the revelers. The entertainment was usually subdued for a few days following an official warning, only to regain its prior momentum by the weekend. The more tawdry nightlife in New York City took place in the Five Points District, in Cow Bay Alley, popularly referred to as "Dickens's Place" because of the author's visit there. However, this nightspot was not owned or operated by women.[72]

Women who ran "bawdy houses" used the daytime hours to frequent open-air markets, replacing their stock and preparing meals for nightly clientele. A few enterprising women maintained these houses at night and worked as laundresses, peddlers, or seamstresses during the day. Since their day jobs offered meager income, the evening cash business improved one's life substantially. Although these women were frowned upon and ostracized by devout churchgoers and those who ran "respectable" boardinghouses or "hincty" (snobbish) upwardly mobile neighbors, those with combined labor activities frequently gained some measure of respectability because of their cross section of influence and networking in some spheres of white society. "Bawdy house" keepers, who became prosperous at this endeavor or at least had access to cash, could win a degree of influence in the black community by providing small loans to women who had very marginal family budgets, donating to the African Dorcas Society, or soliciting funds from their clientele for community projects. Frequently, these women served in the role as moneylenders, providing capital for fledging business ventures. Tarnished reputation or not, "bawdy house" keepers were perceived, albeit many times reluctantly by religious devotees, as vital economic contributors to the community.

BROAD-BASED ECONOMIC COLLECTIVES

Other economic vehicles for black women were small or large organized collectives where women mastered the many facets of large-scale business ownership. Women became skilled at negotiating and purchasing products wholesale or in bulk; preparing small and large orders for individuals, organizations, and churches; creating attractive and appealing item displays; bookkeeping procedures; basic managerial techniques regarding business operations; and attempting to produce a consistent profit margin for the business. The advantage of several members owning a shop would be the lower initial capitalization expenses per individual member, the networking and contacts that members brought that was vital to the business collective, and the expertise of each member to enrich the range of services that the establishment offered. Hamilton, Newton, and Hamilton, a small black female collective in Brooklyn, owned and operated a dressmaking shop offering dressmaking, embroidery, shirtmaking, and quilting. Very large collectives of black female entrepreneurs were rare but did occur. In New York City, a hundred black women jointly owned and operated a large, well-stocked grocery store, the Female Trading Association, perhaps more closely akin to the minisupermarket in most contemporary neighborhoods. While their stock included coffee, chocolate, cocoa, tea, ham, pork, beef, the staples of grits, peas, beans, brooms, and brushes, all of their items were sold at a discount, indicating an extensive knowledge of wholesale purchasing, negotiating prices, and management skills.[73] While the Female Trading Association appears to have been short-lived, black women were clearly interested in owning and operating their own businesses. They regarded economic collectives as a viable method that included brainstorming, the constant sharing of ideas, limited financial risk, and ongoing business opportunities.

BLACK FEMALE ENTREPRENEURSHIP AND POLITICAL ACTIVISM

Several black female entrepreneurs meshed their business acumen with their political and social activism. Hence, they pursued a three-fold purpose: owning and operating an independent business enterprise; developing an apprenticeship program for young women in the community; and supporting the growing abolitionist movement. These businesses offered comprehensive services, advertised for helpers in the black press or abolitionist tracts and journals, and, when financially able, took on female apprentices. Women who possessed a skill earned more money and had several more options than did unskilled women. Often, the completion of an apprenticeship program led to a better job or to the establishment of one's own business. Many apprentices who studied the techniques and skills under a seamstress viewed it as a stepping stone to a more lucrative income in the future. S. R. Given, the proprietor of a dressmaking shop in Philadelphia, advertised in the black newspaper the *Weekly Anglo-African,* seeking young female apprentices.[74] By training these apprentices in the operation of a sewing machine, Given passed her skills and techniques on to young black women. Given and others who took on female trainees created a new pool of skilled seamstresses, demonstrating not only their social commitment by helping others in the community but also passing on vital experience, skills, techniques, contacts, and expertise to young black women in Philadelphia. For black females, this intergenerational bonding that ensured one's survival was reminiscent of the intergenerational bonding that Deborah Gray White contends was an integral feature of the female slave networking apparatus.[75]

Several black female entrepreneurs whose families had been in the cities for a generation or more connected their economic enterprises to their family's social activism. By making a larger public commitment to the liberation of the slaves, which black community residents perceived to be a community goal, these female entrepreneurs garnered business from their regular customers and from politically oriented customers who saw it as a social commitment to use their services. If their families were well-known abolitionists, these entrepreneurs had less difficulty in establishing their business reputation and garnering a steady pool of customers. As previously noted, Grace Bustill Douglass of Philadelphia operated a home-based millinery business. Undoubtedly, Douglass benefited from her father's reputation as a baker, as well as from her family's connection to progressive programs in the black community, including their well-known antislavery activities. Other black businesswomen also intertwined their political and economic activities. In Brooklyn, realtor Elizabeth Gloucester utilized some of her profits to contribute to John Brown's radical antislavery efforts. Other entrepreneurs, such as three of the Remond sisters—Cecilia Remond Babcock, Caroline Remond Putnam, and Maritcha Remond—known throughout the abolitionist movement and particularly in Salem, Massachusetts, where they lived, operated the largest wig factory in the state. Although their sister Sarah Parker Remond was an international abolitionist noted for her crusade in Scotland, Ireland, and England, another sister, Susan Remond, had a reputation as a pastry chef and ran a small eating room that featured her desserts. Susan benefited from her culinary talents and from her family's abolitionist tradition, and "her kitchen was a Mecca where gathered radicals, free thinkers, abolitionists, female suffragists, fugitives."[76] Black female entrepreneurs found innumerable ways to bridge the gap between their abilities to earn a living and the twin goals of the abolitionists that emphasized the liberation of the slaves and the improvement of the lives of free blacks.[77]

THE INTERDEPENDENCE OF ECONOMIC ACTIVITY

Black women's economic activity was an interdependent process connecting their lives to the development of black communities and to their social and political consciousness. Woven inextricably into capitalist expansion, although tangential to main centers of commodity production and in most instances operating segregated economic enterprises, free antebellum black women strove to transcend the social, economic, and political barriers and engaged in a continuous process of contouring and defining their own economic space. Creating a sense of economic space and, from a historical perspective, free labor space contributed ultimately to a sense of self. This amalgam of resistive patterns of inner consciousness forged during slavery, black women's marginalization from the main industrial centers, and their racial stigmatization owing partly to the slave legacy and partly to the entrenched Northern racial attitudes intrinsic to capitalist expansion all proved factors in black women's developing political consciousness. Their empowerment, a dual consciousness of their inner space and outer material realities, informed their own definitions of black womanhood and their thought and political activism.

In confronting the perils of freedom in urban areas, black female workers relied, as they had done in slavery, upon their labor power as a source within themselves of survival and strength in the midst of chaos and social instability. While the roots of the endurance and survival of black women lay in their African-derived spirituality, the autonomy, racial pride, and solidarity of black communities were sustainable components in their lives. In pragmatic terms, the creation of an alternative economic structure located in black communities, enforced by racial segregation, provided the impetus for their economic initiatives. Independence and autonomy, critical elements of black women's labor activity, were gained through wage work and independent economic initiatives. As the industrialization and market economy expanded and black female workers experienced a greater alienation as more male and female white workers were drawn into the economy, their material world appreciably enhanced their political consciousness.

Forced to the periphery of the marketplace, black female workers, utilizing alternative economic vehicles that they developed and expanded, saw the urban marketplace as a place where they could survive, gain a measure of dignity, and yet defy a system of oppression. Their economic activity may be intrusive subversion at its best. Within this limited autonomous space, black women paralleled their slave experience by imposing their labor will upon their workplace and reconstituting the space to address their social needs and political aspirations. In carving out their workspace, black female workers broadened the foundation for economic activity and social activism in black communities.

The critical position of their labor activity in families became an empowerment tool that black women employed for community-based activities. Black women's invisibility and historic role as laborers (while it flew in the face of conventional gender norms of female domesticity) ironically paved their way into the larger black communities as active participants, making them an acknowledged social force in community life. Their community activism, which emerged initially from their economic roles, informed and politicized black communities and undergirded the larger abolitionist movement, which in turn fueled their own political and social activism. For black women, the trajectory of social and political activism was inherent in their economic relationship to the community and the intrinsic value their labor served in the larger society.

PART 3

Collective Consciousness

CHAPTER 5

Shaking the Tree of Liberty

Alienation and Activism

> The condition of our people, the wants of our children, and the welfare of our race demand the aid of every helping hand.
> FRANCES ELLEN WATKINS HARPER, 1852

IN 1854, FRANCES ELLEN WATKINS HARPER, AN AVOWED BLACK abolitionist-feminist, penned an essay entitled "The Colored People in America." In it, she writes: "Having been placed by a dominant race in circumstances over which we have had no control, we have been the butt of ridicule and the mark of oppression. Identified with a people over whom weary ages of degradation have passed, whatever concerns them, as a race, concerns me." Harper's critique on the status of black people placed black women squarely in the center of the intertwining struggles of abolitionism and the battles for racial equality. The conflation of Harper's analysis, the racial oppression of blacks, the centering of the racial dynamic in antebellum culture and politics, and her "personal commitment to a common struggle" pointed to the critical challenges that lay ahead for free black women.[1] Sarah Forten, a poet and essayist, was also a passionate abolitionist from the well-known Forten clan of Philadelphia. Writing under the pen name of "Magawisca" in the *Liberator,* Forten spoke of spiritual redemption, criticized America's tenuous ideals of freedom, and embraced black protest when she called on America to remember that God "is just, and his anger will not always slumber. He will wipe the tear from Ethiopia's eye; He will shake the tree of liberty."[2] Together, these two black female activists captured the political and social dimensions of black protest, the intrinsic alienation of black women in society, and the powerful faith that they had in a victorious struggle. Harper and Forten wrote with voices that had been shaped by their community activism.

The confluences of several critical dimensions contoured black women's political and social alienation and, simultaneously, their social and political activism. On the one hand, industrialization caused their total estrangement from the American polity and, on the other, created the political and economic space for black women's social and political activism to lay the foundation of black urban resistance. Largely from their participation in community self-improvement and reform societies and associations, black women became the shapers of their political identity by honing a collective consciousness as well as pragmatic organizational skills. As Anne Boylan states, "Their organizers wrote constitutions and bylaws, chose officers, met regularly, raised funds, and established programs." Black women's associations and societies, regardless of the intentional focus, were multidimensional, serving benevolent causes, self-improvement concerns, and reform activities. These were identified as major areas in thwarting notions of black inferiority and effecting the quest for social equality. Black women like "Hester Lane, former slave, manager of the African Dorcas Association, and nominee for the Executive Committee of the American Anti-Slavery Society, readily combined benevolence with reform work."[3]

Susan Paul, a well-known abolitionist and daughter of Thomas Paul, a leading Baptist minister in the Boston community, also combined community commitments with antislavery activism. Paul assumed an extraordinary load. On the community level, Paul was a seamstress and an educator, forced to do both to support her family and her deceased sister's children. Still, she found the time to "recruit a Garrison Junior Choir, which sang at abolitionist gatherings," as well as assume the office of secretary in the local temperance society, and she was selected as one of the delegates to the American Anti-Slavery Convention in New York from the interracial Boston Female Anti-Slavery Society, where she was an active member.[4] Black women's social commitment, their discipline shaped by being a part of the industrial labor force, and their organizational expertise garnered from their literary societies made them vital assets to the larger antislavery movement. "Some of the most able officers of the women's antislavery conventions, such as Sarah Mapp Douglass and Hetty Burr, served their apprenticeship in Philadelphia's female literary societies."[5] Black women's political expression and activism encompassed three areas: community activism, evangelicalism (see chapter 6), and abolitionism (see chapter 7). Estranged from electoral politics, black women were key players in nonelectoral politics that formed the basis for political and social reform activities initially in black communities and, subsequently, the larger society.

BLACK WOMEN'S ALIENATION

Deeply intertwined in black women's alienation from the body politic have been the confluences and devastating consequences of racial caste, gender discrimination, and urban impoverishment. These factors were common in the lives of black women in urban areas by the 1830s and 1840s, as they struggled with increasingly high levels of physical and mental stress. The three-dimensional character of their oppression was already taking on the heavily laden texture that sociologist Deborah K. King posits as the "multiplier effect," which "refers not only to several simultaneous oppressions but to the multiplicative relationships among them as well. In other words, the equivalent formulation is racism multiplied by sexism multiplied by classism."[6]

Black women's political and social alienation, which embodied their estrangement from the political, economic, and social life of the city, was a complex phenomenon. It was not wholly a divorce from the controls and logistics of commodity production and, via that process, from other workers, families, and ultimately self.[7] Black women were experiencing a deliberate apartheid policy and an increasingly systematic removal by the intent of the government or the active or passive support of white citizens, from all facets of political, social, and economic life. To the extent that nascent capitalism gained some measure of stability in the antebellum era, black women's marginalization in commodity production was entrenched. With this marginalization in industrial centers, black women were locked out of any possible fraternity of workers or labor coalitions. In relegating black women solely to menial labor, early industrialization was a direct impediment to their socioeconomic progress.

In the midst of the spiraling wealth accumulation noticeable by the 1840s in urban centers such as New York City, black women were firmly in place as permanent members of an emerging underclass. "New York City's African-American population did not share in the city's economic bounty, nor did it obtain any greater social or political acceptance."[8] The encroachment of laws, public policy, and white citizens who viewed black laborers as eroding white economic privilege and industrialization all worked together to exclude black women from society's collective memory and historical consciousness. This denial of black women's experiences in American society essentially made them invisible members of the urban landscape.

Thus black women's alienation was contextualized by the infinitely more inclusive "embeddedness and relationality of race, class, and gender and the multiplicative nature of these relationships" within the context of the governmental apparatus and citizen support of the disparate labor systems that anchored their lives.[9] Black women's estrangement from social relations and labor production were readily apparent in both antebellum labor systems and established an interactive pattern of oppression. Whether slave or free, black female workers provided the labor for two economic systems to flourish, although these women were separated from the products and capital that they created. The centrality of their agricultural labor in the cash crop commodity production of slavery fueled the development of the slave economic system, the emerging industrialization of Northern cities, and the larger transnational economy of Great Britain and the United States. While female slaves labored in creating the domestic and international markets, free black female workers sustained the nascent capitalist system and its interlocking dependencies on slaves and industrial workers.

Harper saw this collusion of slavery and capital, declaring, "Oh, could slavery exist long if it did not sit on a commercial throne?"[10] As urban workers, particularly household workers, free black women buttressed the specificity of gender roles in the industrial order by providing the labor that sustained the sexual differentiation. The capitalist system, the white middle-class women who increasingly had leisure time to engage in political and social activities, and, ironically, the complementary slave system that circumscribed the lives of black people all benefited from black female workers. Although black women were alienated from the multifaceted market arena, they were providing a constant and consistent labor supply, adding enormous surplus value to the two economic systems that engulfed their lives.

Within the complexities of black women's alienation, race and racial discrimination—a shared oppression of black men and women—was a major node in the larger scope and depth of existing inequalities. Northeastern cities, for all of their touting of freedom and equality, were moving steadily toward a caste society determining laws and treatment specifically for black people. In 1821, Massachusetts legislators, "panic-stricken" over a black population increase of three individuals despite a corresponding increase of over 50,000 whites in the second decade, appointed a committee to study the "increase of a species of population which threatened to become both injurious and burdensome."[11] Daniel Curry, writing on the development of New York City in 1853, made an apt observation on the social alienation of black New Yorkers. "Though they have since ceased to be slaves they are still a wholly-distinct and an outcast class in the community."[12]

Black women were making similar observations about their political plight. Harriet Brent Jacobs, a fugitive living in New York City, observed that "everywhere I found the same manifestations of that cruel prejudice, which so discourages the feelings, and represses the energies of the colored people."[13] Maria W. Stewart, the fiery black abolitionist, also informed her audience at Franklin Hall in Boston about the plight of black women, making the connection between racial discrimination and black women's work: "I am also one of the wretched and miserable daughters of the descendants of fallen Africa . . . look at many of the most worthy and most interesting of us doomed to spend our lives in gentlemen's kitchens."[14]

Despite a tenuous free status, blacks were clearly not welcome in these cities, particularly as white immigrants began to arrive in great numbers, facilitating the transition from a slave to an industrial economy. Irish workers, quickly mastering the racial hierarchy, resented black labor competition in servile occupations. "All the more obnoxious to the Irish were indications of a preference for the Negro."[15] One traveler to New York City gained a sense of the racial antipathies among the white working classes, commenting that "I am satisfied that some of these people would shoot a black man with as little regard to moral consequences as they would a wild hog."[16] In the wake of the European waves of immigration, black men and women were confined to menial labor and were rapidly losing the few citizenship rights that they possessed.

Aldon Morris views these racial exclusionary practices that made black women vulnerable in urban areas as integral to the "tripartite system of racial domination." Although Morris's primary focus is on the race relations in Southern cities in the 1950s, his argument of race formation and the racial forces that determined urban black existence were already evident in northeastern antebellum cities. For Morris, this "tripartite system of racial domination" and control effectively "protected the privileges of white society and generated tremendous human suffering for blacks," rendering them "economically, politically, and personally" powerless.[17] Seeds of this system of domination and control of blacks in cities were being planted in the antebellum era, locating these mechanisms of power and the oppression of blacks well within the development of early northeastern urbanity. For black women, the "tripartite system of racial domination" served as an extension of their servitude and universalized their oppression as free women. In effect, black women and men were trapped behind a "cotton curtain" where all the burdens and negative consequences of slavery, created and developed by the avarice of financiers, merchants, and planters, were theirs to bear.

Although northeastern cities were recognized havens or sanctuaries for slave fugitives and recently emancipated blacks, antebellum culture shaped a political climate hostile to black women. Mired in the northeastern slave trade and the marketing of slave products that were sold throughout the cities, as opposed to the harder to find products of free laborers that blacks and some white abolitionists endeavored to purchase, black women had to maintain a constant vigilance against the bounty hunters. "It was more profitable for Southern plantation owners to have their agents kidnap free blacks off New York City streets for transport to Southern plantations than to pay auction-block prices."[18] Jacobs, who was in constant fear of being re-enslaved by her master, Dr. Flint, believed that the summertime created a heightened sense of fear for black women. "Hot weather brings out snakes and slaveholders, and I like one class of the venomous creatures as little as I do the others." Black women's vulnerability was increased by their critical need to work, and, in most cases, the kind of work that they did placed them in daily contact with the larger society, thereby increasing their exposure and risk of capture and re-enslavement. Employed as a nurse by Mrs. Bruce for her daughter, Mary, Jacobs dreaded taking the child outside. "It was necessary for me to take little Mary out daily, for exercise and fresh air, and the city was swarming with Southerners, some of whom might recognize me."[19]

Black women in Boston also lived in fear of being captured, re-enslaved, and sold to Southern planters. In a blink of an eye, a black woman's long journey toward freedom could be subverted by slaveholders, kidnappers, and police officials, all acting in concert in the slave-trafficking enterprise. In *The First Annual Report of the New York Committee of Vigilance for the Year 1837,* radical abolitionists, who believed in rescuing fugitive slaves from their abductors and providing them with safe passage, reported that the "pro-slavery spirit pervaded the free states."[20] In Boston, the Vigilance Committee had approximately 168 black and white members. Regardless of membership status, however, black women played key roles in all efforts on behalf of fugitives. "The records of the Boston Vigilance Committee . . . reveal that many black women provided aid to fugitives through the committee even though they were not members."[21] Because the fear on the part of the black community was palpable concerning the immediate loss of their freedom or the constant disappearance of loved ones, black women could quickly become mobilized into a rescue team. These mobilization efforts demonstrated the level of political activity as well as the deep level of political disaffection and resistance that was a subterranean part of black women's lives.

When, in the summer of 1836, Eliza Small and Polly Ann Bates, fugitives from Baltimore, were captured by slave hunters and brought before a judge to be returned to their master, blacks acted to save them. On a given signal, a group of black women rushed into the courtroom, whisked the runaways out of the building to a waiting carriage, and escaped the city. In this action a key role was played by a black cleaning woman "of great size," who subdued an officer long enough for the rescue to be effected. This daring rescue, which caused great excitement and raised spirits in the black community, came to be known as the Abolition Riot. Neither the fugitives nor the rescuers were ever captured.[22]

Contributing to black women's political and social alienation was the legal and political sanctions that defined the boundaries of their exterior lives. Although black women understood clearly what had to be done when fugitives were in danger of being caught, legal and political sanctions placed their whole question of freedom on a tenuous foundation. If any black could be captured, regardless of status, and re-enslaved, then no black was really safe, and black women could be stolen at any time. "A man comes with his affidavits from the South and hurries me before a commissioner; upon that evidence ex parte and alone he hitches me to the car of slavery and trails my womanhood in the dust."[23] Proscriptions circumscribing the lives of black women had a negative impact that was both immediate and enduring. White citizens, depending on how they viewed privilege and racial subordination, lessened or extended the boundaries of these laws and statutes by their thoughts and participation in black women's lives. James Fenimore Cooper, for example, the most famous American author of the period, believed that free blacks were "a body of men who had been nurtured in the habits of slavery, with all their ignorance and animal qualities."[24] One can safely assume that Cooper possessed similar feelings regarding black women. Other white citizens supported black disenfranchisement through the electoral process and the informal sanctions of community.

The conflation of the state and society—which institutionalized and legitimized slavery and black disenfranchisement as well as perpetuated the multiple oppression of black women—subordinated black women's political and social aspirations. Clearly, they were deprived of the full range of citizenship rights including suffrage, jury participation, testifying against whites in court, and participation on any level of the electoral process, constituting the crux of their political alienation. "Forbidding Black women to vote, excluding African-Americans and women from public office . . . all substantiate the political subordination of Black women."[25] Still, it was the total estrangement of black women from all facets of society, compounded by the multifaceted oppression and exploitation, that comprised the material realities of their alienation.

ANTEBELLUM POLITICS, CULTURE, AND BLACK WOMEN

Intrinsic to the formation of black women's social relations were antebellum culture and politics, which were major contributing factors to black women's alienation. Under the material gloss of industrial expansion, mass market consumption, and rising opulence, there was another layer where the collusion of politicians and capitalists made blacks the caricatures of the new industrial age. "Black imagery, caricature, and blackface minstrelsy was [sic] embedded in the cultural lore and evinced the racism of the period. In the bastardization and appropriation by white men of black folk culture for commercial success, they thwarted 'the development of Negro public arts and generated an enduring racist ideology—a historical process by which an entire people has been made the bearer of another people's "folk culture."' "By society deflecting the attentions of white workers away from the fluctuations of the labor market, the perennial hunt for jobs, the routinization of factory labor, and competition with black workers, it obfuscated "the extent to which it (black imagery, caricature, and blackface minstrelsy) was the racial politics of the time" and provided an outlet for labor-related tensions.[26] "Whites in blackface appeared on the streets as well as on the stage." Black women frequently bore the humiliation of this debasement. In Philadelphia, part of the Christmas celebrations by "the late 1820s were young white men (who) began dressing as black women they called 'Aunt Sallys.'"[27] A lethal combination of the prevailing notion of white superiority and black imagery could diffuse job tensions with ridicule or lead to the more insidious confrontations in the streets or to antiblack riots. "Whatever the economic transitions, adjustment to new ways was frequently difficult or often associated with fears and frustrations that could easily be released on black scapegoats."[28]

Such factors as the rise of the two-party system in northeastern cities and its racially based political strategies, antiblack riots, and black imagery and caricature determined the customary treatment of urban blacks. In Philadelphia, urbanization brought "a new edge of tension, a hint of lawlessness and hostility that was echoed in street brawling and conflicts over public space."[29] As these factors became culturally ingrained into the collective psyche of white society, they had profound and pragmatic implications for black women not only as features of the cultural lore but also in their vulnerability in the city streets. Black women were subjected to physical assaults by white gangs, random acts of violence, and discriminatory practices by white urbanites on the streets or public conveyances. Daily taunts, jeers, and racist name-calling were a part of everyday existence. Even foreigners were quickly "schooled" on the pecking order. In New York City, a "foreigner who spoke courteously to a black woman was pitted with brickbats," aptly reflecting the future treatment of foreigners who forgot Northern "social etiquette" as well as the tenuous status and treatment of black women in urban environments.[30] George Thompson, the British abolitionist who referred to blacks as "brethren and sisters," had encountered frequent mob violence during his stay in the United States, causing Susan Paul to write to him, "I cannot describe the emotions of my soul in view of the wicked murderous and fiend-like disposition exhibited toward you."[31]

Although black women were excluded from mainstream electoral politics, the racial discrimination inculcated into its development had a decisive impact upon their lives. In creating racially centered strategies to gain and maintain supporters, political parties reinforced the existing racism in city life. "Indeed, Tammany Hall claimed to publicly advance immigrants' interests by actively promoting the idea that Southern slavery created jobs for New Yorkers."[32] Despite the hoopla and the racial epithets hurled between parties at election time and journalists weighing in with critical commentary, blacks were the only group resolute in the struggle to abolish slavery or participate in the equal suffrage campaign. Black women were as zealous as black men in the suffrage campaign, and they "fully expected to be included in the politics of their community, and saw the ballot as community property, even if cast only by men."[33] In this early period, blacks were always to the left of contending parties, although they supported the Whig Party in the 1830s, the Liberty Party in the late 1840s and early 1850s, and the Free Soil movement in the 1850s, as well as forming their own New York Suffrage Association in 1855, in order to influence the electorate in their cause. "This [latter] group intended to act as a political party and to serve as a balance of power in close elections."[34] By 1856, blacks, led by Henry Highland Garnet at the black state convention of New York, were endorsing the Republican Party because "it did come closest to positions on suffrage and slavery favored by blacks."[35]

While all political parties employed racial strategies to either support slavery, exclude black men from suffrage, or as propaganda to gain supporters and contributors, the Democratic Party was consistently proslavery and antiblack in the cities where there was a significant black population. Appealing to a multiethnic working-class base of disaffected workers and artisans who found their status being eroded by the new factory system, the party's emphasis on the "common man," its proslavery stance, and democratic republicanism gained a broad-based constituency. "The Republicans had to be portrayed as a party that would be 'soft' on the race issue, as a pro-amalgamation, 'nigger-loving' political conglomeration bent on raising Negroes to full legal and social equality with whites."[36]

Prominent among the strategies employed by the Democratic Party was the scapegoating of blacks to "vent indignation upon the most visible of scapegoats—free blacks—so that after 1830, social segregation intensified in New York City . . . And so did the support for slavery."[37] Black scapegoating also fostered white hostility in Philadelphia, where "northern free blacks were condemned for inciting the slaves" in the Nat Turner rebellion in Southampton County, Virginia.[38] Even labor unions with a developing workers' consciousness, third-party formations, and splinter groups from the larger dominant parties that formed to challenge the two-party system were threatened by the abolition of slavery in the South, fearing that it would lead to a large influx of black laborers competing for their jobs. The Workingman's Party, followed by the LocoFoco Party, believing that the two dominant parties did not advocate the interests of workers, were in concert with the Democratic Party and, for that matter, Southern planters on racial matters. "Indeed racism was a peculiarly useful issue, for while Northern Democrats found it more and more difficult to agree with their Southern counterparts on the manner of slavery's expansion into the west, they certainly could find some common ground in their contempt for the black race."[39] Black men and women caught up in this political strife understood at the most basic level that political scapegoating, race-baiting politics, proslavery sentiments expressed by all politicians and most labor leaders, and restrictions on their rights as citizens would, in the near-term and long-term, exclude them from the American polity.

Antebellum politics was intertwined with the larger tapestry of racial, gender, ethnicity, and class subordination, making effective use of the symbolic lore of myths and caricatures that were intrinsic to popular culture. Urbiculture proved instrumental in universalizing black women's oppression by weaving derogatory images of black women into the industrializing and urbanizing process. As urbiculture was packaged for mass consumption among city dwellers, foreigners and rural folk also sought the urbane, more cosmopolitan ways of the city dwellers and embraced those caricatures that defined black women. "The stereotype of the black pervaded even areas where blacks were virtually unknown."[40] The appropriation of symbols, myths, and caricatures of black women had their origins in the economic and sexual exploitation of slavery and became intertwined in the Northern acceptance of slavery, the migration of free blacks to northeastern cities, industrialization, and disaffected white workers' psychological need for scapegoating. The "Mammy" and the "Jezebel" images, migrating to northeastern cities, were integral to the social, political, and economic degradation of free black women. Free black women found that the planter's tentacles had a long reach and that "the Old South's image of slave womanhood emerge[d] as a powerful weapon of white male domination over both free and enslaved women."[41]

Images of black women underwent muted shades of meanings in the new urbiculture. In the doting portrayals of the "Mammy" image dressed in city garments, while "Mammy" was still viewed with superordinate strength and powers of nurturance, black women now were "industrialized" and "marketed" for the developing affluent society. In the construction of the urban "Mammy," black women, serving the political, economic, and social functions of the new industrial system, were billed as still possessing physical endurance and stamina, but for the new wealthy classes. For many black women, domestic service was a lateral move from slavery to freedom. Consequently, the servant-mistress relationship replicated the stereotypical notions of planter aristocracy. When white abolitionist Ellis Gray Loring was seeking employment for some recently emancipated black women, he described them as "strong and healthy," indicating the kind of labor that they were suited for and would perform well.[42] Meeting the needs and desires of the more affluent classes, black women were now perceived as the substrata of the labor force, working as domestics to perform household labor for the affluent, caring for their children, creating leisure time for the women of the household, and providing overall security through constant labor on the family's behalf. "In this way, the devaluation of black womanhood reflected and perpetuated the 'power distance' between whites and blacks."[43]

But the dual imagery of black women from slavery also persisted, and this, too, served a political function.[44] Black women still had to combat the powerful sexual imagery of their promiscuity. In city life, they were perceived as "loose women," women who were readily available and desirous of chance sexual encounters. "The image of the 'bad' black women, in particular, which has persisted into the twentieth century, portrays her as sexually promiscuous."[45] Angela Y. Davis posits that the imagery of black men as rapists complements the image of the black woman as chronically promiscuous.[46] For the urban culture, the notion of black female promiscuity provided sexual fantasies and release of sexual tensions for white men of disparate classes. The not-so-hidden message that black women, due to their lascivious nature, could not be raped made them vulnerable and victimized on city streets, in their workspaces as domestics, and in happenstance encounters by lewd men. The dual imagery permeated the culture, became embedded in the rise of industrial capitalism, and has endured until the contemporary period. Black female imagery, a political and social mechanism for tensions and aggressions in the marketplace, was coeval with the debasement of black women in all facets of life. Black female imagery became popular at a time when leisure-time activities were being developed for disaffected factory workers.

Striking at the heart of black women's symbolism in popular culture were its subversive political and social meanings. Black women's imagery emerged in the Northern industrial order at the time when the nation was forging a national identity and determining who would be incorporated into its collective memory. In the marginalization of black women in free urban centers and in the dislodging of them from the historical center in the American collective consciousness, the society made a deliberate choice to mythologize American and black women's history. By deliberately reconstructing the historical memory, the limitations and shortcomings of the democratic ideals that the nation espoused became readily apparent.[47] For black women, as they were being erased from the historical memory and, consequently, historical sources, the transforming of the American racial landscape in antebellum culture was critical in establishing a basis in free society by which the political, economic, and social status of black women would be determined. Black women's political and economic status varied little throughout the nineteenth century. Most telling is that black women's imagery, socially constructed and packaged for mass consumption, was simultaneously being deconstructed of their womanhood and biographies of self. In this deconstruction process, the attempt was to alienate black women from their natural allies, as during slavery, by eroding their psychological, economic, and political agency, which was the power of their thought and activism in engendering social and political change.

BLACK WOMEN'S CONSCIOUSNESS AND PRAXIS

Alienation was the prevailing catalyst for the development of black women's political consciousness in northeastern cities. Transformed from its incipient beginnings under slavery, where women established a networking system of survival and laid the foundation for a culture of resistance to emerge, black women's political consciousness evolved to a more "conscious" state in northeastern cities, mobilizing black communities for political and social change. Ironically, the slave experience, whether it was urban, rural, or agricultural, prepared black women for alienation and the pervasive racial, gender, and class subordination that comprised city life. In contrast, however, one of the many salient features that freedom and the urban environment did offer antebellum black women was the new marketplace of exchange, a cross-fertilization of ideas, strategies, and goal-setting behavior.[48] Black communities were continuously holding public forums and debates, usually in black churches, on critical issues that impacted upon their lives.

Since black women were unable to participate in mainstream electoral politics that surrounded their daily lives in the city, church organizations, community associations, evangelicalism, and community-based and regional abolitionism offered a venue for black women to expand the political and social dimensions of their lives. Starting with the earlier benevolent societies, the Female Benevolent Society of St. Thomas founded in 1793; the Benevolent Daughters of Philadelphia founded in 1796; the African Female Benevolent Society of Newport, Rhode Island, organized in 1809; the American Female Bond Benevolent Society of Bethel Church, established in 1817; and the Colored Female Religious and Moral Society of Salem, Massachusetts, formed in 1818, black women desired autonomous organizations that reflected their concerns.

By the 1820s, 1830s, and 1840s, black women had a plethora of these societies and associations in northeastern cities.[49] "Through these organizations black women not only contributed to the welfare of their communities, they also participated in the political discussions of the day, a role unfamiliar to most American women of the time."[50] These venues were conducive for not only reform activities that aided the multidimensional aspects of black community life, but they also served as "organizing centers" for all phases of social activism. Black women received training, organizing, and fund-raising skills; learned how to articulate their grievances; created an informal leadership cadre in black communities; and laid the foundation for abolitionism to gain its broad-based currency. The subterranean components of black women's resistance were often found, organized, and promoted in their volunteerism. "In a climate where any type of political opposition might result in life-threatening retaliation by whites, black women organized and collectively promoted reforms through their voluntary organizations and clubs."[51]

Black women's political consciousness was refined via their multifaceted organizational development in the antebellum period. Though starting in the early nineteenth century, by the mid-1840s, black women had developed a vast social and political network of societies, associations, ad hoc community committees, lyceums, and organizations, many with overlapping purposes, cross-fertilization of ideas and membership, and invariably common agendas and goals. While middle-class free black women or women who were members of families of social activists were more active in community life, church and community-based societies encouraged those with little time to give to work on specific projects, as well as those women who sustained the larger antislavery movement. The black press also encouraged and supported black women's social commitment. In 1837, the *Weekly Advocate* made a special plea to black women: "In any enterprise for the improvement of our people—either moral or mental, our hands would be palsied without women's influence. We ask then for the exertion of her influence. It is now needed."[52]

Black women's community activism, however, was a double-edged sword, and some black men and women were in a dilemma about black women maintaining middle-class notions of conventional "womanhood" and respectability in community activities. This dilemma was exacerbated and made particularly poignant by the negative black female imagery that was integral to antebellum culture. "But there were other reasons why organized black women felt that they had to be extremely careful about appearances and behavior. They knew that racist stereotypes made them, like their slave sisters, vulnerable to sexual and moral debasement."[53] Inherent in this dilemma was the notion that black women should stifle their leadership capabilities and remain subordinate to black men in sacred and secular activism. Paralleling middle-class white male and female roles, this would ensure black women's status, confine them within the boundaries of conventional womanhood, and allow black men to play a dominant role in black community activism. Both the black church and press encouraged the conventional standards of womanhood for black women. Samuel Cornish, a renowned abolitionist, Presbyterian minister, and editor of the *Colored American,* cautioned black women who were taking the leadership reins in some community activities by warning them against "masculine views and measures." Cornish argued that "woman was created to be the 'helpmeet' . . . with all the intellectual, moral and physical requisites for her important place."[54] Mary Still, a black educator, also saw the value of black female domesticity in the home and community. "The moral or degraded condition of society depends solely upon the influence of woman, if she be virtuous, pious and industrious, her feet abiding in her own house, ruling her family as well."[55]

Even though black women were receiving contradictory messages about their roles of womanhood, the praxis of black female activism was in supporting the conventions in the home and in the community while simultaneously subverting the existing political environment in the community and society by their creation of a grassroots resistance movement. On the one hand, black women became the mainstay of family and community life; on the other hand, they were contraconventional in expanding the boundaries of community activism, challenging ecclesiastical sexism, developing autonomous entrepreneurial activities, and creating political space for their participation in the abolitionist movement. The combination of conventional and contraconventional vehicles of black women's participation in social and political activities was one of the ways that black women found of coping with and yet challenging their oppression at the same time. For example, Emma Gloucester, who was the wife of the well-known black clergyman J. N. Gloucester of New York City, headed charity benefits for the New York Colored Orphan Asylum, while she sent monies to her friend, John Brown, to finance his raid at Harpers Ferry in his grandiose plan to liberate the slaves.[56]

Despite the admonitions of the black church and press against women pursuing business or politics, black women expanded their entrepreneurial activities, making such a decisive impact in the community that it launched their community activism. Too, black women used their organizations to send a clear message about their political and gender positions. It is within this context that Maria W. Stewart was invited to lecture at the Afric-American Female Intelligence Society in 1832, when only a year earlier she had asked, "How long shall the daughters of Africa be compelled to bury their minds and talents beneath a load of iron pots and kettles?"[57] While Stewart's stinging criticism of black men would soon motivate her "to shake the dust of Boston from her shoes and move to New York," she had obviously planted the seeds of consciousness with black Bostonian women.[58] Stewart also encouraged black women to take their rightful place in the public discourse on racism by "striv[ing], by their own example both in public and private, to assist those who are endeavoring to stop the strong current of prejudice that flows so profusely against us at present."[59]

Grassroots activism on the part of black women was also evident in their direct participation in slave rescues. Slave rescues in northeastern cities brought black women in direct confrontation with white male authority and sometimes black public criticism. The Abolition Riot demonstrated that black women could mobilize and pursue an independent course of political action to effect immediate change. There were similar efforts in the Boston community. Nancy Prince and a group of black women and children in Boston removed a slavecatcher from a neighbor's home by "dragg[ing] him to the door and thrust[ing] him out of the house." The women then gave hot pursuit, with "their numbers constantly increasing" as they chased him down the street.[60] Abolitionist "Sarah Remond was one of those involved in the bizarre effort to free Henry 'Box' Brown, who escaped from slavery in a box mailed to Philadelphia via Railway Express." In New York City, black women participated in a slave rescue attempt only to be criticized by the Colored American for their heroic actions. "Everlasting shame and remorse seize upon those females that so degraded themselves yesterday. We beg their husbands to keep them at home."[61] This subterranean grassroots activity indicated that black communities were multilayered and that black women continued to create political and economic spaces for their independent protest strategies.

Black women created, shaped, and determined their political space in the building of the collective "we." This claiming of political space by black women was the beginning of a collective political identity. Of necessity, black women were transformed by this collective identity and honed their political skills on their increasing political and social activities.

Black female community activists painted a diverse body of organizations with the broad brush of abolitionism and black protest, viewing the emancipation of the slaves, the collective improvement of the black community, and the education and eradication of sexism as inseparable issues. The evolving political consciousness and praxis were most pronounced in the mobilization of organizations toward collective goals. Limited in available resources—that is, finances, power, influence, and contacts—the utilization of their labor power and these manifold organizations became the political resources and tools that transformed black women's individual powerlessness into powerful collectives for social change. In this sense, black women were empowering themselves. The conflation, however, of alienation, the free flow of ideas, the sanction of militant action, and organizational development was an empowering process that placed black women way beyond conventional boundaries of female activism. These community organizations centered black women in the larger protest and abolitionist struggles.

BLACK WOMEN AND THE MICROMOBILIZATION OF COMMUNITIES

Black women's micromobilization of black communities was driven by a conglomerate of oppressive forces. Transhistorically, scholars have viewed race and color as well as the deliberate exclusion of blacks from the American polity as the dominant factors in black community mobilization. Political scientist Marguerite Ross Barnett, in commenting on racism, observes that "racism emerged as a rationalization for slavery" and notes the protracted influence of racial ideology upon black communities: "racism is a pervasive ideology that ranks Blacks as a group below all others because it assumes the inherent genetic inferiority of Blacks."[62] Other scholars discuss the role that historical relations played in towns and cities that provided the context for black mobilization to occur.[63] In antebellum northeastern cities, blacks began to mobilize around their group-centered oppression. Charles Tilly views this type of mobilization as "defensive mobilization [that occurs when] a threat from outside induces the members of a group to pool their resources to fight off the enemy."[64] Early black communities perceived the threat to be the local, state, and regional governments; the law; the police apparatus; Southern planters in collusion with capitalists; and the customary treatment of blacks. Initially, these communities mobilized their resistance against these oppressive forces through the black church. V. P. Franklin argues that the independent church movement among free blacks was the initial step of resistance. "From this independent religious base, free blacks moved into other areas and organized or supported resistance campaigns against the political and social oppression of Afro-Americans."[65]

Driving much of the collective mobilization of black communities were the micromobilization efforts of black women that politicized black communities, creating a "network of resistance" or culture of resistance that brought community members together around important concerns. Black women's "protest activity [was] the result of a combination of expanding political opportunities and indigenous organization" that was micromanaged by the women themselves.[66] Temma Kaplan notes that women in Barcelona, Spain, in seeking to enlarge their sphere of influence, politicized the entire community around critical issues. Other scholars have noted that these types of political activities contribute to the formulation of a collective identity and group consciousness.[67] Black women were able to reinforce the existing racial solidarity of urban blacks. Although all were interconnected by the common threads of abolition and liberation, the autonomous societies and organizations could also be viewed as "political units" in the broader framework of urban black resistance.

For black women, their alienation in the society and "the twin demons of history and memory" of enslavement, as well as the ever-present reminder that approximately 90 percent of blacks were still slaves, remained a guiding force behind their social activism.[68] Black women played a pivotal role in black communities in politicizing and recruiting members for political and social participation. They formed the majority of the black population in these port cities and were the main conduits for newcomers looking for work, lodging, and social ties. Boardinghouse keepers were another important resource to help newcomers acclimate themselves to the community and to refer them to key members of community life. Black women also formed the majority of church parishioners and were members of auxiliaries that served both the church and the community. These women, then, had an informal knowledge of families in stress and overall community concerns. As laborers and entrepreneurs, black women moved about the community and the city acquiring information through their work. They also developed substantial public patronage through word of mouth. This data gathering and dissemination of information and ideas were important resources in the community, linking a vast informal network of residents to common sources of information.

Black women's formal organizational development was the canopy that overarched this network of resistance and vast interactive pattern of newsgathering as a major node in planning their community activities. The daily organizing, promotion of critical events, dates and times of fund-raisers, and recruitment efforts relied on these informal community contacts. Ad hoc committees, benevolent associations, literary societies, and church auxiliaries laid the foundation for community residents to become involved, either on a single project or on an ongoing basis, in community activities.[69] For black women, their organizational development paralleled the culture of resistance that they created as nexus women in slave communities. These nexus women in freedom brought disparate members of the community together, facilitated intergenerational bonding and socialization, and sustained the notion of resistance and protest against oppression. Such women may be an earlier version of Belinda Robnett's depiction of black women as "bridge leaders" during the civil rights movement. As activists, black women "created a particular substructure of leadership, which became a critical recruitment and mobilization force for the movement."[70] The material realities of alienation dictated that black women utilize a method of "intrusive resistance" in their micromobilization efforts.

COMMUNITY-BASED ACTIVISM

Permeating the organizational development of black women in the 1820s and 1830s was their sense of spirituality and the intertwining goals of the collective advancement of free blacks and the abolition of slavery. The latter two goals were later adopted as the goals of the larger abolitionist movement. Black women supported the contention, pervasive in black communities, that the areas of benevolence, education, temperance, and morality were all indices of self-improvement that would enhance the quality of life of free blacks, advance their quest for social equality, and in the long run combat notions held by whites of blacks' genetic inferiority. Interconnected with this theme of black socioeconomic progress was the theme calling for the immediate emancipation of the slaves. Black women knew, as did all blacks, that one segment of the population could not succeed without the other. While both of these goals appeared insurmountable, black women were centered in a spirituality that linked their fate to the cosmos, and, empowered by God, they were waging a righteous struggle. For Maria W. Stewart, the battle lines were clearly drawn

ing black women's course of action: "We will not come out
ou with swords and staves, as against a thief (Matthew 26:55);
..._ ..._ vill tell you that our souls are fired with the same love of liberty
and independence with which your souls are fired."[71]

In actualizing their goals, black women employed a number of
strategies, in effect, combining their more conventional roles of female
domesticity and expectations with those that were contraconventional
and sure to arouse the ire of more conservative members of the black
community. A prominent feature of black women's community activism
was the varied roles that they played in the black church. Although black
males dominated the hierarchical structure of the black church, depending on the church affiliation, black women did participate on major decision-making committees regarding the ministerial leadership and the
functioning of the church. Some black women were instrumental in the
founding of churches. "In 1847 six members of Manhattan's Abyssinian
Baptist Church who lived in Brooklyn met at the home of Maria Hampton on Fair Street. Their mission was to create a Baptist church in their
own community."[72] Black women's subordinate role in the black church,
however, did not obfuscate their organizational skills, knowledge, and
commitment, and these women were critical to the institutions' survival.
Mary Still, a black educator, admonished those who criticized female participation in the church in an obvious attempt to stifle their leadership
potential: "We are sometimes told that females should have nothing to
do with the business of the Church. But they have yet to learn that when
female labor is withdrawn the Church must cease to exist."[73] Women
who believed that "God had called them to preach" and were rebuffed
by male ministers took their spiritual calling to the people by becoming
evangelists. These women, who wanted to become spiritual leaders in the
black church, reinforced the dramatic tension in black churches over
female leadership and role diversity and, in their wake, created a new
political dimension in evangelicalism.

A more conventional activity for black women, however, was the
development of autonomous benevolent societies. Reinforcing their spiritual or Christian ethic, these societies allowed black women to carry out
"good deeds" in the church and community, combining the sacred and
the secular and immeasurably assisting those in need. Providing both
financial and spiritual support, benevolent societies such as the Daughters of Zion Angolian Ethiopian Society and the Female Beneficial Philanthropic Society of Zoar focused on the needy in Philadelphia's black
community. Other societies, such as the aforementioned African Female

Bond Benevolent Society of Bethel Church and its New York affiliate, the New York Benevolent Branch of Bethel, and the Daughters of Tapsico, also of Mother Bethel Church, focused on caring for indigent church members and on providing for funeral expenses and financial support for widows and children. Similarly, the female branch of Zion in New York City provided comparable coverage for its members.[74] While daily life in the urban environment was hard for blacks and black women especially needed the unemployment coverage, the rituals of funerals and funeral expenses were part of a long African tradition. "Perhaps the strongest link between the African societies in America and the African heritage of their members was the centrality of burial benefits among their various functions."[75]

These church groups were also important in promoting critical fund-raising events, viewed as a strength of black women's organizations and perceived as conventional women's work. While a conventional tool, black women's fund-raising efforts spearheaded much of community-based activism. "Black women carried on activities which made much of the community work possible, particularly fund-raising. Through the church, in independent bazaars and community fairs, black women collected thousands of dollars."[76] These fund-raisers, however, honed the organizational skills of black women and provided them with critical expertise in the concomitant and subsequent abolitionist activities. Black churches were sustained financially by a variety of fund-raising activities, such as church suppers, public forums, lectures, concerts, bake sales, used-clothing drives, and holiday fairs. "In 1837, for example, female members of the African Methodist Episcopal Church in New York City held a fair at which they offered for sale 'a general assortment of Fancy Articles, Dry Goods, Toys, Confectionery.'"[77] The United Daughters of Conference, an auxiliary to the African Methodist Episcopal Zion Church, and the Female Education Society at the First Colored Presbyterian Church used their fund-raisers largely for ministerial support. Other societies like New York Benevolent Daughters of Esther Association, a church affiliate of the Abyssinian Baptist Church, used its incoming dues to fund crisis and medical care for its members and others who were indigent.

Although black women often integrated sacred and secular activities, there were many organizations and associations that reflected a secular focus and hence drew on a larger membership. Mutual aid and benevolent societies, by far the most prevalent societies among black women, evinced a broad spectrum of participation. However, what was of great importance in these autonomous organizations was the fact that black women were running them themselves, and, as workers, black women were continually seeking ways to cushion family stress in periods of unemployment. The Daughters of Africa, founded in 1821 in Philadelphia, handled sensitive negotiations between contentious members, chastised wayward society members, and penalized those women who were "disorderly and improper in the Extreme."[78] In this sense, the society, by providing methods of adjudication, consistently reinforcing the obligations and expectations of its members, and serving as a place where one's grievances were legitimized and validated in egregious disputes, strengthened the entire collective.

Black women, as individuals and as members of societies, contained the hopes and dreams of community residents that their children would achieve an education and become contributing members of society. Education, long denied to blacks, was intrinsically valued for creating an independent and liberated individual who would continue the traditions of building the black community's infrastructure and become a viable member of the antislavery cause. The community's stress on education led most educated black women to become educators. Too, it was a conventional and "respectable" occupation for women, and educated black women were severely restricted in their occupational choices, but black communities shared a source of racial pride when their children were taught by black teachers. "In black communities throughout the North, black women started and maintained schools for children and adults."[79] Charlotte Forten's life typified the high expectations, unrealistic or not, of many urban black parents. When Forten was attending school and experiencing some anxiety over reading her compositions before strangers, through a conscious effort on her part, she was able to overcome her fears and reinforce her political commitment. "If I were to tell Mrs. R[emond] this, I know she would ask how I could expect to become what I often say I should like to be—an Anti-Slavery lecturer. But I think that I should then trust to the inspiration of the subject."[80] In 1862, Forten, as a young woman, went to Port Royal, South Carolina, to teach the newly emancipated slaves. Following the Civil War, Forten spent the rest of her life as a teacher, writer, and civil rights activist.

Alongside the Institute for Colored Youth in Philadelphia and African schools for boys and girls in New York City and Boston, black women operated independent schools. Since racially segregated black schools, where they existed, were woefully inadequate and inferior to white schools in these areas, black parents were eager to send their children to schools operated by black educators, although the tuition and fees were often an insurmountable hardship. Sarah Mapps Douglass, an educator and abolitionist, established the only high school academy for young black girls in Philadelphia. Operating on a shoestring budget, Douglass was able to maintain the school for several years through her contact with Margaretta, Harriet, and Sarah Forten, who held critical positions in the interracial Philadelphia Female Antislavery Society.[81] Other black women trained black youngsters in specific areas of study. The renowned opera singer Elizabeth Taylor Greenfield, dubbed "The Black Swan," "returned to America in the 1850s, from a triumphant concert tour of Europe, which included an audience with Queen Victoria, and settled into teaching music to young Philadelphians."[82] Societies like Boston's Garrison Society established a Garrison Juvenile Society for black girls to train them in sewing. By providing these quasi-apprenticeship programs, not only would these young girls have a trade, but black women were connecting the next generation of women to their obligations and expectations as women as well as evincing an early commitment to the abolitionist cause.

Wherever there was a significant black population, black women founded an African Dorcas Association.[83] While principally to help the destitute, the function and emphasis of the association were different from city to city. In Philadelphia, the association concentrated on distributing food to the poor, providing clothing, and, in emergencies, offering limited financial support. The New York Dorcas Association, however, operated as an educational support service by providing clothing for schoolchildren. Pragmatically, black women realized that a number of children who had significant absenteeism may have had inadequate clothing, and the association pledged to "afford relief in clothing, hats, and shoes, as far as our means may enable us, to such children as regularly attend the schools belonging to the Manumission Society."[84] Although the impetus behind the founding and maintenance of the New York Dorcas Association came from black ministers and a few white businessmen who supervised the association's activities, the women did the actual work of running the organization as well as the sewing and mending of garments for schoolchildren. Similarly, black and white reformers were instrumental in maintaining the Colored Orphan Asylum for children and the Colored Home for the Aged in New York City.

Black women also participated in ad hoc collectives for specific projects. These projects provided another venue for women to become involved in community activism on a short-term basis. In Boston, a group of black women "decided that something must be done about the loud noise the children made going to and from school" and organized "a patrol to curb the disturbances."[85] Other women used ad hoc collectives as a vehicle to foster black upliftment. In most instances, since these involved fund-raising initiatives, black women brought their fund-raising skills to replenish scarce institutional or community resources.

One of their endeavors was to support the abolitionist press. These women thought that the abolitionist press provided a salient contribution to black upliftment, "believing that the success of our cause depends mainly upon Self-Exertion and that the Press and Public Lecturer are the most powerful means by which an end so desirable can be attained."[86] The abolitionist press, black or white, was a fledgling enterprise at best. Some of the black women who organized the Women's Association of Philadelphia had previously raised monies for the antislavery journal the *Liberator* and were now organizing benefits to raise funds for Frederick Douglass's journal, the *North Star.* Not to be outdone, black women in New York City also formed a North Star Association and made similar contributions to aid Douglass's financially strapped weekly.[87]

Self-improvement societies among black women reflected the need and desire for independence and ambition typical of urban dwellers. Temperance, education, and the free produce movement were subsumed under the broader rubric of the collective elevation of the black community. With these societies, black women emphasized their desire to acquire knowledge, expand their intellectual endeavors, and reinforce the abolitionism that permeated organizational life in black communities. Reality also dictated for black women that they could actualize skills that could be used in labor productivity. On different education levels, a broad spectrum of black women found a venue in self-improvement societies that reaffirmed a sense of themselves, contributed to their wholeness of being, and contoured their political consciousness. Black women who had few skills found a sanctuary where they could improve and advance rudimentary training. Black female abolitionists like Sarah Forten of Philadelphia, Henrietta Green Regulus Ray of New York City, and Maria W. Stewart of Boston and later New York City also had a venue for essays, works in progress, or protest concepts and ideas. Some women may have been perfecting basic skills; others were honing their leadership potential by gathering a new body of knowledge from the lectures, readings, and new contacts; and still others may have been utilizing this political space for social criticism. The dynamics of these groups agitated struggle and expanded the boundaries of community activism.

The grounding of abolitionism in black women's organizations spearheaded the quest for full citizenship for free blacks. Declarative statements of goals to eradicate racism were embodied in the constitutions of black female organizations and in their political activities. One self-improvement society, the Female Literary Association of Philadelphia, founded in 1831, meshed the goal of educational endeavors for its members to the fight for racial justice. "As daughters of a despised race," it was their "duty . . . to cultivate the talents . . . that by so doing, we may break down the strong barrier of prejudice."[88] Sarah Forten, Sarah Mapps Douglass, and several other black female activists were the impetus behind the institutional formation of the society. Although the "mental feasts" included readings, essays, and works in progress anonymously submitted, the members hoped to spread this enlightening process to black women in other cities by having their constitution, poetry, and prose published in the *Liberator*.

Character development was an integral part of the aims of self-improvement societies. Women believed that education and morality not only empowered their own lives but also facilitated their role as parents in raising their children. The Edgeworth Literary Association and the Female Minervan Association, both of Philadelphia and founded soon after the Female Literary Society, modeled themselves on the latter, with an emphasis on sponsoring educational programs and forums for ongoing works from society members. The Ladies Literary Society of the City of New York had a different focus. Women in this society demonstrated their political commitment by furnishing monies to sustain the black newspaper the *Colored American,* an institutional voice for black communities. The society also consistently channeled funds to support the New York Committee of Vigilance so that the monies could be used by David Ruggles for harboring fugitives and supplying them with food, clothing, shelter, safe passage, and, when necessary, temporary employment.[89] This subterranean component of black women's societies, deploying resources into critical areas of resistance and abolitionism, speaks volumes about black women's political consciousness and commitment to social change.

The seedlings of black women's political consciousness were firmly planted before the nascency of modern abolitionism in the antebellum era. Shaped and nurtured by the protest tradition that arose with the founding of the black church, by the material realities that forged their oppression with the Northern black migration of the early 1800s, and by the contemporary black abolitionism and protest in Northern black communities, black women were a part of the political struggle that challenged the political hegemony in American society in the early 1830s. Having their political awareness continuously refined in both crisis and struggle, antebellum black women, individually and collectively, protested against the forces of slavery, racism, sexism, and impoverishment that circumscribed their lives. Much of their consciousness was attributed to the chameleon-like effects of oppression, which placed antebellum black communities at the mercy of varying political currents characterized chiefly by white supremacy and economic exploitation. Counteractively, the political strategies and methods of resistance of these black communities that were in perpetual crisis varied with the level, type, and intensity of the political repression. At the heart of the black liberation struggle for survival, freedom, and political equality lay community activism, giving the struggle its resiliency and vibrancy.

Alienation and activism were dialectical in the lives of black women. While political and social activism would have undoubtedly been a strong factor in black women's lives, particularly since the philosophy of self-determination permeated black thought, the alienation of black women from the American polity did contour the ongoing struggle for black equality and abolitionism. In the creation and maintenance of the community's infrastructure, they addressed not only their needs as community residents but also the issues and concerns of all of the community members. Black women constructed a network and culture of resistance via their autonomous societies that defined their path of political development. The application of both conventional and contraconventional venues of political and social activism were germane to their overall participation and effectiveness. Their community activism was the incipient stage of their political development in northeastern cities, and their use of varied strategies allowed them to expand these boundaries and paved the way for their broader influence in evangelicalism and the larger abolitionist movement.

CHAPTER 6

Hallowed Fire

*The Gospel Politics of Black
Female Evangelists*

> Many will suffer for pleading the cause of oppressed Africa, and I
> shall glory in being one of her martyrs; for I am firmly persuaded,
> that the God in whom I trust is able to protect me from the rage and
> malice of mine enemies.
> MARIA W. STEWART, Boston, 1831

THE SPIRITUAL CONSCIOUSNESS OF EARLY BLACK FEMALE EVAN-
gelists emerged in concert with the anomie and deracination of people
losing their religious anchor in the changing political and social landscape following the American Revolution. Within this transitional period
came the Second Great Awakening, circa 1787–1845 ("awakenings are
the means by which cultures adapt themselves to traumatic social
change"), bringing evangelical fervor, inner stability, and vast societal
transformations. Evangelical Christianity, in this multidimensional
capacity, became a catalyst for social and moral regeneration.[1] The
gospel mission of early black female evangelists pivoted as much on the
spiritual strivings of people amid societal upheavals as it did on the social
oppression dominating black lives. In reclaiming their personal identities
and their family lives, they were plagued, as were all blacks, with the
material realities of slavery and racial and sexual discrimination as they
struggled for their spiritual center in order to spread the gospel and serve
their God. Hence, early black female evangelists such as Jarena Lee, Elizabeth, Zilpha Elaw, Rebecca Cox Jackson, Sojourner Truth, Nancy
Prince, and Julia A. J. Foote sat astride contrasting worlds, a transcendental one where there was a perennial search for inner peace and a temporal world full of turbulence, strife, and uncertainty. "They all testified

to God's providential care for an independent black woman in a racist as well as sexist society."[2] Believing that they were "called to preach the gospel," anointed by God to spread God's Word on earth, these itinerant preachers saw beyond the temporal plane as they embraced the transcendental aspects of their divine mission.[3] The social and pious construction of these early black female Evangelicals' divine missions, of necessity, integrated the spiritual evolutionary path of their consciousness with the material realities that emanated from their oppression as black women.

Morally armed with their faith, evangelical fervor, and a passion for justice, Lee, Elizabeth, and Elaw moved into the public sphere in the early 1800s. In claiming their sacred ground, these gospel ministers preached mainly across the northern and western regions of the United States, although Elizabeth and Elaw frequently went south, believing that, among whites as well as slaves, there was a strong potential harvest of souls. Although most of these Evangelicals drew their converts from such disparate venues as rural camp meetings, frontier homes, and town meetings, they could also be found conducting prayer meetings, classes, and spontaneous exhortations in women's homes, bonding with potential converts and the "chosen" as they spread God's Word. Evangelical Christianity quickly gained adherents, proving to be a passionate faith offering fortitude and spiritual salvation for true believers. Resonating with many blacks was the egalitarian ethos in the doctrine of Arminianism, that Christ died so that all may achieve salvation; the immensely appealing charismatic sermons; and the overall joy of the worship service. "The egalitarian tendency of evangelical revivals to level the souls of all men before God had been one of the major attractions to black converts in the first place."[4]

In spite of its widespread appeal among the masses, philosophical egalitarianism, and broad societal criticism, evangelicalism did not produce enduring changes in racial relations. Underpinning the Second Great Awakening were the same racist sentiments that were evident in the First Great Awakening (1725–1770s), where white ministers were chagrined that "Negroes (had) even taken upon themselves the business of preaching."[5] By the time of John Wesley's death in 1791, white evangelists were already compromising their religious tenets with slavery, racism, and sexism. "The evangelicals' accommodation to slavery in the 1740s and 1750s led to the development of a paternalistic ethos and created a legacy for future generations." By the movement's compromise with slavery and racism and white Evangelicals embracing the doctrine of white supremacy, the dynamics were set in motion for a separate path of spiritual development for black and white converts.[6] Fueling the impetus was the estrangement already felt by black parishioners in Northern churches, which quickly led to the desire, on the part of blacks, to institutionalize black religious development.

Black female evangelists did not emerge unscathed from the estrangement process but were rendered far more vulnerable. As itinerant ministers, they were not officially recognized by any institutional body and were seen at the camp meetings they frequented as a "transient phenomenon outside the mainstream of institutionalized religion."[7] Undaunted and resolute, black female evangelists preached to vast interracial audiences as a part of their ministry, "claim[ing] their own power and operat[ing] from the margins, outside of the boundaries of traditional church rule."[8] In spite of their marginalization in the hierarchy of black churches, their tedious schedules, and prolonged absences from home for months at a time, they chose their "home" church to be one of the independent Northern black churches in the communities in which they lived.

For the most part, the spiritual maturation of black female evangelists took place in Northern cities and towns, where many groups of religious enthusiasts had shared their spiritual messages. Julia Foote "grew up in western New York's notorious 'Burned Over District,' where waves of revivalism had left in their backwash numerous sects devoted to the attainment of Christian perfection."[9] Jarena Lee's first religious encounter was with a Presbyterian missionary in southern New Jersey in 1804. Zilpha Elaw was associated with the Methodists outside of Philadelphia in the early 1800s, and despite her recollections about the historical period, there was a growing number of Methodists in the area by that time.[10] Although Sojourner Truth's freedom in 1826 and subsequent evangelicalism occurred a decade or so later, she, too, was deeply involved in Methodism. "Isabella [Sojourner Truth], being poor and fervent, belonged to the holiness tendency within New York Methodism."[11] But Truth's spiritual trajectory provides a vastly different contrast to most black female evangelists who anchored themselves as members in Northern black churches. Flirting briefly with African Zionism in the early 1830s, Truth, emerging as an evangelist, was instead attracted to the predominantly white revival cult of Prophet Matthias, and by the 1840s had become a Millerite, a member of a group of religious enthusiasts who preached that the beginning of the millennium would occur in 1843. While other black female evangelists, like Zilpha Elaw, embraced this doomsday prophecy, what distinguishes Truth from these other black women is that her spiritual evolution was centered among white revivalists.[12] The material conditions of most of these black evangelists, however, were strikingly similar—Truth and Elizabeth both had been slaves; Lee, Elaw, and Foote were bound out as servant girls in their youth; and still others, like Nancy Prince, were impoverished but free—paralleling the racial and economic oppression typical of free black Northerners.

Black female Evangelicals viewed their divine mission in universal and humanist terms, carrying the gospel to homes, churches, communities, and neighboring countries. Those who heard a more distant call for their gospel labors served as preachers or missionaries in foreign countries. Betsey Stockton, for example, a recently emancipated slave from Princeton, New Jersey, served as a Presbyterian missionary to Hawaii in 1822. First a slave and then a domestic servant of Ashbel Green, "Betsey took advantage of her freedom and surroundings to educate herself." Coming with Stockton's spiritual awakening in the "revival that swept through the College of New Jersey in 1815" was a commitment to become a missionary in Africa. Having those plans thwarted, Stockton did accept an invitation by the American Board of Commissioners for Foreign Missions to become a missionary in Hawaii, where she remained until 1825. After a brief return to the United States, Stockton "was sent to Canada . . . where she established a school for Indians." By 1830, Stockton had once again returned to the United States, where she founded a school for black infants in Philadelphia, subsequently duplicating those same efforts in Princeton.[13]

Some black women became missionaries after serious unfortunate circumstances occurred in their lives that triggered old dreams, desires, and goals. Nancy Prince became a missionary after spending nine years in Russia with her husband, where she owned and operated her own infant clothing business catering to the Royal Court. Unable to endure the Russian winters any longer, Prince soon returned to the United States to recover her health. Following her recovery, Prince's missionary work took her to Jamaica, where she worked with the newly emancipated blacks in the early 1840s. "My mind, after the emancipation in the West Indies, was bent upon going to Jamaica. A field of usefulness seemed spread out before me."[14] Other Evangelicals, like Zilpha Elaw, whose itinerant ministry kept her stateside for most of her life, responded to inner visions and messages from God to preach abroad. "I there heard the voice of the Almighty, saying, 'I have a message for her to go with upon the high seas, and she will go.'"[15] According to her narrative, although somewhat tenuous at this point, Elaw preached in England for at least five years. Remarkably, these evangelists-missionaries, responding to their innermost spiritual thoughts and feelings, were not constrained by either the geographical borders of the United States or the conditional emancipation that defined free black existence. Their spirituality, permeating their entire lives, proved to be a critical source of their empowerment.

Most black female Evangelicals developed their ministry in the United States and, in seeking to escape the racism and sexism pervasive in white evangelical Christianity, found their missionary efforts to be vastly different from their white counterparts.' As black female evangelists preached the gospel, they formed interracial spiritual ties to the larger evangelical community and often used these opportunities to speak out against slavery, racism, and sexism. Despite these connections to the larger evangelical community, however, black evangelists frequently reflected in their exhortations the priestly function and prophetic traditions of the black church. Nor did they retreat on those issues that confounded black women's lives. Singular in their religious resolve, black female evangelists challenged the social inequities that oppressed them as black women. "Female converts to the cause later became some of the most outspoken social reformers of the age."[16] They embraced contra-conventional views on women in the ministry, believing that God, not men, determined who was "called" to preach the gospel and out of necessity became active combatants in challenging ecclesiastical sexism. When Elizabeth was sharply criticized for her preaching, which black church elders viewed as "contrary to the discipline—[she] being a woman," Elizabeth, giving as good as she got, retorted with what "makes them think they are qualified to be judges of the ministry, . . . judging of the revelations that are given to others, while they have received none themselves."[17] With equal religious fervor, these gospel pioneers challenged Southern slavery and Northern racial discrimination, holding society up to the same moral barometer by which they guided their own lives. In seeking liberation for their spiritual voices in the ministry, it was by spiritual extension that these evangelists spearheaded the challenge to sexism within the black church.[18] This tedious, often acrimonious challenge by female itinerant preachers to the male-dominated black church hierarchy has been noted by Nellie Y. McKay, who comments that "in its political and revolutionary significance, their long struggle against the church fathers is second only to their struggles, alongside their men, against slavery and white racism."[19]

The moral prism of these preaching women formed a buffer against worldly criticism, giving them agency through their faith. Motivated by their faith, these gospel pioneers possessed individual and collective voices against all forms of societal injustices. Sporadically, Lee and Elaw shared their spiritual mission together, copartnering in their ministry and hence empowering each other's social consciousness. Their spiritual narratives evinced their "feminist ideals sanctioned by evangelical Christianity."[20]

What marks the early resistance of these evangelists was the double dynamic of a personal desire to control their freedom and a fledging consciousness to end their condition of servitude or indentured labor. In struggling to claim themselves, these female evangelists as youngsters, which may give us a fuller picture of resistance among slave children and free black youngsters, sought agency over their spiritual and material lives. This political sense of spirituality was common to many female evangelists, where as youngsters the process of merging their social consciousness with their piety had begun. Serving as the major impetus for these defiant evangelists was not only the empowering sense of their spiritual awakenings but also the close kinship ties or historical memories of family life. The separation from their families and the keen longing to be home exacerbated the challenges to their new environment; spiritual awakening was the instrument by which they empowered themselves. Lee was separated from her family at seven years of age; Elizabeth was sold before she was ten years of age; and Foote became a servant girl at ten years of age. Despite the adverse circumstances affecting their lives and the obvious impoverishment, their families served as a buffer between them and their surrounding material conditions, mitigating some of the harshness of black existence. Even though the families were powerless to effect social change, they still provided those enriching intangibles, such as love and security, for their members. The active ingredients of love and security became contributing factors in providing the youngsters with fortitude and courage.

These women followed in the tradition of black female religious leaders in slave communities by refining the resistance tradition in freedom with the utilization of their gospel labors in fortifying their inner spirits, bringing the masses to salvation, and protesting against oppression. The common thread between the resistance of slave women and black female Evangelicals lay in the economic realities that shaped the contours of their oppression. For most black female evangelists, slavery and indentured labor had been an inescapable factor in their lives, and it was within the perils of servitude that these women, as youngsters, had demonstrated their own resistance, giving their oppression voices. Thus, for many slave women who were emancipated by the antebellum era, their resistance started in their formative years and was transformed as they confronted the exigencies of free black community life.

Captured in their spiritual narratives were some of the power and energy that must have emanated from their sermons, testimonies, prayers, and spontaneous exhortations, all bearing witness to their state of divine grace. But these narratives also provided living testimonies of the racial as well as the ecclesiastical and societal sexual discrimination that were living entities in black women's lives. Zilpha Elaw was preaching in a small town when the service was interrupted by a gang of ruffians. Elaw recounted that the leader "came close up to me, making a demonstration as if he intended to seize or strike me, but this producing no impression upon me, he stood over me as if he would take my life; but God was with me, and I felt no fear."[21] Confronted continuously by men who sought to place them in the more traditional gender spheres, the moral prism through which they lived their lives reinforced and buttressed their atypical gender roles in society. The state of divine grace for black female evangelists, most particularly evinced by the sanctification experiences, proved a transformative vehicle of empowerment, self-confidence, and self-esteem that only the anointed possessed. Within these moral parameters, black female evangelists' divine mission encompassed an embryonic consciousness of the oppression of African Americans; a fledging political critique of slavery, racial caste, and sexism; and political and social activism in the sacred and secular spheres. By intertwining the sacred and secular spheres, black female evangelists became important tributaries of the early protest movement gaining momentum in nascent Northern black communities.

MORAL CENTERS OF LEADERSHIP

The evangelical ethos permeating the country in the early 1800s, the parallel institutionalization of the black church, and blacks claiming public space for kindred historical community celebrations in such cities as Philadelphia, Boston, and New York were all contributing factors to the spiritual development of black female evangelists and their entry into the public sphere.[22] As these gospel pioneers, steeped in piety and imbued with their own sense of divine power, forged a public redemptive path, they became the moral centers of leadership for the intellectual discourse and political praxis of black women mobilizing for social change. More than spreading the gospel, black female evangelists gave black women's political activism moral agency. For example, morality intertwined with justice drove black female evangelists' activism: "Morality was also central to the material world-view of antebellum Black women and was at the core of their political activism. Black women viewed their morality, aspirations, and political commitment all through a religious prism. It was their spiritual consciousness that defined the parameters of their political action."[23]

By constructing moral parameters around black female discourse and political activism, black female evangelists strove to dislodge the contemporary negative images of black women, alternatively the "Mammy" or "Jezebel" images, and the growing antebellum caricatures of black women that were increasingly gaining in popularity, resulting from their victimization in slavery. Although partly commercialized to detract workers from class and labor tensions and obfuscate worker alienation in the capitalist economy, degrading racial images of blacks provided a source of entertainment affording the white working-class a sense of superiority and complacency with their material world.[24] A patriarchal construction, these images blamed black women for their sexual exploitation during slavery and made them vulnerable to all forms of harassment as free women.

While the intent of negative black women's images was to deflect the responsibility away from white slaveholders for the sexual and physical exploitation of black women, they also absolved society from its responsibility and complicity in the maintenance and perpetuation of the institution of slavery itself. Negative black female imagery fueled society's complacency with slavery and, subsequently, all patriarchal forms of gender oppression. The inculcation of negative black female imagery into antebellum culture not only rationalized the institution of slavery and its degradation of free blacks but also eroded the essence of the society's humanitarian ethos. For black female evangelists, the morality inherent in their divine mission evinced a flawed society that was in need of spiritual redemption. Just as compelling for these itinerant ministers was that their moral prism empowered black women, providing the context for their protest and mobilization.

Traveling hundreds of miles annually in their spiritual efforts, black female evangelists operationalized their divine mission via the vehicle of their gospel labors, enlarging the boundaries of black women's influence in the public sphere beyond their initial community-based activism. In so doing, they contributed to the broadening of the sphere of black women's political activism, which ultimately included international abolitionism. With their gospel message, black female evangelists reached deep into society's core, challenging slavery, racism, and sexism on their own moral terms and confronting black and white authorities that sought to stifle their fledging ministries. These gospel pioneers spread the intertwining sacred and secular message of the black church, of protest and providence, far beyond the borders of black communities.

SPIRITUAL AWAKENINGS AND EMPOWERMENT

The empowering process for black female evangelists, operating in tandem with their spiritual awakenings, began in the early stages of their lives. Common and somewhat deceptive to the spiritual narratives of many black female evangelists was the tangential homage that they paid to these formative years, often characterized by their precondition to worldly sin and then followed by a more intense concentration on the spiritual forces and gospel labors that dominated the major portions of their lives. Having already been seasoned by religious conversion, followed by sanctification several years later, and years of an itinerant ministry, these evangelists recounted their lives, ennobling their state of divine grace while diminishing those years that impacted upon their character formation. But it was at the incipient stage of their spiritual journey that black female evangelists, as youngsters, began to defy their labor-intensive environment, expand the boundaries of their lives, and reclaim themselves.

One primary characteristic that black female evangelists experienced in their formative years was an inchoate spiritual awakening that had a profound effect in determining their resistance to their oppression. Frequently viewed as a "spiritual essence," or identifying these evangelists with an early predilection toward godliness, such a spiritual awakening was often unique to their familial environment. In these instances, when the spiritual essence permeated the lives of these evangelists, God was viewed as the final arbiter in all of their real or perceived transgressions. There was a range of familial experiences in that some of these evangelists who experienced early spiritual stirrings came from pious families; others had received formal or informal religious instruction; and others had encountered no religious experiences before this period.

Jarena Lee (1783–185?) recounts in her spiritual narrative, *The Life and Religious Experience of Jarena Lee, a Coloured Lady, Giving an Account of Her Call to Preach the Gospel,* that she developed her spiritual essence in 1790 at seven years of age. Lee had been sent "to live as a servant maid," and it was in conjunction with her rebelliousness at her new labor assignments that her initial spiritual stirrings emerged. Despite the fact that her "parents" were "wholly ignorant of the knowledge of God," Lee still felt a spiritual force piquing her conscience on an occasion when she lied about an assigned task. "At this awful point, in my early history, the spirit of God moved in power through my conscience, and told me I was a wretched sinner."[25]

Elizabeth (1766–1867), a black female evangelist who was a former slave, makes a connection between her early spiritual awareness and her family's when she shares with her audience that her slave parents, steeped in piety, belonged to the Methodist Society and provided consistent religious instruction for their children. According to her narrative, *Elizabeth, a Colored Minister of the Gospel, Born in Slavery,* her spiritual essence was piqued at five years of age. "I often felt the overshadowing of the Lord's Spirit, without at all understanding what it meant."[26]

Similar to Jarena Lee and Elizabeth, the widely known evangelist Julia A. J. Foote (1823–1900), who penned the narrative *A Brand Plucked from the Fire,* also experienced "distinct religious impression[s]" at an early age. For Foote, her earliest spiritual stirrings were at the "big meeting" held at the segregated Methodist Episcopal Church to which her family belonged.[27] These spiritual awakenings, which signaled God as a significant presence in the lives of black female evangelists, were also the initial stages in their spiritual journey, leading ultimately to their call to preach the gospel.

Following their spiritual awakening, black female evangelists were empowered in initiating acts of resistance against the oppressive forces controlling their young lives. These defiant acts centered on the labor-intensive schedule that they were forced to maintain either as slaves or servant girls that consumed their existence. Since all of the labor was coerced, regimented, exacting, and most often routinized, these youngsters were alienated from both the mode of labor as well as the hostile environment that engendered their labor productivity. As youngsters, some evangelists engaged in covert resistance, while others were openly defiant, displaying singular acts of raw courage, as they sought to alter the power relationships within their lives.

In 1777, at age eleven, Elizabeth was sold and separated from her family. Overcome with the loneliness and loss of her family, Elizabeth requested permission from the overseer to visit her mother. "I asked the overseer if I might go, but being positively denied, I concluded to go without his knowledge." At that time, opting for disobedience and defiance, Elizabeth disobeyed the overseer, walked twenty miles to visit her mother on another plantation, stayed for several days, and then returned home to await her fate with her overseer, who was angered by her disobedience and absence. "He tied me with a rope, and gave me some stripes, of which I carried the marks for weeks."[28]

Elizabeth's act of defiance was far more overt than Jarena Lee's. Lee's act of lying to her mistress about the completion of an assigned task was a more covert form of resistance, falling into the stereotypical norm that slaveholders and domestic employers had come to expect of blacks. Lee's behavior, which continued for some time, was probably viewed more as an aberration of blacks or a prickly annoyance on the part of her mistress as opposed to a confrontation with her mistress's authority. Elizabeth's behavior, however, was openly defiant and confrontational, and her punishment for disobeying the authority of her white overseer also provided an example for others, particularly other children, who might display the same courage and tenacity. Once these youngsters had defied the economic system that held them in bondage, they had empowered themselves in their freedom's journey. Emanating from the same rebellious centers of the spirit against domination, resistance, whether it was overt like Elizabeth's or covert like Jarena Lee's, most often depended on the environment, the individuals, the authority figures, and a critical assessment of the reprisals.

Foote's path to spiritual redemption was shaped just as much by political and social forces as it was by her early religious impressions. One senses immediately that it is her proud claim that she was the daughter of proud parents who were slaves and had worked and purchased their freedom that shapes the context of her spiritual evolution, defiance, and resistance. In 1833, at the age of ten, when Foote was sent to work as a servant girl, she took her initial fledgling steps of resistance. In this instance, Foote was accused by Mrs. Prime, the woman for whom she worked, of eating some pound cakes that had been prepared for dinner guests. Although Foote denied that she had taken the cakes, she was beaten with a piece of rawhide to make her confess to her "crime." Finding Foote silent during and after the beating, Mrs. Prime then threatened that Foote would be beaten again, as she was determined to elicit a verbal confession from the girl. This incident precipitated Foote displaying a singular act of courage and resistance. Waiting for Mrs. Prime to go out one afternoon, Foote records that "I carried the rawhide out to the woodpile, took the axe, and cut it up into small pieces, which I threw away, determined not to be whipped with that thing again." Once displaying her courage and emboldened by her initial act of resistance, Foote followed her defiant act with another challenge to her oppressive environment. At the age of twelve, Foote left the Primes of her own volition and returned home. Having taken control of her young life, Foote recalled that "the experience of that last year made me quite a hardened sinner."[29]

Foote's first act of defiance was against the debased conditions of her servitude. Similar to both Lee's and Elizabeth's experience, Foote's act also made her more defiant, as she sought ways to mitigate her oppression but nurture her spiritual growth as well. Enmeshed in the racial and gender conventions of the time, the first tentative steps of claiming agency over one's life may have precipitated, on the part of these youngsters, the search for transcendental forces to buffer their early resistance. The inner struggle of spirituality of black female evangelists was always confounded by their material realities. For these women, material oppression formed a contextual factor in their spiritual experiences and became the dialectical force in contouring their spiritual journey. As black adolescents, these evangelists were acutely aware of the social inequities of the world, and once having claimed agency over their lives, they sought the dictates of a divine presence as a source of empowerment.

Black female evangelists' defiance often created a period of inner turmoil where the conflict between secular resistance and transcendental awakening was resolved in religious conversion. Lee, for example, struggled with her spirituality and the oppressive material reality that shaped her life for a period of fourteen years. She recounts that in this period of turmoil, when she continued to challenge and defy her environment, "the Lord never entirely forsook me, but continued mercifully striving with me until his gracious power converted my soul."[30] In 1804, at twenty-one years of age, Lee experienced a religious conversion, followed by sanctification several years later. Throughout this religious experience, Lee continued to challenge her environment, confronting ecclesiastical sexism and slavery.

Elizabeth's inner turmoil and conflict began after being beaten by the overseer for her rebelliousness and disobedience by visiting her mother on another plantation. When Elizabeth sought consolation from her mother following her beating, she was told, somewhat comfortingly, that she had "nobody in the wide world to look to but God," and Elizabeth became increasingly aware of her own as well as her mother's powerlessness to alter the circumstances of their lives. But Elizabeth then realized that God, as an omnipotent force, could mutate the circumstances of those powerful forces that controlled her freedom and separated her from her family. Seeking consolation in prayer, Elizabeth's prayer vigil lasted six months where she, like Lee, acknowledged her transgressions while imploring God's mercy. "Still it was my fervent desire that the Lord would pardon me."[31] Undoubtedly, for Elizabeth, God's pardon meant that her transgressions would not only be forgiven but also that God would provide freedom from slavery and the reunification of her family. It was in prayer that Elizabeth had a visionary experience culminating immediately in her religious conversion. This conversion marked a six-year period, from five to eleven years of age, that defined Elizabeth's grappling with both her spiritual and material condition. Elizabeth's religious conversion was followed by sanctification some years later.

Julia A. J. Foote's spiritual journey and defiance against countervailing forces in her life stem from the slave and subsequent freedom legacy of her parents.[32] Foote's spiritual journey was an intense struggle comprising the worldly pleasures in which she engaged, her spirited defiance, an early religious conversion experience, a crisis of faith, and a second, more dramatic religious conversion. In contrast to the religious conversion experiences of Jarena Lee and Elizabeth, where the dramatic impact of the experience was singular and enduring, Foote required more spiritual nourishment to sustain her faith. Foote recalls that as a youth, a woman visiting her home taught her the Lord's Prayer. This experience was so profound that Foote states that it "seemed to me that I was converted at this time." Foote adds, somewhat wryly, however, that because she was deprived of proper religious instruction, her zeal was short-lived.

But Foote was to experience spiritual renewal when her family moved to Albany and started attending an African Methodist Episcopal Church. Attempting to serve God and follow the doctrinal interpretations of the Scriptures by the black church, Foote found that worldly pleasures once more led her astray. On one occasion when Foote had gone dancing, she felt the presence of a "heavy hand" pulling her from the dance floor. At the cajoling of other dancers to try again, Foote, ignoring the warning signs, advanced to the dance floor a second time. "Being shamed into it, I did try it again, but I had taken only a few steps, when I was seized with a smothering sensation, and felt the same heavy grasp upon my arm, and in my ears a voice kept saying, 'Repent! repent!'"[33]

Following the dance episode, Foote was beleaguered with turmoil and confusion and sought peace in constant prayer. Her spiritual resolve was again weakened, however, when her family persuaded her to go to a party. Although this party was uneventful, Foote believed that it marked a turning point in her prayer vigil and her search for spiritual peace. In 1838, at fifteen years of age, Foote experienced religious conversion. This religious conversion marked a seven-year spiritual struggle between the conflicted desires of the contemporary world, her search for inner spiritual renewal, and her own defiance and resistance over societal forces.

This spiritual gestation period—one of inner turmoil, confusion, and the beginnings of political consciousness—was a spiritual and social awakening of the individual freedom yearnings in conflict with the individual's subordinate status in the contemporary world. As these black evangelists encountered more traumatic experiences in the contemporary world that engendered their spiritual conflict, they continually sought refuge in the spiritual realm where they could redefine themselves and, by extension, imbue a mirror of social conscience to the larger society. This spiritual realm engendered a gradual retreat not only from worldly pleasures but from material possessions as well. It was not just to prepare their spiritual selves for the religious conversion experience that made this retreat necessary; rather, it was that the conflict with the world had reached a new transitional stage where activism was necessary in order to bring resolution between the inner spirit and the outer world. The retreat, therefore, was dynamic in nature, serving to fortify the individual psychologically and spiritually while it simultaneously prepared one to be spiritually combative in the material world. In concert, then, the soul, spirit, and political awareness in seeking harmony effected a transformation of spiritual essence, becoming a vehicle whereby the evangelists could engage life as political and religious change agents liberated from the mundane dictates of gender conventions promoted by men.

RELIGIOUS CONVERSION AND SANCTIFICATION EXPERIENCES

In the space created between the contentious worldly struggle and divine grace lay the religious conversion and sanctification experiences of believers. For the faithful, the duality of the religious conversion and sanctification experiences served as the conduits by which black female

Evangelicals obtained spiritual wholeness and divine grace. The contention between the transcendental plane, where the individual strives toward perfection and oneness with the Holy Spirit, and the temporal plane, with its earthly temptations, social alienation, and worldly sin, augured piety and ongoing spiritual struggle. Since material realities provided the moral barometer by which these Evangelicals refined their continuous spiritual struggle toward perfection, they had to directly engage contemporary life, which in turn provided the dynamism for that struggle to take place. Hence, the transcendental and temporal planes served to mutually reinforce one another. For black female evangelists, religious conversion and sanctification experiences were not merely spiritual balms but were more radical vehicles that could be used as catalysts for social reform and moral regeneration. "Beyond survival, as leaders . . . became more sophisticated about how to use religion, it has helped them to free themselves, first from slavery, then from civil inequality and subordination, to go on to greater heights of personal and group achievement."[34]

Religious conversion enabled the convert to begin a spiritual journey with forgiveness for past transgressions, while the higher spiritual plateau of sanctification immersed the spirit in totality with God's will. In this two-fold transformative process of spiritual striving, where God's will is in total concert with the individual spirit, the individual experiences the ultimate achievement of earthly spiritual perfection, or "holiness." Seeking "justification from sin" according to Christian dogma, purifying the soul and spirit, these new visionaries would now be found worthy of divine grace. Once liberated from intentional sin, black female Evangelicals experienced the inner peace of the spirit and the outer tranquility that comes with the knowledge and power that, for believers, is inherent in God's providential care. The combination of religious conversion and sanctification was a blessed spiritual event in the lives of these believers, for it came with the recognition that the Lord had touched and empowered this human spirit with both forgiveness and divine grace. For these black Evangelicals, the "walk with God" was a powerful healing force, and it imbued them with power and the righteousness of their social cause. John Wesley, the founder of Methodism, contended that this select status was the Christian's inner source of power; surely for black female evangelists, the empowerment was the wellspring of their spiritual and social consciousness.[35]

Black female evangelists honed their skills for their ministry by making spiritual cause with other women, thereby empowering themselves and these other women. Indicative of the scope of these gendered activities were black female prayer bands, where testimonies, preaching, prayers, and spontaneous exhortations were opportunities for female participation, networking, and bonding. Black female evangelists, perceived as leaders in the spiritual community among black women, often led these groups in spiritual rejuvenation. These informal prayer bands proved to be training grounds for the future ministry for African American female evangelists, who were excluded from formalized instruction because they were women. Jarena Lee was upset when her marriage caused her to relocate outside of Philadelphia away from "those who composed the band of which I was one."[36] Although frequently regarded as a threat by black male elders from the church, black community women continuously sought out these female "soul" centers for spiritual healing. Here women bonded, shared their spiritual and secular experiences, energized each other by validating their temporal lives, prayed together, and felt "the power of the Spirit calling."[37]

Black female Evangelicals also relied upon a plethora of supernatural abilities as sources of their spiritual and social empowerment. A broad constellation of visions, voices, signs, and out-of-body experiences were perceived as commonplace to the black female evangelist, who viewed these events as her "gifts of power" and "a part of her heritage as a black Methodist woman."[38] These heavenly "signs" were also experienced by people of various religious faiths vastly different from Methodism. For these evangelists, however, their visionary experiences were defining moments of their faith, reinforcing their divine power and grace. These special gifts ennobling black female Evangelicals also empowered them in challenging their opponents. Elaw, believing that she was on divine ground, saw those who were skeptical as lacking in spiritual knowledge and experience: "There are many skeptical persons who conceitly [*sic*], rashly, and idly scoff at the idea of apparition and angelic appearances; but they ignorantly do it in the face of the most extensive experience, instinct, belief, and credible testimony of persons of every nation, and of all ages, as well as the inspired statements of the Scriptures."[39]

As evangelists became reconciled to their spiritual mission, followed by an increased desire for biblical knowledge, the quest for the sanctification experience itself culminated the inner spiritual journey. The "signs" of spiritual ecstasy, starting when most evangelists were quite young, were integral to the religious conversion experience and frequently occurred in the intervening period between the conversion and sanctification experiences. Lee, Foote, Elaw, and Jackson recounted their visionary experiences that were induced by personal crises, traumas, or intense religious struggle. As the gospel labors of black female Evangelicals intensified following sanctification, the "signs" became more commonplace in assisting these women in their daily spiritual activities or as portents for the future.

Jarena Lee recounted that she was immediately renewed by God's spirit following her forgiveness of an individual who had disparaged her reputation: "That instant, it appeared to me, as if a garment, which had entirely enveloped my whole person, even to my finger ends, split at the crown of my head, and was stripped away from me, passing like a shadow, from my sight-when the glory of God seemed to cover me in its stead . . . That moment, though hundreds were present, I did leap to my feet, and declare that God, for Christ's sake, had pardoned the sins of my soul." Wrestling with her spirituality four years later, when Lee's personal traumas had even led her to contemplate suicide, she prayed for "the entire sanctification of my soul to God." For Lee at that moment, the confluence of prayer and sanctification was instantaneous. "That very instant, as if lightning had darted through me, I sprang to my feet, and cried, 'The Lord has sanctified my soul!'"[40]

The visions, prayers, and voices engendered by Foote's religious struggles that culminated in her sanctification experience were not her first visionary encounters. Prior to that defining moment, Foote had a vision followed by her religious conversion in a religious collective. While some black female evangelists had religious conversion experiences in private settings, Foote's took place in the emotional ethos of the black church. One Sunday evening, Foote fell unconscious in church from the power of the minister's sermon. Taken home to bed by several parishioners who remained "to pray her through," Foote heard a voice in the darkness accusing her of being a sinner. Foote prayed to the Lord for forgiveness: "The voice which had been crying in my ears ceased at once, and a ray of light flashed across my eyes, accompanied by a sound of far distant singing; the light grew brighter and brighter, and the singing more distinct, and soon I caught the words: 'This is the new song—redeemed, redeemed!' . . . Such joy and peace as filled my heart, when I felt that I was redeemed and could sing the new song."[41]

Foote, as did other female evangelists, had an intervening period of doubtful reflection, living a very erratic existence for a year or more following her religious experience until she received the joys of "sanctification and holiness in this life."

Following her sanctification, Jarena Lee recalled that "Satan was there, I knew; for no sooner had I cried out, 'The Lord has sanctified my soul,' than there seemed another voice behind me, saying, 'No, it is too great a work to be done.'"[42] Zilpha Elaw stated that doubt immediately set in following her sanctification experience, when "Satan . . . succeeded in producing a cloud over my mind . . . damping the delightful ardours of my soul in these blessed labours."[43]

Although Foote experienced her religious experiences primarily in the group catharsis of the black church, other evangelists' religious conversion experiences occurred in a variety of settings. Rebecca Cox Jackson, the black Shaker eldress known throughout the Shaker and black communities of Philadelphia, experienced her "secret conversion during [a] thunderstorm, followed six months later by her public experience of sanctification during a neighborhood revival."[44] After a period of frustration over her sinfulness, Elaw saw an apparition while milking a cow. In this instance, Jesus Christ came to her, arms open to receive her, smiled, and then disappeared.[45] Her religious conversion followed this vision, and for Elaw the joy of the event lasted three years.

Despite Elaw's new family responsibilities, marrying in 1810 and giving birth to a daughter a year later, she continued her spiritual activities with a women's prayer group near her home and attended worship services at the nearby African Methodist Episcopal Church in Burlington, New Jersey. Elaw sanctified her spiritual vows in 1817 at a camp meeting. "There many thousands assemble in the open air, and beneath the overspreading bowers, to own and worship our common Lord." Induced by the spiritual intensity of this mass of believers, Elaw fell into a trance-like state. "When I recovered from the trance or ecstasy into which I had fallen, the first thing I observed was, that hundreds of persons were standing around me weeping."[46]

Visionary experiences of empowerment were frequently intertwined in black female evangelists receiving the call to preach the gospel. Doubt often ensued as these Evangelicals struggled with the enormity of their mission, very much aware of the fact that they were adopting a contra-conventional advocacy for women in the society and were inviting repercussions from their families and black men in the church community, as well as the harassment of whites in the larger society. When Jarena Lee heard the voice that told her to "Go preach the Gospel!" she immediately replied, "No one will believe me." The voice, seeking to reassure her, countered her fears with, "Preach the Gospel; I will put words in your mouth, and will turn your enemies to become your friends." When seeking further assurances, "there appeared to my view the form and figure of a pulpit, with a Bible lying thereon."[47] Her visionary experience convinced Lee that she was "called" and chosen by God for a divine mission.

Elaw first got the "sign" on her sickbed that she was "called to preach the Gospel" when "a human figure in appearance, came and stood by my bedside" saying, "Be of good cheer, for thou shall yet see another camp-meeting; and at that meeting thou shall know the will of God concerning thee." Recovering from a near-death illness that lasted two years, Elaw did go to a camp meeting, where she responded to inner voices to exhort spontaneously. "After I had finished my exhortation . . . there appeared a light shining round about me as well as within me, above the brightness of the sun . . . and the same identical voice . . . said, 'Now thou knowest the will of God concerning thee; thou must preach the gospel; and thou must travel far and wide.'"[48]

The highly spirited Foote, who "had always been opposed to the preaching of women, and had spoken against it, though, I acknowledge, without foundation," initially shrank from the possibility of preaching, pleading, "Lord, I cannot go!" Despite her entreaties and grave reluctance, Foote continued to experience visions and voices of spiritual encouragement. On one occasion, "what seemed to be an angel, made his appearance" with "a scroll, on which were these words: 'Thee have I chosen to preach my Gospel without delay.'" Foote still found the mission insurmountable, "I could not give up and obey." One night when Foote was imploring "the dear Lord to remove this burden from me there appeared the same angel . . . on his breast were these words: 'You are lost unless you obey God's righteous commands.'"[49] The reluctance of these women to defy conventional standards of womanhood necessitated an inner struggle where divine forces, the woman's own personal issues, and material gender realities were all engaged in the spiritual commitment.

To reinforce their spiritual growth and commitment, out-of-body experiences frequently operated in tandem with other visionary or religious experiences, appearing to have been fairly common for black female Evangelicals. A few evangelists recorded their out-of-body experiences as integral components of their divine encounters. Enmeshed in Elaw's sanctification experience at the camp meeting, she commented, "Whether I was in the body, or whether I was out of the body, on that auspicious day, I cannot say." Following her trance, Elaw did not move, and she noted, "for the space of several hours I appeared not to be on earth, but far above all earthly things." In recalling one of her out-of-body experiences, Rebecca Cox Jackson "soars, lifts, leaps easily into the sky, flies through the air, looks down from a great height, and can see things never visible from such a perspective before."[50]

The recounting of these visionary experiences supported these black female Evangelicals' claims of divine power and grace as well as having a special calling to embrace their holy mission. But these visionary experiences also provided them with the inner fortitude to confront the material world as members of an oppressed group. Expecting and receiving sexual harassment and racial ridicule, the knowledge of their spiritual powers, commitment, and visionary experiences emphasized their abilities to transcend the temporal plane so adversarial to their divine energy. In defining their sacred space and their right to preach the gospel, black female itinerant preachers had the inner certainty that they were also chosen to be in communion with the saints.

Black female evangelists' eternal quest for spiritual purification and oneness with the Holy Spirit placed them beyond the conventional powers of mortals. Their visionary experiences brought them peace and empowerment, "and looking upwards, the Lord opened my eyes, and I distinctly saw five angels hovering above and engaged in the praises of God."[51] The degree to which certainty was represented by sanctification was the degree to which these evangelists embraced sanctification as a deification of their existence. For these black women, however, who were still enmeshed in the conventional gender trappings of the early 1800s, one cannot readily dismiss the psychological function of sanctifying grace as a buffer in confronting racial and sexual subordination. To be spiritually free meant that their state of divine grace provided a plateau from which to reconcile their dignity and material being in a pragmatic society. This inner spiritual transformation empowered their mission in remolding the social world in moral chaos around them.

POLITICS, RESISTANCE, AND THE DIVINE MISSION

Empowered by their own spiritual transformation, black female gospel messengers used this new moral plateau in assessing the world's shortcomings from the province of God's divine plan as revealed by God's Word and their own intimate visionary and divine experiences.[52] This prophetic tradition, comparing the transcendental plan to the temporal mores of contemporary society, underpinned the spiritual activism of black female evangelists, bringing them in concert with the leadership within the black church and its "agitation from pulpit, press, and platform against slavery and oppression."[53] From this moral stance, black female evangelists created a secular reality as close to their definition of moral perfection as possible. "Among free black religious spokesmen, it was almost universally held that moral improvement was possible only if one became a true Christian."[54] The merging of the evangelists' sacred journey and secular commitment, while challenging the norms of society, paved the way for their dual mission. "Thus for black Evangelicals, doing good and avoiding evil were proofs of racial equality as well as signs of justification or sanctification."[55] With an intimate knowledge of God's divine plan, black female evangelists transmuted their mission of saving souls into moral reform, righteousness, and justice for the downtrodden.

With the dual mission of converting souls and spearheading a new social consciousness that reflected more of African Americans' views of Christianity, black female evangelists took on the task of proselytizing and protest in the larger society. "Blacks could accept Christianity because they rejected the white version with its trappings of slavery and caste for a purer and more authentic gospel."[56] The spiritual transformation process of black female evangelists was centered in the material realities of their oppression, and justification and sanctification fortified them in preserving their dignity as black women and engaging the society in a moral challenge to itself. God's work of moral reform demonstrated Christian virtues and grace in blacks, and the promulgation of moral reform by black ministers also affirmed the right of spiritual redemption and consequently social equality for all African Americans. Embarking on this mission, these ministers were armed with a gospel of salvation for their people. "Such a gospel, it was believed, not only offered the key to spiritual salvation but would also enable blacks to overcome the negative effects which were the legacy of slavery and caste."[57]

By the early 1820s, Jarena Lee, Elizabeth Cole, and Zilpha Elaw were seasoned spiritual veterans. One could speculate that Maria W. Stewart, who also merged her spirituality with her gender consciousness and ardent abolitionism, reflected the activism of black evangelists who had entered the public sphere a decade earlier. Stewart made a more dramatic appearance, historically at least, in 1832 as a speaker at the Afric-American Female Intelligence Society, where she raised the consciousness of the black women by advocating black moral redemption, the political activism of black women in the freedom struggle, and the liberation of African peoples. Sojourner Truth, a contemporary, also emerged in public life in the 1830s in New York City, a city rapidly acquiring a reputation for extremes. There was the burgeoning capitalism and newly acquired wealth, on one the hand, and the struggling laborers, poverty, and racism, on the other. Truth, a still-impoverished former slave who became part of an enclave of white upper-middle-class religious enthusiasts in the city, in a sense typified these contrasts. Known both for her preaching and singing abilities, Truth would continue to evolve into her evangelical mission. "She had the magnetism and ascetism [sic] that characterized New York perfectionism, and her physical stature, fervor, eloquence, and singing were making her reputation."[58] In the next decade, Foote would also emerge in the public sphere with her spiritual redemptive work, as a part of the women's rights and abolitionist movements. But it was the pioneering ministries of Lee, Cole, and Elaw, by their actions and sermons, that facilitated the entry of black women into the public sphere with an articulate voice of moral redemption and oppression.

Empowered by their own personal transformations, these women crisscrossed the land preaching and saving souls. Zilpha Elaw, for example, spent several months away from her home, bringing hope to those in bondage. Often, particularly since some of these black female Evangelicals traveled in slave states, they created a degree of excitement and a disquieting presence in the communities where they carried their spiritual message. Elaw's memories of one of these experiences illuminates not only her courage in risking her life and freedom, but her very presence as a free black woman, completely mobile, was rich with symbolism and inspiration: "I was then in a small town in one of the slave states; and the news of a coloured female preaching to the slaves had already been spread widely throughout the neighborhood; the novelty of the thing had produced an immense excitement and the people were collecting from every quarter, to gaze at the unexampled prodigy of a coloured female preacher."[59]

Although black female Evangelicals appeared to be largely undaunted by the material obstacles impeding their ministry, meeting with "recurrent opposition from those who felt women's preaching to be either unscriptural or unseemly," they were obviously relying on God's divine intervention on a daily basis.[60] The breadth of black female Evangelicals' itinerant ministries afforded them substantial interracial contact. Elaw observed that "the number of white brethren and sisters who flocked to my ministry increased daily."[61] As they garnered broad reputations for their ministries, black female Evangelicals consciously made a decisive impact with their critique of society's oppression.

DISCRIMINATION, PROTEST, AND GOSPEL POLITICS

One frequent problem that black female Evangelicals confronted was the racial discrimination and harassment by hostile whites on all public conveyances. These daily racial barriers reinforced the racial conscious-ness of these evangelists, who found that, after preaching, exhortation, and rendering testimony of the Holy Word to hundreds of potential con-verts, the exigencies of black womanhood prevailed in their daily lives. A joyful day could immediately disintegrate into pure chaos when blacks had to move about the city or travel to regional areas. "But how could they get from one place to another in cities, visit friends or relatives, even get to work at the servile jobs open to blacks, without using the public transportation facilities?"[62] In some instances, African Americans attempting to ride omnibuses were ignored by conductors and drivers or were not permitted to board the vehicle. In other instances, once securing passage, they might be relegated to "Jim Crow" sections, as in Boston, although the practices were common throughout Northern states. By the late 1850s, when streetcars replaced the omnibuses in Northern cities such as Philadelphia, for example, blacks had to con-front the same racial prohibitions as they did on other vehicles: "The proprietors wish it to be understood that PEOPLE OF COLOR ARE NOT PERMITTED TO ENTER, EXCEPT WHEN IN ATTENDANCE UPON CHILDREN AND FAMILIES."[63] Black passengers frequently experienced harassment from other passengers or conductors who were hostile to their presence. Black women and the difficulties that they experienced with public transportation services was a long-standing problem up until the civil rights movement of the 1950s and 1960s.

Since black female Evangelicals traveled internationally and domes-tically, preaching in rural areas, camp meetings, frontier homes, urban cities, and predominantly white churches, they experienced the entire spectrum of racial discrimination on public transportation systems. Often, upon arriving at their destination, particularly in Southern or bor-der states, evangelists were subjected to tedious examinations and searches for identifying marks of slavery. "Upon our arrival there [Balti-more] we were closely questioned as to our freedom, and carefully exam-ined for marks on our persons by which to identify us if we should prove to be runaways." Traveling in free states proved just as discriminatory, and evangelists were frequently harassed by hostile passengers. "The next night the boat stopped at a village [New York], and the captain procured lodging for me at an inn. Thus I escaped further abuse from that ungodly man."[64]

Water transportation often proved to be the bane of black northern travelers. In 1827, the editors of *Freedom's Journal* commented that "the conduct of officers of steamboats and packets to coloured people has been cruel in the extreme."[65] Traveling on a steamer from Philadelphia to New York, Mrs. Wright, the wife of the black Presbyterian abolitionist, Reverend Theodore S. Wright, found that her illness was exacerbated when she was refused space below deck, leading to her death shortly after she disembarked. Elaw, attempting to board a steamer going from Utica to downstate New York, also encountered racial discrimination. Denying her access to the steamer, the captain told her that there was no room for additional passengers, "though my complexion appeared to be the chief reason of his refusal."[66]

Upon returning from Jamaica in 1841, Nancy Prince was confronted with a conundrum of ambiguous legalities of free blacks, racial discrimination, and obvious duplicity on the part of the captain and several other white passengers on board. The captain, in lieu of embarking for New York, dropped anchor in Key West, ostensibly for ship repairs. There, an attempt was made to induce Prince and other free blacks to go ashore, more than likely to be captured and eventually sold into slavery. Prince indicates that a "law had just been passed there that every free colored person coming there, should be put in custody on their going ashore."[67] These racial incidents on public conveyances served as continuous reminders of the tenuous status of freedom for free blacks.

Whenever possible, black female evangelists met harassment on public transportation with resistance. Journeying in upstate New York on a steamer, Foote was ordered to move from her berth because a white man, not finding space in the men's cabin, decided to sleep in the women's cabin and wanted the berth that she occupied. The man rationalized this by insisting that his family, who was expecting to board the boat the next day, would "not come where a nigger is." After a heated discussion, during which Foote was not only prepared for physical confrontation but also made it clear that she would only be moved by force, she was eventually left alone.[68] Similarly, Sojourner Truth was prepared for physical confrontation on the transportation system in Washington, D.C., where she was working to aid the newly emancipated slaves following the Civil War. When ignored by the streetcar conductor, Truth overtook and boarded the car when it stopped for other passengers to board. The conductor, undoubtedly angry at her not only for overtaking the vehicle but also for chiding him publicly, threatened to remove Truth if she said another word. When he moved toward her threateningly to deliver on his promise, Truth stood her ground, telling him, "If you attempt that, it will cost you more than your car and horses are worth."[69] Truth remained on the streetcar until she arrived at her destination. Truth's, Foote's, and other's resistance against racial indignities on public conveyances throughout the antebellum era contributed to the eventual elimination of segregated transportation in many Northern cities.

For all of its manifold problems of humiliation, segregated transportation and harassment on public conveyances merely represented a microcosmic view of the larger racial subordination of blacks in a predominantly white society. Black female Evangelicals, in concert with other blacks in the public sphere, reflected their political ties to the black community in their efforts to combat racism. Elaw frequently provided a critique on racial relations. "The pride of a white skin is a bauble of great value with many in some parts of the United States, who readily sacrifice their intelligence to their prejudices, and possess more knowledge than wisdom."[70]

Black female Evangelicals also employed more direct methods of racial protest. One strategy was the refusal by evangelists to preach in predominantly white churches that excluded other blacks from the worship services. Foote encountered this racial exclusionary practice when she brought her ministry to Chillicothe, Ohio. There, a white Methodist congregation invited her to preach but refused to admit other blacks. "The white Methodists invited me to speak for them, but did not want the colored people to attend the meeting. I would not agree to any such arrangement, and, therefore, I did not speak for them." Foote remained firm on her stance against racial prejudice, refusing to preach in places where "prejudice had closed the door of their sanctuary against the colored people of the place, virtually saying: 'The Gospel shall not be free to all.'"[71] By consistently challenging these racial patterns and maneuvers by white congregations, evangelists represented a unified force against ecclesiastical racism.

Although black female evangelists were unsuccessful in moving into the hierarchical black church structures, which were the exclusive preserves of black men, they were openly combative in challenging this form of ecclesiastical sexism. It proved one of the ways in which black female evangelists protested against sexism and simultaneously advanced the cause of women's rights before the coalescing of that movement in the late 1840s. Most black female evangelists, having already developed a well-honed itinerant ministry and at ease with preaching to large audiences, wanted to become recognized preachers of the black church, enabling them to preach in the churches and the homes of black parishioners and lead classes and prayer groups in black communities without being threatened by black clergy for challenging the religious status quo. Whether women were denied the right to preach because of gender or because of their pervasive influence in the black community, which threatened the male authority and thereby male domination and control of the black church, the genesis was sexism aimed at keeping women in subordinate positions in the church's hierarchy.

When Jarena Lee was denied the right to preach because of the African Methodist Episcopal (AME) Church's stance against women preaching, she confronted Richard Allen, the founder of the church: "If the man may preach, because the Savior died for him, why not the woman, seeing he died for her also? Is he not a whole Savior, instead of a half one, as those who hold it wrong for a woman to preach would seem to make it appear?"[72] In 1841, Foote found that her preaching and undoubtedly her growing influence in the black community in Boston put her at odds with the African Methodist Episcopal Zion (AMEZ) Church there, and her strident resistance to male criticism led to her excommunication from that body. When attempts at reinstatement proved futile, the spirited Foote crystallized black women's struggle: "Even ministers of Christ did not feel that woman had any rights which they were bound to respect."[73] In this masterful stroke, Foote not only challenged the prevailing ecclesiastical sexism within the black church, but by paraphrasing Chief Justice Roger B. Taney's majority opinion of the Supreme Court in the Dred Scott decision of 1857, united the twin evils of racism and sexism that plagued black women's lives. On the whole, however, black female evangelists were combating the forces of sexism in the sacred and secular arenas that threatened to obfuscate their quest for women's equality.

The multifaceted complexities of racial degradation of black Americans would not be resolved in the antebellum era. Hopeful African Americans, however, through such vehicles as the black church, press, mutual benevolent societies, and antislavery societies, were calling for the abolition of slavery, the elevation of the conditions of free blacks, and mobilizing free black communities for social reform.[74] Black female Evangelicals viewed the abolition of slavery as a part of their divine mission to liberate all humanity from oppression. This philosophical perspective often led them into antislavery protest in slaveholding states where the hostile climate was particularly dangerous to free blacks. Zilpha Elaw spoke of the influence of "Satan's fear" and the threat to her personal safety in the Southern states. "When I arrived in the slave states, Satan much worried and distressed my soul with the fear of being arrested and sold for a slave, which their laws would have warranted, on account of my complexion and features." This trepidation, however, did not prevent her critical comments on slavery as she toured the region. In 1828, in Annapolis, Maryland, after witnessing several distressing incidents, Elaw stated that in "every case of slavery, however lenient its inflictions and mitigated its atrocities, indicates an oppressor, the oppressed, and the oppression."[75]

Elizabeth's preaching in the slave states eventually netted her an open confrontation with Virginia officials: "they strove to imprison me because I spoke against slavery." When the Virginia officials could not intimidate Elizabeth, they attempted to gain leverage by questioning her authority to preach the gospel. Of course, this was obviously a ruse. The officials feared her antislavery message and influence among the Virginia slaves, and their tactics of intimidation were designed to make her leave the state. But Elizabeth responded to their challenges wrapped in the mantle of a higher power. "I have not been commissioned by men's hands, if the Lord has ordained me, I need nothing better."[76] Apparently, the answers Elizabeth gave silenced her opponents because she was not imprisoned. She continued her itinerant ministry well into her eighties, preaching in slave and free states and protesting against slavery whenever the opportunity arose.

Some evangelists sought to raise the consciousness of those around them about slavery. Nancy Prince, en route to New York on a sinking steamer that had stopped for repairs in Texas, declined a proposal to have her trip rerouted through the States, feeling that she could not "see my fellow-creatures suffering without a rebuke." Stranded for several days in Texas, she protested to the captain and all others against the constant slave traffic at the docks "and that awful sight I see in the streets." Prince's adamant protest soon caused her to be threatened by slave traders regarding her own freedom, but she refused to stifle her criticism.[77]

Other evangelists also had their freedom jeopardized because of their antislavery protest. In 1862, Sojourner Truth's antislavery crusade in the Midwest caused her to run afoul of Indiana's legal covenants regarding blacks. Indiana, a strong proslavery state, had passed a law forbidding the entrance of blacks into or remaining in the state. Although the law was frequently ignored, Truth was arrested for both offenses. With astute counsel, Truth emerged free from that ordeal, although friends cautioned her to take a pistol for protection if she wished to continue her antislavery meetings. "I carry no weapon; the Lord will [p]reserve me without weapons. I feel safe even in the midst of my enemies; for the truth is powerful and will prevail."[78] Truth's resolve was in keeping with other evangelists who believed that divine power was the only protection necessary against their enemies.

Abolitionism reinforced the political and spiritual resolve of black female evangelists and their inherent belief that all humanity must be redeemed. For many blacks, abolitionism was seen in its dual context of emancipating slaves from bondage and the liberation of free blacks from oppression, keeping it the center of black protest.[79] While these Evangelicals embraced the spiritual side of abolitionism, espousing that slavery was morally wrong and that, ultimately, the antislavery movement would prick the conscience of slaveholders, causing them to free their chattel property, they did not sidestep the political issue of freedom and liberation for all blacks. Black female evangelists participated in the various organizational strategies of the abolitionist movement. Some of these women participated in the larger, predominantly white movement by affiliating with the American Anti-Slavery Society under the aegis of William Lloyd Garrison, while others sought all-black antislavery groups that were conduits and ancillaries to the larger struggle.

Typifying the commitment to abolitionism, in 1840 Jarena Lee joined the American Anti-Slavery Society, hoping that the gospel, via abolitionism, "will have free course to every nation." Elaw also participated in the antislavery meetings that were held in the Boston area. Foote attended meetings in Geneva, New York, for the purpose of forming a chapter of the American Moral Reform Society, an ancillary abolitionist and reform society founded in the mid-1830s as "an all-Negro group which hopefully, but unsuccessfully, opened its doors to whites and discountenanced separate action by black men."[80] Nancy Prince, returning to the United States in 1833 after living in Russia, participated in the early American Anti-Slavery Society meetings in Boston until dissension broke out among the participants. She poignantly describes her disappointment, "for the weight of prejudice has again oppressed me, and were it not for the promises of God, one's heart would fail."[81]

By the 1850s, Truth was widely recognized by most reformers for her political activism and her deeply abiding spirituality that provided a context for understanding not only her crusading abolitionism but the passion that black female Evangelicals brought to the cause of freedom and justice. Nell Painter notes that evangelicalism, abolitionism, and feminism comprised "the major chapters in Truth's life," and in the interweaving of all three facets of her life is evinced the philosophical humanism of black female Evangelicals that lay the foundation for their political activism.[82] At each stage of this evolutionary cycle of her life, far more complex that it appears on the surface, Truth gains in the rediscovery and reclamation of herself, which marked her self-liberation and then her larger divine mission "and the Lord gave me Truth, because I was to declare the truth to the people."[83] Truth's crusading abolitionism leading to the emancipation of the slaves, women's rights, and the social progress of freedpersons after the Civil War comprised her divine mission. In sounding the clarion call of social injustices in society, Truth, like all other black female Evangelicals, hoped to lead both black and white Americans to spiritual redemption. What thwarted these women's efforts was that the liberation of both groups was inextricably linked to each other. America's regenerative powers could only come about in the redemption process of African Americans.

The centeredness of spirituality in the lives of these gospel pioneers allowed them to transcend all of the conventional bonds of womanhood, imbuing them with vision, courage, and fortitude. Inured to worldly criticism, their spiritual journey, by placing them at counterpoint with contemporary society, also forced their confrontation with the abnormal variants—slavery, sexism, racism, and impoverishment—that dominated the antebellum era. Fortified, however, by their spirituality and, ultimately, their divine mission and honed by the impact of the material world, evangelists forged a tradition of black feminine political protest that underpinned their gospel message. While the evangelists' goal was the conversion of souls and their divine mission was touched by the Holy Spirit, theirs was also a crusade for justice in American society. Thus black female Evangelicals entered the public sphere challenging the racial and sexual practices of segregated transportation, racism, abolition of slavery, and ecclesiastical sexism that engulfed black lives. As individuals, these itinerant preachers' defiant acts of resistance bore an organic relationship to the collective African American voice of protest. Their dual mission, however, contoured and defined the terrain of black women's discourse and activism against injustice. Tied to the collective voice of protest, black female evangelists' incipient political consciousness reinforced African Americans' organized resistance.

CHAPTER 7

Rocking the Bastille

Black Women's Abolitionism

> This is a common cause; and if there is any burden to be borne in
> the Anti-Slavery cause-anything to be done to weaken our hateful
> chains or assert our manhood and womanhood, I have a right to do
> my share of the work. The humblest and feeblest of us can do some-
> thing; . . . if there is common rough work to be done, call on me.
>   FRANCES ELLEN WATKINS HARPER, 1859

T HE COMMUNITY ACTIVISM AND EVANGELICALISM OF BLACK
women rested upon the sacred and secular dimensions that defined their
historical consciousness of both Africa and the New World. In a dialectical sense, oppression and resistance were the driving forces behind
black women's historical consciousness and their living memories of
slavery, exploitation, and alienation. These simultaneously existed with
the spirituality that anchored their sanity, slave resistance, and evolving
urban political identities. Drawing upon their own legacy of organizational experience, black women organized their own collectives around
issues of political and economic inequality. These associations for women
served as springboards for their political activism and resistance. In the
implementation and praxis of political activities, black women's cohesiveness as a political cadre was developed. This politicization often led
to community mobilization—particularly around slavery, racial discrimination, and economic issues—and ultimately resistance to the superordinate power structure that circumscribed their lives. Patricia Hill Collins
states that black women's resistance emanated from a "shared standpoint
among Black women about the meaning of oppression."[1] By directly
challenging institutional oppression, black women were in open defiance
against the existing social structure. In the process of challenge, black
women reconstructed a political consciousness and identity.

Black women's political consciousness was also driven by the emergence of black nationalism in black communities, with its tenets of racial solidarity, spiritual redemption, and self-determination. This nationalist belief system emphasized the positive shared experiences of African Americans throughout the diaspora, namely history and culture, as well as the vicious systems of slavery and the oppression of Africans in New World societies.[2] African American women also viewed nationalism as a strategy to counter gender oppression and promote collective female consciousness. Emanating from this nationalist base, black women's evolving political consciousness included a developing praxis, along with their analysis of the realities of slavery, racism, sexism, and impoverishment that were the common plight of African Americans. Derived from antebellum material realities, this nationalist consciousness provided the political spark for black women's resistance. With the political mobilization of urban African American communities, black women's collective involvement sensitized them to their shared political oppression. As community activism evolved, centering on spiritual regeneration, political protest, and social reform, activists effectively transmuted black nationalism into collective self-help organizational strategies in black communities to effect social change.

As an ideology, antebellum black nationalism proved compatible with black women's consciousness because it identified racial solidarity and class consciousness as oppressive elements common to all African Americans. Black women, in utilizing this ideological framework for developing consciousness and praxis, broadened black nationalism to include their peculiar condition. For the community, then, black women's activism provided the economic, political, and social stabilization of black family and community life; a community organizational infrastructure for ongoing social and political change; and the development of political consciousness and resistance among black women. Community activism, the path by which black women defined their collective voice in political struggle, also provided the transitional political function of moving black women into the larger arena of the abolitionist struggle.

As black female activists made the transition to the public sphere, they broadened their protest terrain while widening the circles of their political, social, and religious influence. In concert with shared community ideals for emancipation and social change, black female activists mobilized around a community-based agenda that they also inculcated in biracial local antislavery societies. As members of interracial female antislavery societies, black female activists promoted an independent course of political and social action that had been sharpened by years of community activism. As Naples notes in speaking of contemporary female activists, "community activists develop their political sensibilities in community with others and . . . the process of politicization is influenced by . . . the social networks in which they circulate as they age."[3] As activists, and sometimes belonging to families where several generations of family members were activists, these black women had already developed reputations as informal community leaders, with abolitionism as an essential component of their lives. By employing a conscious use of self and their labor will, black female activists spearheaded a collective agenda in interracial antislavery societies that reflected their community concerns and a broader vision of abolitionism and liberation.

Hetty Reckless, Hetty Burr, Sarah Mapps Douglass, the Forten women, Susan Paul, Frances Ellen Watkins Harper, Julia A. J. Foote, Nancy Prince, and Maria W. Stewart were all recognized community activists before they became noted participants in the larger abolitionist struggle. This prior centering of black female activists in the ecopolitics of black communities meant that the emancipation of the slaves and the issues within free black communities would be top priorities in the antislavery societies in which they became members. Black women took a combative stance against racism and sexism, and their quest for women's equality would be shaped by the legacy of their experiences. Because this quest was inextricably tied to the goals of emancipation and racial equality, it obfuscated the fact that they were consistently creating political space where they could diligently pursue their dual agenda.[4]

Pragmatically, black women's political actions were largely determined by the political environment that circumscribed black communities and by the women themselves deciding on an independent course of action based on an analysis of resources, issues, and events. From their expanding political base, black female activism evolved in two complementary directions. The most popular was the overt direction, where black women participated in community associations, ad hoc collectives, church organizations, community-based reform societies, and biracial antislavery societies. Intertwined with most of these societies were the diligent efforts of abolitionists, to whom monies could be funneled in support of antislavery journals or more subversive activities. One black female association, the Women's Association of Philadelphia, whose participants came from a number of local societies, organized fund-raising events for Garrison's journal, the *Liberator,* and Frederick Douglass's weekly, the *North Star.* Similarly, in New York, black females organized a collective called the North Star Association that held annual fund-raisers to underwrite Douglass's newspaper.[5] The movement, always bereft of funds, depended upon the singular contributions from noted abolitionists like Arthur and Lewis Tappan and Gerrit Smith and from the female antislavery societies' annual fund-raisers. In black communities, black women could always be counted upon to hold a plethora of fund-raisers during the course of the year to add to the movement's coffers and to contribute to the more subversive activities of the underground as well.

This dual approach to abolitionism in black women's organizations created a vehicle for the covert direction of black female activism. This covert direction was the illegal participation of black female activists in dramatic slave rescues, vigilance committees, protests, raising monies, and the multifarious operations on the Underground Railroad. Black female activists who participated in this more radical abolitionism went beyond the philosophical stance of immediate abolitionism, viewing it as a direct-action strategy of slave and urban resistance.[6] Black abolitionists viewed abolitionism with a greater urgency than did white abolitionists and believed that aiding fugitive slaves struck a direct blow at the institution of slavery. Black female activists, already members of organizations where the allocation of funds and resources to aid fugitive slaves became commonplace, readily expanded their political activities to include this facet of subversive activism.

Black women's roles in antislavery societies was to challenge the inherent racial bias of white abolitionists while they expanded the boundaries and restrictive interpretations of white female abolitionists about abolitionism. White abolitionists held diverse viewpoints on how and when slaves should be liberated, while most shied away from black community uplift. "They tirelessly proclaimed such equality, but for most of them projects directly aimed at improving black people became only a side issue, if they were interested in them at all."[7] Initially, black female activists gained their organizational experience in community organizations, societies, and associations. This was usually followed by a group of black female abolitionists recruited by the larger interracial society's black members to ensure a black presence.[8]

Black women joined female antislavery societies as founding members, as members serving in some official capacity, or as active participants. As a smaller group within the larger female body, black female activists served as nexus women, linking the antislavery society to black community endeavors via financial contributions and community assignments. Black female abolitionists spearheaded the continuous development of the community infrastructure by serving simultaneously in both the larger antislavery society and in the community projects where some of the resources from these antislavery societies were allocated. Whenever possible, black female abolitionists resisted taking sides when schisms broke out in the antislavery movement, fearing that the internal hostilities, whatever the merits, would deflect attention away from the abolitionist agenda. For black female activists, the expansion of their political activities into these larger female antislavery societies provided them with additional networking contacts for community improvement projects as well as with funds for their subversive activities. Since female antislavery societies were acknowledged proving grounds for the later women's rights movement, black female activists, who were already combating racism and sexism on a daily basis, expanded their consciousness as society members in the quest for women's rights. These biracial female antislavery societies were critical in gaining adherents to the cause and placing the emancipation of slaves on the national political agenda.

BLACK FEMALE ABOLITIONISM
AND ANTISLAVERY SOCIETIES

Although the modern abolitionist movement moved both black and white women into the forefront of the international struggle for the abolition of slavery, black female abolitionists, except for a noted few, played a subordinate role to white female abolitionists. In most female antislavery societies, white female abolitionists dominated the slate of officers as well as the board of managers, paralleling the male-dominated parent societies. Most often, if one or two black women held official positions, white female abolitionists convinced themselves that they were not racially prejudiced. This "racial arrangement" was prevalent throughout male and female antislavery societies that encouraged black participation. Although black male abolitionists held more official positions than did black women, they were not in major decision-making roles, and this obvious inequality was a source of rancor for Frederick Douglass and others who shared his views. Black abolitionists charged white abolitionists with racial bias, abstract theorizing about abolition, segregated meetings and hiring practices, and paternalism.[9] "Black abolitionists attended antislavery meetings as full-fledged participating members, served on committees of antislavery societies, wrote pamphlets and delivered speeches for the cause; yet it probably is true that white abolitionists in general did not accept Blacks as full partners in the antislavery crusade and did not admit them fully to decision making."[10]

Principally, black communities' common goals—of the immediate emancipation of the slaves and black political and social progress—were culled by the American Anti-Slavery Society. There were always abolitionist interests in black communities. Two early groups, the Massachusetts General Colored Association, founded in 1826, and National Negro Convention Movement, founded in 1831, formally mobilized around the abolitionist cause.[11] Too, the institutions of resistance—that is, the black church, the black press, self-improvement associations, and antislavery organizations—already spoke to blacks' commitment to abolitionism. However, under the aegis of its principal founder, William Lloyd Garrison, the abolitionist goals of the American Anti-Slavery Society gained broader mass appeal among white reformers, and its new organizational apparatus was superimposed upon the black community's existing infrastructure. The majority of societies and organizations in black communities became antislavery societies, in form if not in fact, generating funds, apprentices, or speakers for the antislavery effort. Female antislavery societies, serving as auxiliaries to the male societies, developed in the early 1830s. Black women, in pivotal positions in community affairs, became active members of these antislavery societies, where they refined and broadened their political consciousness.

The Philadelphia Female Anti-Slavery Society (PFASS), which was founded in 1833 and encouraged women of diverse backgrounds and races to become members, was remarkably different from the small band of faithful followers that organized and participated in the women's rights convention in Philadelphia in 1854. Over the two decades of its maturation, the society went through decisive shifts in tandem with the political environment that became increasingly hostile to antislavery forces, the schism in the antislavery movement, and the society's internal tensions. Certainly, the antiblack riots in Philadelphia in 1829, 1834, 1835, 1838, and 1842, as well as the burning of Pennsylvania Hall during the four-day meeting of the Pennsylvania State Anti-Slavery Society in May 1838, may have been factors in forcing the society to curtail its recruitment efforts by 1840.

Following the national division in the antislavery movement in 1840, as many abolitionists moved toward party politics with the new Liberty Party, PFASS remained loyal to Garrison's moral suasionist stance, which was already showing signs of failure. In remaining with Garrison, PFASS embraced the more restrictive ideological interpretation of abolitionism.[12]

What PFASS may have sacrificed in terms of the politicalization of its members via membership drives, party politics, petition campaigns, and protest meetings over the decades, they gained in maintaining an autonomous base, largely through their prestigious annual fund-raisers, and a critical voice in both the abolitionist and women's movements.

In the 1830s, some of the Forten women, a group of community activists from the same family, became founding members of PFASS. "Mrs. Charlotte Forten, her three oldest daughters, and her prospective daughter-in-law Mary Woods all signed the Philadelphia Female Anti-Slavery Society's charter, which daughter Margaretta Forten had helped to draft." Although there was never a black president of PFASS, black female abolitionists, most particularly three generations of Forten-Purvis women, held official positions, where they could mobilize supporters to promote black community endeavors. "Through key offices they held and through lobbying efforts, they influenced the group's activities and its philosophical direction."[13] In the Forten women's advocacy of community improvement, they were aided by Hetty Burr, Hetty Reckless, Sarah McCrummell, and Grace Douglass and her daughter, Sarah Mapps Douglass, all society members and black community activists. It was this black female base that the Forten women would need to push their community agenda. One may speculate that there were "meetings before the meetings" to formalize their strategies and plans.

One of the early black community initiatives that the group emphasized was coming to the aid of one of its members, Sarah Mapps Douglass, who needed capital to support the operation of her private academy for black girls. Due to the Forten women's influence, "Sarah sat on the female Society's governing board of managers while, as a member of the educational committee, Margaretta supervised specific financial details."[14] PFASS petitioned the state society for approval of providing funds for the school. In the petition, the female society expressed "having seriously felt the want of a suitable room for a female coloured school under the care of Sarah Douglass," was approved, and PFASS operated the school for two years.[15] Two years later, in 1840, despite or because of the zealous involvement of the society in her school's operations, Douglass expressed the desire to regain full autonomy. Although clearly disappointed, the society continued its support with an annual contribution to the school throughout the 1840s.[16] Since the Forten women were effective in mobilizing their educational agenda, it would seem that their support led to the continuous contributions to the school on Douglass's terms.

PFASS and several of the more politically active female antislavery societies, like the Boston Female Anti-Slavery Society (BFASS) in the 1830s, adopted informal pressure-group strategies, hoping to circumvent constitutional and legislative obstruction to slave emancipation. PFASS's extensive petition drives politicized the community to the role of abolition and women in the struggle. The petitions were periodically delivered to the U.S. Congress, although they were undoubtedly filed without comment. Sarah Forten organized a three-year petition drive "to abolish the slave trade in the District of Columbia and to abandon further moves toward annexing Texas," delivering thousands of signatures to the legislature.[17] Society members who engaged in the collection of signatures, canvassing prospective signatories door-to-door, and alerting residents to the antislavery mission and the power of petitions found the work tedious, tiresome, and time-consuming. Despite congressional inactivity regarding the petitions, society members were becoming empowered through the process and were seeking other political options that were not gender-based. Black women's participation in PFASS was instrumental in shaping some of the society's political activities.

The antislavery schism that occurred in 1840 centered on the ideological direction of abolitionism, the role of female abolitionists in the movement, and the rapidly growing Liberty Party, seen by many abolitionists as a political mobilization vehicle for the antislavery movement. For the politically oriented abolitionists, the movement could become a pressure group within the Liberty Party and hold sway over the election of candidates to public office. The schism created two camps, the Garrisonian moral suasionist camp, where political action was discouraged, and the political abolitionists under the aegis of the American and Foreign Anti-Slavery Society, who believed that political agitation would be a more effective strategy. In truth, Garrison was not opposed to political action, but he believed that the immersion of the movement in party politics would cause the movement to lose its focus.[18] The women in PFASS remained loyal to Garrison, although some members who were in favor of political action as a viable strategy for abolition resigned.

While the Forten-Purvis women remained steadfast in their support of Garrison, as did the majority of black women in the antislavery movement, they were similar to other black women in giving lip service to the Garrisonian strategy while actively participating in the subversive activism in the black community's underground. "While the Forten-Purvis women and other members of the Philadelphia Female Anti-Slavery Society publicly professed their adherence to moral suasion as the only acceptable abolition tactic, these women frequently employed a more vigorous action against the peculiar institution."[19] Already utilizing multiple strategies for the liberation of slaves, black women were able to look beyond the ideological factionalism for the moment and support Garrison while they carefully evaluated the conflict. As black "seasoned" female activists knew, most abolitionists who were now in the heat of the controversy would be gone come daylight. For several years following the national schism, the Forten-Purvis women and Hetty Reckless encouraged the society to funnel funds to the two vigilance committees in Philadelphia to aid fugitive slaves while simultaneously advocating that "in the work of abolishing slavery, we rely not on the efficacy of physical force, or political parties but on moral power."[20] For the black female abolitionists in PFASS, this sense of pragmatic politics enabled them to pursue their independent course of action, circumvent political factionalism, and set their own agenda.

Philosophically, black antebellum women embraced the militant black abolitionist stance of the immediate emancipation of the slaves. This militancy, in many cases, countered the general tone of most white abolitionists. Most white abolitionists subscribed to some form of gradual abolitionism, with only a small percentage of radical abolitionists, like Garrison, favoring the more militant position. Whether white abolitionists favored a militant or moderate approach in regards to slave emancipation, rarely did any of them advocate, beyond rhetoric, the political and social equality of free blacks. Consequently, the forbearance and steadfastness of black abolitionists working in integrated, often hostile, abolitionist societies should not be underestimated. The Forten-Purvis women brought supreme dedication to their task, as they had to combat the racism within the society, the racism within the larger abolitionist movement, and the racism that plagued their lives. It was their relentless struggle, however, that moved the PFASS to adopt a more militant stance on abolitionism.[21]

The Forten-Purvis women's involvement in the Philadelphia Female Anti-Slavery Society extended well beyond the life of their membership. Through key offices they held and through lobbying efforts, they influenced the group's activities and its philosophical direction. Working in conjunction with other black members, like Grace Douglass and her daughter, Sarah, and with liberal whites, like Lucretia Mott, the Forten women often enabled this predominantly white organization to reflect a black abolitionist perspective, a perspective

equally dedicated to the abolition of slavery and to the triu
racial justice in America but a perspective usually more militani.

New York City's female antislavery societies, which were more conservative than affiliates in Philadelphia and Boston, excluded black females
as members. Although the waves of religious revivalism sweeping New
York and the New England states in the 1820s and 1830s were the primary impetus behind the formation of antislavery societies in New York
City, these rising, affluent newcomers to city life were determined to
maintain the status quo. With respect to race, white female abolitionists
were in lockstep with other white New Yorkers. Thus although their
humanitarian zeal and Christian benevolence turned upon helping those
less fortunate (and in this context, slavery was viewed as evil), it did not
turn upon social equality between the races. The character of the female
antislavery societies in New York City—the Chatham Street Chapel Society, formed in 1834, and the larger Ladies' New York City Anti-Slavery
Society (LYNCASS), formed a year later—reflected both a conservative
evangelical benevolence that was indicative of the racial schism within
the movement and the subordination of women. "That the women of the
New York society could believe in unity between themselves and slave
women but still exclude black women from their organization reveals
that the members clearly distinguished . . . between social equality with
blacks and social obligation to . . . slavery."[23]

These two societies were not singular in their conservatism. Most
male and female societies had taken a similar stance regarding black
membership. A schism occurred in the Western New York Female Anti-
Slavery society as several members recruited black women to the organization. Black women participated in interracial antislavery societies
whenever those societies encouraged black membership, but since segregation and racial bias were prevalent, they continued to promote abolitionism and community development within their own organizations. In
New York City, black women organized the Manhattan Anti-Slavery
Society, which was an all-black antislavery society with the exception of
white abolitionist Abby Hopper Gibbons. This society promoted abolitionist activities and black community endeavors by working with two
all-black benevolent organizations, the Ladies Literary Society of New
York City and the Rising Daughters of Abyssinia of Abyssinia Baptist
Church. These black women, along with prominent black female abolitionists from PFASS and BFASS—and at the urgings of Angelina Grimké for
the convention to more representative—did participate in the four-day

female antislavery convention in New York City in 1837 hosted by LYN-CASS. Although excluded from the two white antislavery societies in New York City, the abolitionist activities of black female New Yorkers continued apace. One of the benevolent societies that the Manhattan Anti-Slavery Society worked in concert with, which may suggest some overlapping membership, was the Ladies Literary Society of New York City, which was already donating funds to the antislavery journals and the New York Vigilance Committee. The Chatham Street Chapel Society, although having Eliza Ann Day as an active member, was not known for any black community involvement or political initiatives.

Like PFASS, BFASS had a number of black female activists as members. From the founding of BFASS in 1833, shortly before PFASS, the organization had experienced some internal tensions that threatened its solidarity. In fact, it appears that there were definitive racial and class cleavages that, while seemingly benign, prevented the society's members from becoming one cohesive unit. Once Lydia Maria Child and Louisa Loring joined the society and began to establish the society's public political role, the class cleavages were more finely drawn among the society's members. As risk-takers, the wealthiest members of the society were catapulted into the public arena because of their political agenda, positions in the community, contacts, and sense of power. While this group organized antislavery petitions and annual fund-raisers, similar to PFASS's activities, they also attended legislative sessions, speaking as antislavery lecturers, "boycotting proslavery churches, purchasing free-labor goods, and defying customary segregation by seating themselves in areas designated for blacks only."[24] Exhibiting a clear political agenda that was very different from that of the middle-class women in the society, they were in the forefront of women's political activism but risked alienating the more moderate, benevolent-oriented, middle-class society members.

Black female members shared the concerns of both groups in BFASS and participated in the society's broad range of activities, in their own community projects, and in the subversive activities of the Boston's black community under the aegis of the Boston Vigilance Committee. Susan Paul was active in the annual fund-raisers that netted the society thousands of dollars. At the same time, she, like other black female members, was engaged in a number of community projects as well as in the community's more subversive activities. Paul, for instance, operated her elementary school and the Garrison Juvenile Choir. Anna Logan, Margarett Scarlett, and Eunice R. Davis were involved in the black community's efforts to integrate schools in Boston. "By 1835, the onslaught of complaints regarding the poor quality of instruction and poor conditions in the black schools, as compared to those schools serving white children, resulted in the construction of a new school. Dissatisfaction over heavy-handed policymaking was not alleviated by the improved facilities, and many parents whose children were now required to attend black schools became convinced that they had a better idea—integrated schools."[25]

The sustained efforts of BFASS's black members would ultimately lead to the school segregation case *Roberts v. City of Boston* (1850), which would take more than a century for the U.S. Supreme Court to reverse in *Brown v. Board of Education* (1954). Eunice R. Davis and Ann Logan were also active participants in fund-raisers for the African Methodist Episcopal Zion (AMEZ) Church in the 1840s. Nancy Prince, who expressed dissatisfaction with the internal discord within the society—"These meetings I attended with much pleasure until a contention broke out among themselves"—was noted for her evangelical missionary work in the West Indies.[26] What anchored these black female activists was their community commitment, and it braced them for the antislavery schism of 1840.

By the time of the antislavery schism in 1840, several black male leaders, tired of the abstract ideological debates and issues, were considering an all-black antislavery effort.[27] BFASS, unable to sustain its shaky cohesiveness following the intense discussions on ideological perspectives, moved toward dissolution following the national division. Mrs. Jehial C. Beman spoke for black women who, believing that the ideological debates moved abolition offstage, urged reconciliation: "The cause of my enslaved people is the cause of God, and I hope this great and good body will be united in its advancement."[28] But the internal and external discord proved too much for BFASS. Following its dissolution in 1840, society members, obviously still in the heat of passion, reconstituted two societies, the Massachusetts Female Emancipation Society and the new BFASS led by Lydia Maria Child. The majority of black women, "pressured into declaring their allegiances," pledged their loyalty to Garrison by siding with BFASS. But neither group could ever again muster the prominence of the former BFASS, and within a few years both had lost their momentum.

Because of their community activism, which shaped their abolitionism and their independent political action, black women's experiences in the interracial female antislavery societies were not as divisive as they might have been. In stable and enduring organizations like PFASS, black women were able to expand their overt and covert community activities and, in the process, expand the interpretation of abolitionism of many white female abolitionists. When they were excluded from participation in groups like LYNCASS, black women organized their own societies and continued to promote their work through their benevolent societies. In the instance of short-term but prominent organizations like BFASS, black women continued their community work because, unlike the wealthy BFASS members who engaged in intense but abstract ideological debates, the material realities of slavery and its consequences were more immediate to black lives. However, the wealth of contacts, information, networking, and strategies that black female society members gained became integral to their political activism.

BLACK WOMEN'S NATIONAL AND INTERNATIONAL ABOLITIONISM

As national and international speakers on the abolitionist lecture circuit, black female abolitionists were in open defiance of slavery, racism, and contemporary conventional roles of women in the secular sphere. In most instances, black female activists, like Maria W. Stewart, made slavery, racism, and sexism common cause and saw the organic relationship among all three causes. While Stewart's philosophy was heavily influenced by the moral stance that permeated early black nationalism, by placing black women at the center of the black struggle she thereby endowed them with full equality. This empowering process, of sanctioning and legitimizing their rights as women, placed Stewart as one of the forerunners of the women's rights movement.

Before modern abolitionism gained its broad currency, Maria W. Stewart, the first American woman to speak publicly, began to espouse militant black abolitionism in the early 1830s. "Fueled with the same Christian zeal that propelled Zilpha Elaw and Jarena Lee, Maria Stewart felt called upon to address the earthly problems of her people."[29] For Stewart, morality intertwined with black nationalism was at the core of her political activism.[30] Heavily influenced by the militant abolitionist David Walker, Stewart was fired up with the same zeal to "plead the cause of [her] brethren," undergirded by a united sisterhood in struggle. By Stewart uniting black women and black nationalism in struggle and "insisting upon the right of women to take their place in the front ranks of black moral and political leadership," she rescued black nationalism from its male-dominated perch and centered black women as full and equal partners in black activism.

Encouraging black female solidarity, a necessary vehicle for community mobilization, Stewart reminded black women that they would be morally victorious only when "we become united as one, and cultivate among ourselves the pure principles of piety, morality and virtue." For Stewart, a righteous struggle for liberation started with individual morality. Like most black female abolitionists, Stewart believed in the immediate emancipation of the slaves and the collective uplift of blacks. But she was typical of most black female evangelists in believing that the power of her message came from God: "Her sense of having an urgent, divinely inspired mission to the black community allowed Stewart to quickly find her true voice, one full of assurance, spirit, energy, creative imagination, and fervor."[31] It was both the power of her message and her greater sense of urgency that made her audiences, particularly black men, chary of her lecture style.

Stewart advocated a three-phase empowerment process for black women. Initially, she advised, black women must empower themselves with moral fortitude. To Stewart, who saw the world through a moral prism, moral rectitude was a necessary precondition for any active struggle against oppression. Morality would not only shape one's character but would place supplicants in communion with God, who, in turn, would slay their enemies. "You may kill, tyrannize, and oppress as much as you choose, until our cry shall come up before the throne of God; for I am firmly persuaded, that he will not suffer you to quell the proud, fearless and undaunted spirits of the Africans forever."[32]

Second, Stewart endorsed the pragmatic black nationalism of developing economic initiatives in black communities. Black women were encouraged to cultivate business and social enterprises to enhance their business acumen and enrich black community life. To facilitate economic development, Stewart encouraged black women "to pool their economic resources" and to "promote and patronize each other" for financial success.

In keeping with the conventional notions of domesticity, however, Stewart saw women as the primary caretakers of the home and children. The third phase of Stewart's plan was for black women to emphasize the education of the children to ensure the future of the black community: "It is you that must create in the minds of your little girls and boys a thirst for knowledge, the love of virtue, the abhorrence of vice, and the cultivation of a pure heart."[33]

For Stewart, black women could not be good role models until they had educated themselves, developed a sound business plan, and led a moral life. Stewart's three-phase empowerment process was a radical approach to the black woman's condition. Although she emphasized the conventional trappings of morality and childcare, Stewart made a radical departure from the traditional views of women in encouraging black women to move beyond the boundaries of motherhood and become fully participating members in the black struggle for liberation.

In this reconstruction of self, children, and community, and in her belief that black women had the power to change their material circumstances, Stewart was also challenging sexual subordination in society, and she "was never more prophetic, political, or radical than when re-envisioning the world of black women."[34] "O, ye daughters of Africa, awake! awake! arise!" Stewart exclaimed, "No longer sleep nor slumber, but distinguish yourselves. Show forth to the world that ye are endowed with noble and exalted faculties."[35] In urging the passionate transformation of the black woman, Stewart captured the soul of black female abolitionism.

For Stewart, the elevation of black women was in tandem with the liberation of the slaves. While Stewart viewed slavery and the treatment of free blacks as the tyrannical forces of oppression incompatible with liberty and freedom, she also recognized racism in America's foreign policy as well. In 1832, in her lecture at Franklin Hall in Boston, Stewart connected the hypocrisy in both America's foreign and domestic policies with regard to blacks: "You have acknowledged all of the nations of the earth, except Hayti."[36]

In the black nationalist tradition of ridiculing the oppressed, hoping to goad them on in their battle against the oppressors, Stewart challenged black men, already chafing under oppression, to do more for self-liberation. Her sensitive "mixed" audience, particularly to these types of denunciations, had trouble accepting these charges from a woman. "Her gender would indeed underscore what some must have considered the unpalatable nature of her message. Walker, citing armed struggles for liberty around the globe, could dramatically bemoan the failure of manhood among American blacks as a spur to inciting rebellion. It was much less likely that accusations of cowardice, ignorance, and lack of ambition hurled by a woman would rally Stewart's listeners, male or female, to the barricades of social activism."[37]

Eventually, Stewart, who was partially shunned by Boston's black male community, moved to New York City, where she remained politically active and continued her mission of rights for the oppressed. "She joined women's organizations, attended the Women's Anti-Slavery

Convention of 1837, and was an active participant in a black women's literary society."[38] Despite her failings in Boston, Stewart never lost sight of the larger issues that defined black oppression. For Stewart, to be both African and American came with pride, dignity, and a higher calling in urging black women to take their rightful place in the black struggle.

Although the black abolitionist Sarah Parker Remond started out on the antislavery lecture circuit in 1856 in the United States, she was most recognized as part of the influential coterie of black abolitionists, dubbed by Benjamin Quarles as "ministers without portfolio," who spoke abroad to raise monies for their cause. Remond's antislavery beliefs, however, were shaped by such factors as maturing in the segregated city of Salem, Massachusetts; her experiences as a home education student because the separate "African school" had closed; black women's emergence in city life with political voices; and her elder brother's commitment to abolitionism. "The year Sarah Remond was twelve her brother made a significant move: Charles Lenox Remond began his long career as agent for the Massachusetts Anti-Slavery Society."[39] In commenting on Charles's influence upon his sister, Dorothy Porter notes that "Charles Lennox Remond, the first Negro to address American audiences on the abolition of slavery and the best known Negro before the time of Frederick Douglass, probably influenced his sister to become a public lecturer."[40]

Sarah Parker Remond's home soon became a beehive of intellectual activity, with abolitionists as frequent visitors. By 1856, Remond was hired by the American Anti-Slavery Society on the lecture circuit for New York State. Significantly grounded in three years as a lecturer, Remond participated in the international abolitionist campaign in Britain in 1859, seeking to encourage European abolitionists to spearhead the development of antislavery societies and put international pressure on the American government to abolish slavery. Remond always linked the suffering of slaves to the plight of free blacks in America, both of whom, she maintained, were exploited within a common oppressive system buttressed by religious leaders, businessmen, and politicians. As a black woman, however, Remond drew particular attention to the exploitation of black female slaves. Remond argued that the "sufferings and indignities . . . perpetrated on her sisters in America" were intertwined with miscegenation, which she dubbed the "fruits of licentiousness" that created 800,000 mulattoes.[41] Believing that women were the champions of humanity and that this type of sexual exploitation would arouse the ire of her white female audience, Remond particularly appealed to the sisterhood of all European women: "Should not woman take her part in this great work" to mobilize antislavery forces on behalf of oppressed black women in America? "Sisterhood was the bond between speaker and audience. At the close of her talk, one of the women stepped forward to 'acknowledge her as a sister.'"[42]

The material realities of black women being central to the cash crop production was brought home to Remond on her visit to the industrial city of Manchester. The cotton that slaves produced was shipped to Manchester for the manufacturing of cotton garments. Slaves were creating and facilitating England's industrial expansion, which Remond experienced firsthand as she toured the cotton city. Remond realized the extent of the economic collusion between Southern planters and the British owners of industrial mills and understood how deeply the economic base of slavery and capitalism were interconnected. She also criticized the relationship of elitism to cotton production, arguing that slaves and, indirectly, poor Southern whites were both being exploited and were the "victims of slavery." "When I walk through the streets of Manchester, and meet load after load of cotton, I think of those eighty thousand cotton plantations on which was grown the one hundred and twenty-five millions of dollars' worth of cotton which supplies your market, and I remember that not one cent of that money ever reached the hands of the labourers."[43]

Despite England's equivocation on the American Civil War, undoubtedly reflecting the British industrialists' unwillingness to ruin their lively cotton trade, Remond continued her crusade against the cotton industry, knowing that it held the key to Southern cotton commerce in the United States and, just as important, the emancipation of the slaves. "Let not diplomacy of statesmen, no intimidation of slaveholders, no scarcity of cotton, no fear of slave insurrection, prevent the people of Great Britain from maintaining their position as the friend of the oppressed Negro, which they deservedly occupied previous to the disastrous civil war."[44]

Remond returned from her European tour and, following the Civil War, became very active in the universal suffrage campaign. But she soon returned to Europe and made her home in Florence, Italy, and worked as a physician.

Another female black abolitionist, France Ellen Watkins Harper, was a decided favorite on the abolitionist circuit. She was the most popular black poet of her time and was noted for her carefully prepared speeches and gifted rhetorical talent. Like Remond, the confluences of Harper's early antislavery environment shaped her later political role as an abolitionist. Harper's abolitionism was influenced by growing up free in the

slave city of Baltimore, living with her aunt and uncle who were dedicated abolitionists, and being nurtured intellectually by attending the
elite William Watkins Academy for Negro Youth, founded by her uncle,
the Reverend William Watkins. Following the enactment of the Fugitive
Slave Law of 1850, when free blacks were threatened with re-enslavement, Rev. Watkins was forced to give up his home and school and join
thousands of black émigrés in Canada. Harper, however, followed her
own bent, doing a brief stint at teaching in Ohio and Pennsylvania. "In
1853, she moved to Philadelphia in order to devote herself entirely to the
abolitionist cause."[45] After living with William and Letitia Still, who
operated the major node of the Underground Railroad in Philadelphia,
Harper's thinking crystallized into radical abolitionism, where she combined the precepts and philosophy inherent in Garrisonian moral suasionist thought with the more subversive work of aiding fugitive slaves.

By 1854, Harper, employed by the State Anti-Slavery Society of
Maine, was gaining a reputation on the antislavery lecture circuit, causing the black abolitionist and feminist Mary Shadd Cary, who was raising money for her Canadian newspaper, the *Provincial Freeman,* to
remark: "Why the whites and colored people here [Detroit] are just going
crazy with excitement about her. She is the greatest female speaker ever
was here, so wisdom obliges me to keep out of the way as with her prepared lectures there would just be no chance of favorable comparison."[46]

Harper saw the right of liberty and freedom as part of God's divine
law superceding all laws contrived by men. Laws enacted by men undergirded slavery, constituting the key to its preservation, and were responsible for the substantial economic profits derived from the system.[47]
These laws and the slave system, Harper believed, were contrary to both
the Constitution and the democratic tenets of American society: "Oh,
was it not strangely inconsistent that men fresh, so fresh, from the bap-
tism of the [American] Revolution should make such concessions to the
foul spirit of Despotism! that, when fresh from gaining their own liberty,
they could permit the African slave trade."[48] Harper called upon all
morally conscious Americans to challenge oppression by cleansing "the
corrupt fountains of our government by sending men to Congress who
will plead for our down-trodden and oppressed brethren, our crushed
and helpless sisters, whose tears and blood bedew our soil."[49]

Harper steadily came to embrace a more radical abolitionism and by
1857 had departed from the Maine Anti-Slavery Society and returned to
her radical roots in Philadelphia. In keeping with this philosophical
stance, Harper "preached and practiced the politics of Free Produce. That

is, she urged economic boycotts of slave-produced goods."[50] In support of her stance, Harper declared: "I have reason to be thankful that I am able to give a little more for a Free Labor dress, if it is coarser. I can thank God that upon its warp and woof I see no stain of blood and tears."[51]

By the 1850s, the search for the free-labor products of cotton, coffee, sugar, and rice had been a part of the abolitionist campaign for thirty years. While the Colored Free Produce Society of Pennsylvania and the Colored Female Free Produce Society of Pennsylvania had some initial success and garnered a great deal of enthusiasm, the difficulty in obtaining the goods in the United States or abroad proved to be a problem. Yet black female abolitionists like Grace Douglass and Harper were associated with the movement and were able to inspire others to strike an economic blow against slavery. While most abolitionists gave lip service to the idea of free-labor products, the efforts of the American Free Produce Association and other free produce societies notwithstanding, their practice of this aspect of the antislavery cause was far short of the mark.[52] To Harper, however, the free produce movement was reflective of an unwavering commitment to abolition.

Harper's radical abolitionism continued to flourish in Philadelphia. Over the next several years, Harper's abolitionism included lecturing on behalf of the Pennsylvania Anti-Slavery Society and for other antislavery organizations. But Harper welcomed subversive action and contributed most of her proceeds from the sales of her books to the Underground Railroad. In her support of a failed slave rescue attempt by other black radical abolitionists, including her friend William Still, she publicly advocated subversive action: "It is not enough to express our sympathy by words, we should be ready to crystallize it into actions."[53] In a letter to Still in 1859, Harper makes both her financial and political commitment clear: "Do write me every time you write how many come to your house; and, my dear friend, if you have that much in hand of mine from my books, will you please pay the Vigilance Committee two or three dollars for me to help carry on the glorious enterprise."[54] On 12 December 1859 she was again writing Still: "Send me word what I can do for the fugitives. Do you need any money? Do I not owe you on the old bill [pledge]?"[55]

Following in the footsteps of other black female abolitionists, Harper's open resistance and subversive activities were compatible in the causes of abolition and Universal Freedom. In her visit to Toronto, Canada, in 1856, Harper tasted real freedom for the first time, and it provided a sharp contrast to the plight of slaves and free blacks in the United States: "Well, I have gazed for the first time upon Free Land! And would you believe it, tears sprang to my eyes, and I wept. Oh! it was a glorious sight to gaze for the first time on a land where a poor slave, flying from our glorious land of liberty(!), would in a moment find his fetters broken, his shackles loosed, and whatever he was in the land of Washington, beneath the shadow of Bunker Hill Monument, or even Plymouth Rock, here he becomes 'a man and a brother.'"[56]

Harper's belief in Universal Freedom and her major role in subversive activities led her to support John Brown, the fervent abolitionist who believed that slavery had to be countered with warfare. When Brown's raid on Harper's Ferry failed and he and his comrades were captured and awaiting execution in 1859, there was an outpouring of support for him in the black community. Black female activists rallied in support of Brown. "Colored women sent letters of esteem to the jailed Brown. A group of Brooklyn matrons wrote that they would ever hold him in their remembrance, considering him a model of true patriotism because he sacrificed everything for his country's sake." Spearheaded by black women, funds were also raised on a consistent basis in the black community to provide for Mrs. Brown, with heartfelt letters accompanying the contributions. "A group of women from New York, Brooklyn, and Williamsburg sent Mrs. Brown a letter on November 23, its content summarized in the lines, 'Fear not, beloved sister. Trust in the God of Jacob.'"[57]

Harper wrote to John Brown, believing that he had struck a decisive blow against slavery and heightened the national contradictions between slavery and freedom. She thought that the collusion between government and the proslavery forces was unmistakable. "You have rocked the bloody Bastile [sic]; and I hope that from your sad fate great good may arise to the cause of freedom. Already from your prison has come a shout of triumph against the giant sin of our country." For Harper, Brown's crusade was in keeping with the ethos of Universal Freedom that made abolitionism a cause of the righteous: "And, if Universal Freedom is ever to be the dominant power of the land, your bodies may be only her first stepping stones to domination."[58]

BLACK WOMEN AND SUBVERSIVE ACTIVISM

The complementary praxis to free black women's open resistance was their more subversive political activity on behalf of the slaves. Whether black women served in the many capacities that comprised the functioning of the Underground Railroad system, participated in informal slave rescue efforts, or joined the more formalized fugitive aid societies, free black female activists facilitated the slave's journey to freedom. In overtly challenging the hegemony of slavery, free black women were maintaining consanguineous bonds with blacks in slavery, nourishing the slaves' wellspring of hope and culture of resistance while simultaneously paving the way for emancipation.

When Harriet Brent Jacobs, who "had heard that the poor slave had many friends at the north," escaped from slavery, her first encounter with a free black "subversive" woman, Mrs. Durham, was in Philadelphia. "Mrs. Durham met me with a kindly welcome, without asking any questions. I was tired, and her friendly manner was a sweet refreshment. God bless her! I was sure that she had comforted other weary hearts, before I received her sympathy."[59] Free black women's subversive activism did more than strengthen the bond between slave women and themselves. "Black women played important roles in providing shelter, medical aid, and food for fugitives in hiding within the community."[60] In a sense, these women represented a two-sided coin, as the subversive activism of black female abolitionists was coeval with the radical resistance of female runaways. This subversive activity tied slave women and free black urban women together in an ongoing struggle for liberation.

In a bid for freedom to the North or Canada, slave women had to consider such factors as the region and location, the direction of travel, the time of the year, their marital status, the infrastructure on the plantation, and the available resources at their disposal. "Women were reluctant to leave their families, and therefore, a much smaller number of women than men escaped to free states."[61] Most often, the fact that a woman was to be sold to the Deep South or the impending sale of loved ones, particularly children, could be the pragmatic impetus behind her escape plans. Mary Ennis, escaping with her two children, recounted her desire for freedom to William Still: "Long before this mother escaped, thoughts of liberty filled her heart. She was ever watching for an opportunity that would encourage her to hope for safety, when once the attempt should be made. Until, however, she was convinced that her two children were to be sold, she could not quite muster courage to set out on the journey."[62]

Some women adopted ingenious disguises or used the terrain or trusted contacts to aid their plans. Ellen Craft, Maria Weems, and Clarissa Davis donned male attire as part of their escape plans. Ellen Craft, a slave who could pass for white, posed as a young male planter who was traveling to Philadelphia seeking medical attention with his manservant, her husband, William Craft. Her face wrapped to hide the fact that she did not have a beard and her arm in a sling so that she did not have to register at hotels, the couple embarked on a perilous journey to freedom. This bold, improbable scheme moved the Crafts from their plight as Georgian slaves to their freedom in the North and then subsequently to England as abolitionists. "Maria Weems, alias 'Joe Wright,' for two years planned her escape from Washington, D.C. to the free soil of Philadelphia. Traveling on the Underground Railroad as the young black coachman to Dr. T, the fifteen-year old Weems, was finally delivered at the home of the Stills. On delivering up his charge, the Dr. simply remarked to the writer's wife, 'I wish to leave this young lad with you a short while.'" In 1854, Clarissa Davis escaped from Portsmouth, Virginia, dressed in male clothing, which aided the success of her venture: "Dressed in male attire, Clarissa left the miserable coop where she had been almost without light or air for two and a half months, and unmolested, reached the boat safely, and was secreted in a box by Wm. Bagnal, a clever young man who sincerely sympathized with the slave, having a wife in slavery himself, and by him she was safely delivered into the hands of the Vigilance Committee. Clarissa Davis here, by advice of the Committee . . . was christened 'Mary D. Armstead.'"[63]

Lear Green escaped from her owner, James Noble of Baltimore, in a sailor's chest, while Charlotte Giles and Harriet Eglin used the pretext of deep mourning (with heavy veils) to facilitate their escape from Baltimore on a direct train to Philadelphia.[64] Harriet Brent Jacobs and Susan Brooks used water transportation in their flight to freedom. Jacobs, in her attempt to get away from her master, Dr. Flint, had hid in her grandmother's attic for seven years and was finally able to escape north as a stowaway on a ship. "I was to escape in a vessel; but I forebear to mention my further particulars." Susan Brooks used the familiar role of a black woman as a laundress to initiate her flight to freedom:

> In order to avoid suspicion, the woman intending to be secreted, approached the boat with a cleaned ironed shirt on her arm, bare headed and in her usual working dress, looking good-natured of course, and as if she were simply conveying the shirt to one of the men on the boat. The attention of the officer on the watch would not for a moment be attracted by a custom so common as this. Thus safely on the boat, the man whose business it was to put this piece of property in the most safe Underground Rail Road place . . . would quickly arrange matters without being missed from his duties.[65]

Harriet Shephard decided to make her dash for freedom when she could no longer take the thought of her five children being raised as slaves. In addition to carrying all five children with her, Shephard also organized a group of five other slaves and confiscated the master's horses and two carriages to take the group of eleven escapees on the first leg of their journey:

> In 1855, the sleepy, slaveholding neighborhood of Chestertown, Maryland, was doubtless deeply excited on learning that eleven head of slaves, four head of horses, and two carriages were missing ... [Harriet Shephard] was entitled to a great deal of credit for seizing the horses and carriages belonging to her master, as she did it for the liberation of her children . . . the fugitives, under escort, were soon on their way to Kennett Square (a hot bed of abolitionists and stock-holders of the Underground Railroad), which place they reached safely.[66]

Since Southern planters frequently traveled to the North with their slaves for business, vacations, shopping, and other social activities, Underground Railroad operators and vigilance committee members, often one and the same, would apprise the slaves of their legal rights on free soil. Jane Johnson, a slave of the U.S. minister to Nicaragua, John H. Wheeler, was informed by vigilance committee members that she was free, whereupon she took her two children and walked away from the wharf in the company of vigilance committee members, despite the entreaties of her owner.[67] When Cordelia Loney, a slave who was with her mistress in Philadelphia for a short stay, was told of her possible freedom, she decided to "accept the hospitality of the Underground Rail Road, and leave in a quiet way and go to Canada." "Aunt Hannah Moore," en route from Missouri to California with her mistress, had the good fortune to go to a "store in the neighborhood where she was stopping, and to her unspeakable joy she found the proprietor an abolitionist and a friend" who informed her of her legal entitlement to freedom.[68] Moore remained in Philadelphia as a free woman, married, and became a member of "Mother Bethel" Church.

In actualizing their plans, these slave women provided vital connections to their free sisters in urban areas, and each served as a catalyst for the subversive activities of the other. While most fugitives disappeared into the urban community or into the black communities in Canada, they had to always remain vigilant. In New York City, after the passage of the

Fugitive Slave Law of 1850, when there was renewed vigor in capturing fugitives in Northern cities, Jacobs commented that "many a poor washerwoman, who, by hard labor, had made herself a comfortable home, was obliged to sacrifice her furniture, bid a hurried farewell to friends, and seek her fortune among strangers in Canada."[69] Of those that remained in the cities, some joined the antislavery efforts. Since most black women were domestics and most female runaways were employed as domestics, black domestic workers may have played an integral role in the informal slave rescues that were a part of city life. "Generally, women involved directly in fugitive slave rescues were from the working class, including washerwomen and domestic servants."[70] The presence of female runaways contributed to the expansion of free black women's political consciousness, which included subversion as commonplace and intrinsic to the idea of freedom.

For free black women in urban areas who were directly engaged in these illegal activities, subversion included the clandestine activities in black communities that sought to undermine the hegemony of slavery either by crippling those forces that pursued fugitives, providing fugitives with safe passage to free territory, or planning and executing slave rescues from slavenappers or lawful officials. Most often, female activists who openly resisted slavery were also a part of or connected to the underground subversive apparatus in antebellum black communities. "Over a four-year span the colored Women's Association [of Philadelphia] made donations for fugitive slave work, giving $50 in 1851."[71] Creating two realities for survival, overt and covert resistance, black female activists saw the necessity of functioning in both spheres. Yet others who were not activists per se or noted for their activism would engage in spontaneous acts to free fugitives from slave catchers. These women also formed a part of the underground activities and supported the resistance movement in a sporadic fashion.[72] Undoubtedly, it was the strength of both groups of black women, the activists and survivalists, that strengthened this method of political resistance. This covert stage of operations depended most on activities of subterfuge, that is, secret committees and organizations with special purposes, people who volunteered or were carefully recruited, signals, coded letters, secret passwords, and surreptitious hiding places in cities and towns. Additionally, there was a funneling of funds through organizations, a quasi-transportation system of escape routes on land and sea, and the overall appearance of normalcy to obfuscate these activities. Endangering life and limb of all the participants, subversion was a conscious movement by black women against oppression to shape a new reality of consciousness of and resistance to their material conditions.

The most dangerous form of political resistance was the Underground Railroad and the organizational apparatus that arose to carry out its function. Dubbed the Underground Railroad because fugitives seemed to disappear into the system, it was rather a massive networking of way stations, conveyances, committees, and committed abolitionists that moved fugitives from the South en route to the North or Canada. Those who assisted the runaways were called agents, stationmasters, conductors, or operators—employees of a railway system—and were responsible for their "valuable pieces of ebony" reaching the next leg of their freedom journey. Vigilance committees and some members of antislavery societies operated in the Underground Railroad system to ensure the fugitives' safety. Although antislavery societies proliferated throughout Northern communities and their members could be physically abused for their beliefs, the vigilance committees of Boston, New York City, and Philadelphia were illegal operations. Nonetheless, black women participated in vigilantism, in both all-black and interracial groups, in defiance against slavery and oppression and, most specifically, in support of those who were attempting to liberate themselves from bondage.

As members of the resistance, black female activists served in the infrastructure of the Underground Railroad in all capacities. Frances Jane Brown, a former indentured servant, hid fugitives seeking a haven in Cincinnati. When she married Thomas A. Brown, their new home in Pittsburgh became an Underground Railroad station for runaways on their way to Canada. One stationmaster, Elizabeth Barnes, working for a ship captain in Virginia, hid fugitives on ships sailing to Northern ports. Black men and women, as in all phases of the movement, frequently served as husband-and-wife teams on dangerous assignments. John and Mary Jones were operators of an Underground Railroad station in Chicago that housed John Brown and Frederick Douglass before Brown's raid on Harpers Ferry.[73] William and Letitia Still were well-known operators in Philadelphia. William Still kept massive records of the fugitive movement and assisted fugitives in locating their families in freedom. Undoubtedly, his interest in their stories of their slave experiences was the first stage in the healing of their psyches as well. Women conductors, operating alone, also distinguished themselves. As a conductor, "Jane Lewis of New Lebanon, Ohio, rowed fugitives regularly across the Ohio River."[74]

Undoubtedly, the most famous conductor of the Underground was Harriet Tubman, a self-liberated slave whose resistance to the slavocracy included freeing as many slaves as possible. Tubman, traveling and operating in hostile territory alone and mostly on foot, made approximately nineteen trips to the South and was responsible for bringing 300 fugitives to freedom. After her own escape from slavery in 1849, she returned to the South over a period of ten years as a conductor to rescue slaves. Tubman employed several viable strategies on these liberation journeys, including confiscating the master's horses and carriage, which gave the slaves an air of legitimacy when they encountered whites. On those occasions when she believed that her group was in imminent danger, she frequently went south instead of north and then moved in a northerly direction when the coast was clear.[75] To facilitate her plans, Tubman relied on a "network of resistance" in the form of coded letters addressed to key contacts, word-of-mouth, and songs with dual meanings passed from plantation to plantation in the area to alert potential "passengers" before her arrival. Dubbed "Moses" by slaves, Tubman's vast knowledge of the terrain and her preparations for the journey, which included paregoric for babies and a pistol as a gentle persuader for slaves with second thoughts, made her efforts successful. Tedious and fraught with danger and the reality of prison and death, resistance work of any magnitude was only for the most courageous of the freedom fighters.

Free black women were also pivotal in some of the vigilance committees in providing immediate and long-term assistance to escapees. This intense, taxing, and emotionally exacting work more than likely made many female ex-slaves, some who were fugitives themselves, continuously relive their own past slave experiences and hence attack the endeavor with fresh zeal. Since fugitives were fleeing with literally the clothes on their backs, the well-organized vigilance committees in New York City, Boston, Philadelphia, and Cleveland were expected to provide comprehensive services for hundreds of these travelers each year. These services included "boarding and lodging them for a few days, purchasing clothing and medicine for them, providing them with small sums of money, informing them as to their legal rights and giving them legal protection from kidnappers." Fugitives also needed transportation for the next leg of their journey, assistance getting started in a new community, recommendations and other letters of support, small loans, temporary shelter, and jobs, all functions of vigilance committees.[76]

One of the critical functions that black women played was fundraising to help these beleaguered committees, whose main sources of support were "Negroes, a sprinkling of whites, and a corps of women's groups on both sides of the Atlantic."[77] Founded in 1842, the Boston

Vigilance Committee was one of the largest committees of the time. Comprised of both black and white abolitionists, including black women who were members of BFASS and black women such as Isabella and Holmes Snowden, daughters of the abolitionist Rev. Samuel Snowden, the committee engaged in fund-raising and provided financial aid and general assistance to runaways.[78] Owing to the Vigilance Committee's widespread influence in Boston's black community, many black women in the community who were nonmembers also contributed funds to the cause. In the same year, Boston blacks were instrumental in the founding of the New England Association, providing fugitives with food, clothing, and shelter. Two black women were a part of the seven-member leadership cadre of this group. In Cleveland, the all-black Cleveland Vigilance Committee had four women out of nine committee members and boasted of assisting 275 slaves to Canada in nine months.[79]

Although the New York Vigilance Committee was shepherded by the indefatigable David Ruggles, black women furnished housing, food, and clothing for the runaways as well as raising monies desperately needed to keep the organization afloat. "In New York the Negro women held annual fairs at the Broadway Tabernacle for the benefit of the Vigilance Committee." What made black women's fund-raising skills so effective was that they were able to extend their marketing strategies far beyond the abolitionists' circles based on prior community networking that they had developed. "Many of the women who conducted the fair also worked for the committee by collecting a penny a week from friends."[80] In actuality, these women had a long-term approach to fund-raising initiatives that, along with major fund-raising events, ensured a constant source of capital.

In 1838, Philadelphia had its own Female Vigilant Association, where the majority of the women were black. While Mary Bustill, Elizabeth White, Sarah McCrummell, Mary Proctor, and Elizabeth Colly were members of the association and were well known in the Philadelphian black community, Hetty Reckless emerged as the group's guiding light. Through Reckless's efforts, this auxiliary not only worked closely with their male counterpart, the Vigilance Association of Philadelphia, but also with the interracial PFASS. Although McCrummell was a founding member of PFASS, Reckless was influential in keeping the needs of the black community before the group. Like the Forten women who also belonged to PFASS, Reckless persuaded society members to contribute to community projects and to make donations to the vigilance committees to provide fugitives with room and board, clothing, medical assistance, employment, financial aid, and advice concerning their legal rights. Reckless was able to be effective in these undertakings because of her influence in the community and her affiliation with a number of community projects. Like the Forten women, when she joined PFASS her reputation as a community activist had already been established.

Over a number of years, Reckless attempted to imbue a broader interpretation of abolitionism for PFASS by soliciting funds for black community concerns as well as the more subversive components of the antislavery cause. In 1841, Reckless solicited monies for black education to support recently established Sabbath schools in the community. "Hester Reckless informed [us] that through the exertions of the coloured people a Sabbath school had been established." In addition, she sounded the more cautionary note that "the members of the Society were urged to give . . . aid to this work of benevolence." Reckless also solicited monies for the vigilance committees, stressing the urgency of the task. "She reported that since our last meeting they had assisted thirty-five fugitives . . . and that they now had three more under care."[81]

While the society gave monies to black community causes and tried to restrict its giving to a case-by-case basis, some tension was created by this pragmatic abolitionism. Nevertheless, Reckless did persuade the group to make a financial commitment in June 1845 "for the benefit of fugitive slaves."[82] Despite some of the members' reservations, PFASS continued, when pressed, to make sporadic contributions to the underground. While this broader vision of abolitionism caused white abolitionist Lucretia Mott to question whether this was "properly Anti-Slavery Work," black women saw open challenges to the system compatible with subversive strategies to eradicate slavery as the very essence of abolitionism.

Conclusion

Sites of Change

BLACK FEMALE ACTIVISTS DEFIED THE SUBALTERN STATUS imposed on them by the dominant society by forging political roles that sustained an emerging culture of resistance, a shared sense of community, and space in which to challenge their oppressors. Although the political interpretation given by free black women to their race, class, and gender barriers differed from those of slave women, enslaved women and free black women had common bonds of oppression. The cultural templates of enslavement, racial discrimination, and class and gender oppression circumscribed all of their lives. This complex array of factors, which were embedded both in the Southern slave economy and in nascent capitalism, precipitated their mobilization efforts. The political environment nurtured by slave women, which situated the context for resistance, was sustained in freedom. Symbolically, having created this political environment of resistance, slave women had also established a political barometer of what constituted race loyalty and race betrayal to the community. Substantively, the building of slave and free black communities for stability and protest provided the basis for a collective political identity to emerge.

The incipient stage of slave women's political activism was the politicalization of the slave community, the creation of female collectives, and the utilization and activation of their labor will as a political resource for community resistance. The inner source of empowerment developed by slave women, which promoted their labor will, was the continuous reconstruction of African traditions and the relentless tasks associated with cash crop commodity production. Slave women's resistance was hewed out of the labor that informed the daily life experiences of these women. As they struggled to delegitimize the slave system and alter their slave status, slave women transformed themselves into agents of political change in the community.

Contemporary scholars have documented the transformation of black women from being powerless in society to being agents of political change as they press for social reform. In her study of a group of black welfare mothers in Brooklyn, Jackie Pope notes, for example, that in pressing the system for minimum survival benefits, these women recognized that they had a right to challenge the humiliating welfare bureaucracy that controls their lives. In their mobilization efforts, these women were able to claim political and social agency over their lives and, in the process, establish a movement.[1] Similarly, slave women hoped to transform their individual powerlessness into collective resistance to engender a shifting of the power of the hegemony of slavery.

The labor activity of slave women, female cohesiveness, and networking systems on plantations, intertwined with family and community life, not only created the conditions for slave women's incipient stage of political activism to emerge but also maximized their potential as political resources. Slave women, individually and collectively, were able to activate their labor space and inform the community of resistance strategies. Belinda Robnett has observed that in the civil rights movement of the 1960s, the leadership of female activists emerged as they took advantage of "free space" in the movement for maintaining critical contact with community needs and desires.[2] In the same vein, slave women constructed their labor space and slave quarters as sites of resistance and places for potential mobilization. Episodic rebellions, planned and spontaneous escapes, daily resistance, and survival tactics were all critical components of this political environment.

The power of elite white males was superimposed on the labor spaces of black women, devaluating their labor production and womanhood. Although slave women played a central role in cash crop commodity production and the reproduction of the slave population, the devaluation of women in American society and the economic identity of slave women as chattel property contributed to their invisibility as women and as workers. The devaluation of slave women as women and as workers and their atypical labor arrangements reinforced their invisibility to slaveholders and society. At the same time, their invisibility contributed to the formation of female collectives at labor sites of oppression. This antagonism at the labor sites of oppression, although disregarded by the powerful, was the focal point of slave women's resistance. Although slave women often functioned in collectives, there was fluidity in resistance. William Gamson and David Meyer state that "a movement is a field of actors, not a unified entity," allowing for the diverse strategies of slaves.[3]

One may conceivably argue that slave women were engaged in plantation labor struggles and that their politicalization of the slave community was a sign of inchoate grassroots mobilization to alter the conditions of their enslavement. Grassroots mobilization struggles by women are fairly common in the contemporary period, and Norman I. Fainstein and Susan S. Fainstein, Carolyn Howe, Filomina Chioma Steady, Ann Bookman, and Sandra Morgen have all documented the way in which women collectively mobilize at local levels around specific political and economic issues.[4] Female slaves collectively pooled their strength to effect a change in the slave community's political status as chattel property. In so doing, they enjoined the forces of domination at the most vulnerable centers of slaveholders' control.

Slave women's culture of resistance constituted the beginnings of black women's protest in the United States, and slave women's political activism foreshadowed the political agitation of free black women in urban black communities. Michelle D. Wright argues that slave women's resistance also had a measurable effect on the women's rights movement. A major contribution, she contends, "was that of defining extreme and systematic oppression," and white women were able to use female slavery as a framework for their discourse and analysis of oppression.[5]

Slave women's political activism warrants further study. As we continue the retrieval process of slave women's legacy, the roles of slave women in cash crop commodity production will yield different interpretations. Among the larger questions are: How did slave women sustain resistance over a prolonged period of time? What specific conditions in their enslavement led to changes in the nature and mode of their resistance? Because slave communities were dynamically changing entities, at what points were there shifts in the methods employed by slave women in politicizing the community? Finally, how has the recovery of female slave resistance contributed to the overall struggle to dismantle patriarchal institutions and the privilege of whiteness?

Collective political identities were critical to slave survival and resistance. The amalgamation process that transformed disparate African peoples into an African American people also facilitated a collective consciousness of resistance. One obvious manifestation of this resistance was in the slave's religious experience. Although traditional African religions and evangelical Christianity offered succor to the slaves for the horrific oppression that slaves endured, they also provided sources of empowerment and resistance.

FREE BLACK WOMEN'S ACTIVISM

Industrialization and urbanization provided the impetus for free black women's political activism. In this new organizational stage of political development, black women attempted to alter existing relations of power between blacks and whites by creating a power base of established organizations that would sustain black community life as well as a black protest movement. But this organizational dynamic abutted the predetermined templates of race, class, and gender, largely infused into nascent capitalism from the colonial era, causing black women to seek alternative venues of protest. In shaping this organizational dynamic—manifested by the founding of cultural institutions, mutual benevolent and literary societies, and other female collectives—black women established an informal leadership structure in black communities. Circumventing the sexism inherent in traditional black male leadership roles, black women forged a path of political inclusion.

This political shift from the incipient stage of resistance of slave women to the organizational stage of political development of free black women was accompanied by a multiplicity of factors. First, many black women migrating into industrial centers were experiencing a new sense of freedom, and although that euphoria would quickly dim, there was now a family and community cohesiveness that offered protection from the woes of industrial alienation and the legacy of slavery. Second, although nascent capitalism was creating new prospects for white wage earners, economic opportunities for blacks were severely circumscribed. Racial, class, and gender discrimination were rapidly being infused into the economic structure, marginalizing blacks into a reserve labor pool.

Within these material realities shaped by the exigencies of industrialization, black women's economic condition was immediate and critical. Forced to labor outside of the home, black women defied the conventional standards that characterized middle-class white women's lives. But black women's labor created antagonisms on several fronts. Not only did black women encounter antagonism in the workplace, but their relegation to domestic jobs augured resistance on their part against the political system that degraded their economic status, against the elitism of white female workers who supported the denigration of black women, and against the circumscribed racial mores of a society that would not yield. These material realities, which shaped the varied roles of black women as wife, mother, and economic provider, were critical in shaping their political consciousness.

The initial source of empowerment of urban black women came from their economic activities and their ability to expand their labor space. Their negotiations with intransigent employers on wages, the hiring of other family members, and taking their children to the workplace brought marginal successes. Frequently known for their intractability as domestic workers, black women had an advantage in their monopoly in the field during the 1820s, 1830s, and 1840s. Just as they were being supplanted by Irish female domestic workers, black women were exercising other economic incentives by creating a culture and community of independent laborers and entrepreneurs. Although there is a paucity of material on the laboring activity of urban black antebellum women, research into the political and economic ties of black female workers points to a greater understanding of how the masses of black women shaped the early protest movement in cities. The culture or community of female workers was pivotal in merging labor activity and community activism as one continuous action. Patricia Hill Collins and Nancy A. Naples also argue that women integrate work, identity, and struggle in their daily lives.[6]

United under the ideological components of racial solidarity and cultural identity, black women used community activism to fuel their quest for the emancipation of the slaves, for black progress, and for the elimination of racism and sexism. In pragmatic terms, the community infrastructure of cultural institutions, organizations, and societies mobilized black women for social and political participation and for maintaining a combative posture to challenge the status quo; it also provided for the transition in women's political development to the larger spheres of evangelicalism and abolitionism.

The foundation of community activism established by black women promoted the rise of black female evangelists in the public sphere. Just as many black female community activists were circumventing male leadership to gain their political voices, black female evangelists were creating alternative vehicles by which they could preach the word of God. Indirectly, both groups of women were challenging the domination of black male leadership in the community and in the black church. Thus black female evangelists' spiritual journey toward sanctification did not negate the material realities of being a black women in a racist and sexist society. But black female evangelists were empowered by God, and they were chosen to spread the gospel throughout the world. Having a decisive effect on black and white believers, they could now seek moral rectitude on earth. Defying conventional norms with their divine power, black female evangelists challenged the black male church hierarchy, slavery, gender domination in both the church and society, and racism. Expostulating that God, not men, determined justice and equality, they added their voices to the abolitionist cause.

Black women's organizational development secured the foundation for the varied phases of political struggle. This organizational development served to transform the activism of black women and simultaneously to provide a transition to political resistance in the larger abolitionist movement, where they continued their freedom struggle. Just as many black female evangelists were entering the abolitionist movement, so were black female community activists, who were sustaining the movement in the community and in the larger sphere of antislavery societies. Black women came to female antislavery societies with an established agenda and, in addition to contributing their efforts to the society's activities and goals, mobilized a constituency within those societies to achieve black community goals. The movement of black female activists from community-based abolition, to the larger antislavery societies and to the public lecture circuit allowed them to employ both open and subversive political resistance as complementary strategies of liberation. But just as compelling was that these black female activists reached deep within themselves to combine their inner psychological quest for wholeness with their political vision of a just world.

Notes

Introduction. Theoretical Perspectives on Black Women's Political Activism

1. Lucy Stanton, "A Plea for the Oppressed," *Oberlin Evangelist,* December 17, 1850, in *The Three Sarahs: Documents of Antebellum Black College Women,* Ellen NicKenzie Lawson, with Marlene D. Merrill, (New York: Edwin Mellen Press, 1984), 203. Stanton was the first black woman to complete four years of college, becoming a dedicated abolitionist in the 1850s. See Lawson, *The Three Sarahs,* chapter 4, "Lucy Stanton: Pioneering College Graduate."

2. Martin R. Delaney, *The Condition, Elevation, Emigration and Destiny of the Colored People of the United States* (1852; reprint, New York: Arno Press and the New York Times, 1968), 133.

3. Stanton, "A Plea for the Oppressed," 203.

4. Ibid., 205.

5. Ibid.

6. Patricia Hill Collins, *Black Feminist Thought: Knowledge, Consciousness, and the Politics of Empowerment* (New York: Routledge, 1991), 28–29, 203.

7. Carla L. Peterson, *"Doers of the Word": African-American Women Speakers and Writers in the North (1830–1880)* (New York: Oxford University Press, 1995), 7; Anthony Oberschall, *Social Conflict and Social Movements* (Englewood Cliffs, N.J.: Prentice-Hall, 1973), 102.

8. Sterling Stuckey, *Slave Culture: Nationalist Theory and the Foundations of Black America* (New York: Oxford University Press, 1987), chapter 1; Gayraud S. Wilmore, *Black Religion and Black Radicalism: An Interpretation of the Religious History of Afro-American People,* 2nd ed. (New York: Orbis Books, 1983), chapter 1; John W. Blassingame, *The Slave Community: Plantation Life in the Antebellum South,* rev. ed. (New York: Oxford University Press, 1979), chapter 1; Philip D. Morgan, *Slave Counterpoint: Black Culture in the Eighteenth-Century Chesapeake and Lowcountry* (Chapel Hill: University of North Carolina Press, 1998), 559–658.

9. John Mason, "A Crown Is More Than a Hat," 16 November 2000, lecture, Livingston Campus, Rutgers University; Albert Raboteau, *Slave Religion:*

The "Invisible Institution" in the Antebellum South (New York: Oxford University Press, 1978); Wilmore, *Black Religion,* 15–27; Stuckey, *Slave Culture,* 3–37; Theophilus Smith, *Conjuring Culture: Biblical Formations of Black Americans* (New York: Oxford University Press, 1994), 36–45; Peter H. Wood, "Strange New Land 1619–1776," in *To Make Our World Anew: A History of African Americans,* ed. Robin D. G. Kelley and Earl Lewis (New York: Oxford University Press, 2000) 89.

10. Rosalyn Terborg-Penn, "Black Women in Resistance: A Cross-Cultural Perspective," in *In Resistance: Studies in African, Caribbean, and Afro-American History,* ed. Gary Y. Okihiro (Amherst: University of Massachusetts Press, 1986), 189–190; Elizabeth Fox-Genovese "Strategies and Forms of Resistance: Focus on Slave Women in the United States," in Okihiro, *In Resistance,* 148; Michelle D. Wright, "African American Sisterhood: The Impact of the Female Slave Population on American Political Movements," *Western Journal of Black Studies* (spring 1991): 34–35; Collins, *Black Feminist Thought,* 10–13. Note the diaspora context for black women's resistance in Terborg-Penn's article and in Barbara Rush, "The Family Tree Is Not Cut: Women and Cultural Resistance in Slave Family Life in the British Caribbean," in Okihiro, *In Resistance,* 117–132. Note also the role that candomblé played in fostering racial consciousness in Brazil in Kim D. Butler, *Freedoms Given, Freedoms Won: Afro-Brazilians in Post-Abolition São Paulo and Salvador* (New Brunswick, N.J.: Rutgers University Press, 1998), 55–56.

11. Deborah Gray White, *Ar'n't I a Woman?: Female Slaves in the Plantation South* (New York: W. W. Norton, 1985), 68–69, 75–76; Wright, "African American Sisterhood," 34–35, 36; Wood, "Strange New Land," 85.

12. Naples is speaking of the contemporary period of community-based women's activism, although the interplay of roles was very much indicative of slave women's existence. See Nancy A. Naples, ed., *Community Activism and Feminist Politics: Organizing Across Race, Class, and Gender* (New York: Routledge, 1998), 3–4; and Collins, *Black Feminist Thought,* 10.

13. Thomas L. Webber, *Deep Like the Rivers: Education in the Slave Quarter Community, 1831–1865* (New York: W. W. Norton, 1978), 224; Brenda Stevenson, "Slavery," in *Black Women in America: An Historical Encyclopedia,* ed. Darlene Clark Hine (Brooklyn: Carlson Publishing, 1993), 1059.

14. Hanes Walton Jr., *Invisible Politics: Black Political Behavior* (New York: State University of New York Press, 1985), 7.

15. Quoted in Dorothy Sterling, ed., *We Are Your Sisters: Black Women in the Nineteenth Century* (New York: W. W. Norton, 1984), 13.

16. Herbert Blauner, "Internal Conflict and Ghetto Revolt," in *Racial Conflict,* ed. Gary Marx (Boston: Little, Brown, 1971), 54.

17. Angela Y. Davis, "Reflections on the Black Woman's Role in the Community of Slaves," *Black Scholar* (December 1971): 12–14.

18. Charles Tilly, *From Mobilization to Revolution* (Reading, Mass.: Addison-Wesley, 1978), 72; Wood "Strange New Land," 91.

19. White, *Ar'n't I a Woman?* 121–122; Jacqueline Jones, *Labor of Love, Labor of Sorrow: Black Women, Work and the Family, from Slavery to the Present* (New York: Vintage Books, 1985) 29–31; Mary Ellen Obtiko, " 'Custodians of a House of Resistance': Black Women Respond to Slavery," in *Women and Men: The Consequences of Power,* ed. Dana V. Hiller and Robin Ann Sheets (Cincinnati: Office of Women's Studies, University of Cincinnati, 1977), 256–259.

20. Jones, *Labor of Love,* 12.

21. Karen Brodkin Sacks, "Gender and Grassroots Leadership," in *Women and the Politics of Empowerment,* ed. Ann Bookman and Sandra Morgen (Philadelphia: Temple University Press, 1988), 77–94; Belinda Robnett, *How Long? How Long?: African-American Women in the Struggle for Civil Rights* (New York: Oxford University Press, 1997), 7, 17–32. Terry Haywoode argues that working-class women's knowledge of the community facilitates their organizing. Terry Haywoode, "Working Class Feminism: Creating a Politics of Community, Connection, and Concern" (Ph.D. diss., City University of New York, 1991), 183.

22. Cheryl Townsend Gilkes, "The Politics of 'Silence': Dual-Sex Political Systems and Women's Traditions of Conflict in African-American Religion," in *African-American Christianity: Essays in History,* ed. Paul E. Johnson (Berkeley: University of California Press, 1994), 90; John W. Blassingame, "Status and Social Structure in the Slave Community," in *Perspectives and Irony in American Slavery,* ed. Harry P. Owens (Jackson: University Press of Mississippi, 1976), 142. See also Raboteau, *Slave Religion,* 238, 275.

23. Kermit L. Hall, William M. Wiecek, and Paul Finkelman, *American Legal History: Cases and Materials* (New York: Oxford University Press, 1991), 4; White, *Ar'n't I a Woman?* 119. The "configurative effect," according to Hall, Wiecek, and Finkelman, is when the law is shaped by the people as much as the people are shaped by the law. In the slave community, the labor activity of slave women not only facilitated their role as critical actors in the community but also their endeavors' impact upon their lives.

24. Wilma King, *Stolen Childhood: Slave Youth in Nineteenth-Century America* (Bloomington: Indiana University Press, 1995), 120–121.

25. Oscar Handlin, *Boston's Immigrants: A Study of Acculturation* (Cambridge: Belknap Press of Harvard University Press, 1959), 73–80; Robert Ernst, *Immigrant Life in New York City, 1825–1863* (New York: King's Crown Press, 1949), 17–18; Kerby A. Miller, "Class, Culture, and Immigrant Group Identity in the United States: The Case of Irish-American Ethnicity," in *Immigration Reconsidered: History, Sociology, and Politics,* ed. Virginia Yans-McLaughlin (New York: Oxford University Press, 1990), 106–110; Irving Lewis Allen, *The City in Slang: New York Life and Popular Speech* (New York: Oxford University Press, 1993), 21–22.

26. Evelyn Brooks Higginbotham, "African-American Women's History and the Metalanguage of Race," *Signs: Journal of Women in Culture and Society* 17,

no. 2 (1992): 253–254. Note the overview of black feminist scholarship on black women's labor activity in Rose M. Brewer, "Theorizing Race, Class and Gender: The New Scholarship of Black Feminist Intellectuals and Black Women's Labor," in *Theorizing Black Feminisms: The Visionary Pragmatism of Black Women,* ed. Stanlie M. James and Abena P. A. Busia (New York: Routledge, 1993), 13–30.

27. Naples, *Community Activism,* 14.

28. Paula Giddings, *When and Where I Enter: The Impact of Black Women on Race and Sex in America* (New York: Bantam Books, 1984), 48.

29. Sharon Harley, "Northern Black Female Workers: Jacksonian Era," in *The Afro-American Woman: Struggles and Images,* ed. Sharon Harley and Rosalyn Terborg-Penn (Port Washington, N.Y.: Kennikat Press, 1978), 8–10; Julianne Malveaux, " 'Ain't I a Woman': Differences in the Labor Market Status of Black and White Women," in *Racism and Sexism: An Integrated Study,* ed. Paula S. Rothenberg (New York: St. Martin's Press, 1988), 79.

30. Harley, "Northern Black Female Workers," 8–10.

31. Graham Russell Hodges, *Root and Branch: African Americans in New York and East Jersey, 1613–1863* (Chapel Hill: University of North Carolina Press, 1999), 200.

32. Ibid., 202.

33. Oberschall, *Social Conflict,* 102; Gayle T. Tate, "Political Consciousness and Resistance Among Black Antebellum Women," *Women and Politics* 13, no. 1 (1993): 69.

34. Walton, *Invisible Politics,* 66.

35. Bert Klandermans and Sidney Tarrow, "Mobilization into Social Movements: Synthesizing European and American Approaches," in *From Structure to Action: Comparing Social Movement Research Across Cultures,* ed. Bert Klandermans, Hanspeter Kriesi, and Sidney Tarrow. International Social Movement Research, vol. 1 (Greenwich, Conn.: JAI Press, 1988), 1–38.

36. Bettye Collier-Thomas, *Daughters of Thunder: Black Women Preachers and Their Sermons, 1850–1979* (San Francisco: Jossey-Bass, 1998), 17; Peterson, *"Doers of the Word,"* 3.

37. Benjamin Quarles, *Black Abolitionists* (New York: Oxford University Press, 1969), 49.

38. Emma Jones Lapsansky, " 'Since They Got Those Separate Churches': Afro-Americans and Racism in Jacksonian Philadelphia," in *African Americans in Pennsylvania: Shifting Historical Perspectives,* ed. Joe William Trotter Jr. and Eric Ledell Smith (University Park: Pennsylvania State University Press, 1997), 98.

Chapter 1. A Long Ways from Home:
The Context for Oppression and Resistance

1. Marietta Morrissey, *Slave Women in the New World: Gender Stratification in the Caribbean* (Lawrence: University Press of Kansas, 1989), 29–31;

Claire Robertson, "Africa into the Americas? Slavery and Women, the Family, and the Gender Division of Labor," in *More Than Chattel: Black Women and Slavery in the Americas,* ed. David Barry Gaspar and Darlene Clark Hine (Bloomington: Indiana University Press, 1996), 4–8; Leith Mullings, "Women and Economic Change in Africa," in *Women in Africa: Studies in Social and Economic Change,* ed. Nancy J. Hafkin and Edna G. Bay (Stanford, Calif.: Stanford University Press, 1976), 239–264; Jeanne K. Henn, "Women in the Rural Economy: Past, Present, and Future," in *African Women South of the Sahara,* ed. Margaret Jean Hay and Sharon Stichter (New York: Longman, 1984), 1–7.

2. John Hope Franklin and Alfred A. Moss, Jr., *From Slavery to Freedom: A History of Negro Americans,* 6th ed. (New York: Alfred A. Knopf, 1988), 36.

3. Vincent Bakpetu Thompson, *The Making of the African Diaspora in the Americas 1441–1900* (New York: Longman, 1987), 127; see chapter 4, where Thompson discusses African resistance during the middle passage.

4. George P. Rawick, *The American Slave: A Composite Autobiography,* Series 1, Mississippi Narratives, part 4, vol. 9, 1435 (Westport, Conn.: Greenwood Press, 1977), 1435. Note that the style of the language spoken by slaves may not be an accurate reflection of how thy spoke but something imposed by interviewers.

5. *New York Times,* 12 August 1853, 14 November 1848, 19 July 1853; Richard Frucht, ed., *Black Society in the New World* (New York: Random House, 1971), 1; James Oakes, *The Ruling Race: A History of American Slaveholders* (New York: Vintage Books, 1982), 37–68, 123–150; Vincent Harding, *There Is A River: The Black Struggle for Freedom in America* (New York: Harcourt Brace Jovanovich, 1981), 24–51; David Brion Davis, *The Problem of Slavery in Western Culture* (New York: Oxford University Press, 1966), 31–35; Eugene D. Genovese, *The World the Slaveholders Made* (New York: Vintage Books, 1969), 137–150.

6. Oakes, *The Ruling Race,* 81–87, 123–138, 176; note Genovese's discussion on the rise of the southern aristocracy in *The World the Slaveholders Made,* 137–143.

7. Jones, *Labor of Love,* 13.

8. Ibid; Angela Y. Davis, "Reflections on the Black Woman's Role in the Community of Slaves," *Black Scholar* (December 1971): 8; Dorothy Burnham, "The Life of the Afro-American Woman in Slavery," *International Journal of Women's Studies* 1, no. 4 (July/August 1978): 363–367.

9. Austen Steward, *Twenty-two Years a Slave and Forty Years a Freeman, Embracing a Correspondence of Several Years While President of the Wilberforce Colony* (New York: W. Alling, 1856), 14.

10. Quoted in Sterling, *We Are Your Sisters,* 13.

11. Davis, "Reflections," 8.

12. Sterling, *We Are Your Sisters,* 31; see also Joan Kelly, "The Doubled Vision of Feminist Theory: A Postscript to the 'Women and Power' Conference," *Feminist Studies* 5 (spring 1979): 216–227.

13. Robertson, "African into the Americas?" 13–14.

14. Davis, "Reflections," 8–9.

15. "Narrative of James Curry," in *Slave Testimony: Two Centuries of Letters, Speeches, Interviews, and Autobiographies,* ed. John W. Blassingame (Baton Rouge: Louisiana State University Press, 1977, 128.

16. Melton A. McLaurin, *Celia, a Slave* (New York: Avon Books, 1993), 16–37. See also Davis, "Reflections," 12–14.

17. Brenda Stevenson, "Slavery," in Hine, *Black Women in America,* 1050.

18. Robert Harms, "Sustaining the System: Trading Towns along the Middle Zaire," in *Women and Slavery in Africa,* ed. Claire C. Robertson and Martin A. Klein (Madison: University of Wisconsin Press, 1983), 95.

19. Carol P. MacCormack, "Slaves, Slave Owners, and Slave Dealers: Sherbro Coast and Hinterland," in Robertson and Klein, *Women and Slavery in Africa,* 273.

20. Martin A. Klein, "Women in Slavery in the Western Sudan," in Robertson and Klein, *Women and Slavery in Africa,* 85.

21. Sterling Stuckey, *Going through the Storm* (New York: Oxford University Press, 1994), 51.

22. Stevenson, "Slavery," 1050.

23. Blassingame, *Slave Testimony,* 540.

24. Annual Report for the New York Chamber of Commerce of 1861–1862, 40–45, New York Public Library (hereafter cited as NYPL); Philip S. Foner, *Business and Slavery: The New York Merchants and the Irrepressible Conflict* (Chapel Hill: University of North Carolina Press, 1941), 4; Eric Williams, *Capitalism and Slavery* (New York: Capricorn Books, 1966), 98–107, 126–134; Douglass C. North, *The Economic Growth of the United States, 1790–1860* (New York: W. W. Norton, 1966), 154, 166–176.

25. Annual Report of the New York Chamber of Commerce for 1859, 1–10, NYPL.

26. Stephen Colwell, *The Five Cotton States and New York* (Philadelphia, 1861), 23–24. Note the reactions from northeastern newspapers that Colwell's figures were quite conservative: *New York Herald,* 2 February 1860, and *Newark Post,* 12 April 1861.

27. Ruth Bogin, "Sarah Parker Remond: Black Abolitionist from Salem," in Hine, *Black Women in American History,* 141.

28. "Mrs. Armaci Adams," in *Weevils in the Wheat: Interviews with Virginia Ex-Slaves,* ed. Charles L. Perdue Jr., Thomas E. Barden, and Robert K. Phillips (Charlottesville: University Press of Virginia, 1976), 3.

29. "Hannah Davidson, Ex-Slave," in Rawick, *The American Slave,* Series 1, Ohio Narratives, vol. 16, 29.

30. Robertson, "Africa into the Americas?" 9.

31. "Liza McGhee, Ex-Slave," in Rawick, *The American Slave,* Series 1, Mississippi Narratives, part 4, vol. 9, 1403.

32. Doug McAdam, *Political Process and the Development of Black Insurgency* (Chicago: University of Chicago Press, 1985), 41–44.

33. Webber, *Deep Like the Rivers*, 71.

34. Tilly, *From Mobilization to Revolution*, 73; Paula Giddings, *When and Where I Enter: The Impact of Black Women on Race and Sex in America* (New York: Bantam Books, 1984), 39–46; King, *Stolen Childhood*, 115–139. Note also McLaurin, *Celia*, where Celia, a young slave woman, murdered her master who had molested her over a period of several years and stood trial for the crime.

35. "Harriet Miller, Ex-Slave," in Rawick, *The American Slave*, Series 1, Mississippi Narratives, part 4, vol. 9, 1501.

36. "Josephine Howard, Ex-Slave," in Rawick, *The American Slave*, Series 1, Texas Narratives, part 4, vol.5, 163.

37. William Still, *The Underground Railroad* (1872; reprint, Chicago: Johnson Publishing Company, 1970), 210, 311–313.

38. Quoted in Webber, *Deep Like the Rivers*, 165.

39. Ibid.

40. King, *Stolen Childhood*, 120.

41. Linda Brent, *Incidents in the Life of a Slave Girl* (New York: Harcourt Brace Jovanovich, 1973), 99–103, 117–120, 121, 134, 154–157.

42. Quoted in King, *Stolen Childhood*, 120, 121.

43. White, *Ar'n't I a Woman?* 119–141.

44. Naples, *Community Activism and Feminist Politics*, 332.

45. Oakes, *The Ruling Race*, 23.

46. Giddings, *When and Where I Enter*, 39; Stevenson, "Slavery," 1057–1058.

47. Webber, *Deep Like the Rivers*, 106.

48. When Frederick Douglass was a slave, he observed that the most submissive slaves were the ones who were most often beaten. See Frederick Douglass, *Life and Times of Frederick Douglass* (1892 rev. ed; reprint, New York: Collier Books, 1962), 52.

49. Ophelia Settle Egypt, J. Masuoka, Charles S. Johnson, "Unwritten History of Slavery, Autobiographical Accounts of Negro Ex-Slaves," Social Science Document No. 1. Nashville: Fisk University, Social Science Institute, 1945), 284.

50. Harding, *There Is a River*, 57, 180.

51. Collins, *Black Feminist Thought*, 24–25.

52. Webber, *Deep Like the Rivers*, 237–238.

53. "Leah Garret, Ex-Slave," in Rawick, *The American Slave*, Supplement Series 1, Georgia Narratives, Part 2, vol. 4, 14–15.

54. Webber, *Deep Like the Rivers*, 236.

55. Oakes, *The Ruling Race*, 107.

56. Steward, *Twenty-two Years a Slave*, 107.

Chapter 2. Troubled Waters:
Invisible Boundaries of Resistance

1. "Chaney Mack, Ex-Slave" in Rawick, *The American Slave,* Series 1, Mississippi Narratives, part 4, vol. 9, 1415.

2. Eugene Genovese, *Roll, Jordan, Roll: The World the Slaves Made* (New York: Pantheon Books, 1974), 3–4; Frederick Douglass, "Prejudice Against Color," *North Star,* 13 June 1850; Robertson, "Africa into the Americas?" 16; Paul D. Escott, *Slavery Remembered: A Record of Twentieth-Century Slave Narratives* (Chapel Hill: University of North Carolina Press, 1979), 97–99.

3. Webber, *Deep Like the Rivers,* 163.

4. Stuckey, *Slave Culture,* 43.

5. White, *Ar'n't I a Woman?* 119–141.

6. Ibid.

7. Solomon Northup, *Twelve Years a Slave,* ed. Sue Eakin and Joseph Logsdon (Baton Rouge: Louisiana State University Press, 1968), 191.

8. "Ellen Cragin," in *Bullwhip Days: The Slaves Remember,* ed. James Mellon (New York: Weidenfeld and Nicolson, 1988), 236–237.

9. "Lulu Wilson," in Mellon, *Bullwhip Days,* 324.

10. V. P. Franklin, *Black Self-Determination: A Cultural History of African-American Resistance,* rev. ed. (New York: Lawrence Hill Books, 1992), 83.

11. Several scholars have examined the extent of African retentiveness among the slaves and free blacks in America, using for their framework of analysis a component of African cultural traditions such as religion, music, or folklore in demonstrating the connection between Africans in Africa and those in the diaspora. These scholars include Blassingame, *The Slave Community;* Lawrence W. Levine, *Black Culture and Black Consciousness* (New York: Oxford University Press, 1977); Raboteau, *Slave Religion;* Stuckey, *Slave Culture;* Wilmore, *Black Religion;* and Joseph E. Harris, ed., *Global Dimensions of the African Diaspora* (Washington, D.C.: Howard University Press, 1982).

12. Webber, *Deep Like the Rivers,* 163–164.

13. Blassingame, *The Slave Community,* 39.

14. Stuckey, *Slave Culture,* 41, chapter 1; Blassingame, *The Slave Community,* 22–24; Webber, *Deep Like the Rivers,* 198–199, 234–236, 207–223; Raboteau, *Slave Religion,* 79–128; Theophus H. Smith, *Conjuring Culture: Biblical Formations of Black America* (New York: Oxford University Press, 1994), 116–118.

15. "Chaney Mack," 1418.

16. Blassingame, *The Slave Community,* 32.

17. "Annie Reed," in Mellon, *Bullwhip Days,* 48.

18. Smith, *Conjuring Culture,* 152–153, and note the more comprehensive discussion of High John the Conqueror (151–155).

19. Webber, *Deep Like the Rivers,* 220–221.

20. For a full discussion of Charles Joyner's "magical shamanism," a term interchangeable with "conjure," see Charles Joyner, " 'Believer I Know': The Emergence of African-American Christianity," in Johnson, *African-American Christianity,* 18–46.

21. "Marrinda Jane Singleton," in Perdue, Barden, and Phillips, *Weevils in the Wheat,* 267.

22. "Sarah Hatley," in Mellon, *Bullwhip Days,* 85.

23. " 'Ma' Stevens," in Mellon, *Bullwhip Days,* 100.

24. Smith, *Conjuring Culture,* 31.

25. Joyner, " 'Believer I Know,'" 34–36.

26. W. E. B. DuBois, "The Religion of the American Negro," *New World* 9 (December 1900): 618.

27. Gayle T. Tate, "Black Nationalism and Spiritual Redemption," *Western Journal of Black Studies* 15, no. 4 (1991): 214. See also John S. Mbiti, *African Religions and Philosophy* (1969; reprint, London: Heinemann, 1988), 75–91; Raboteau, *Slave Religion,* 5–13; and Josiah U. Young, *Black and African Theologies: Siblings or Distant Cousins?* (Maryknoll, N.Y.: Orbis Books, 1986), 63–69.

28. Wilmore *Black Religion,* 27.

29. Mbiti, *African Religions,* 10–13, 15–36, 39–43; Wilmore, *Black Religion,* 15–19; Raboteau, *Slave Religion,* 5–16; Webber, *Deep Like the Rivers,* 118–130; Smith, *Conjuring Culture,* 35–45.

30. Wilmore, *Black Religion,* 15.

31. Raboteau, *Slave Religion,* 7–8; Tate, "Black Nationalism," 214–215; Smith, *Conjuring Culture,* 36–37.

32. E. W. Fashole-Luke, "Ancestor Veneration and the Communion of Saints," in *New Testament Christianity for Africa and the World,* ed. Mark E. Glasswell and Edward W. Fashole-Luke (London: S.P.C.K., 1974), 213.

33. Paul Radin, foreword to *God Struck Me Dead: Religious Conversion Experiences and Autobiographies of Ex-Slaves,* ed. Clifton H. Johnson (Philadelphia: Pilgrim Press, 1969), ix.

34. Ibid.,; Raboteau, *Slave Religion,* 55–92; Wilmore, *Black Religion,* 15–28; Young, *Black and African Theologies,* 70–79; Stuckey, *Slave Culture,* 83–97; Joyner, " 'Believer I Know,'" 19.

35. Thomas J. O'Dea, *The Sociology of Religion* (Englewood Cliffs, N.J.: Prentice-Hall, 1966), 14; William B. McClain, "Free Style and a Closer Relationship to Life," in *The Black Experience in Religion,* ed. C. Eric Lincoln (New York: Anchor Press, 1974), 5; Wilmore, *Black Religion,* 10.

36. Donald G. Matthews, *Slavery and Methodism: A Chapter in American Morality* (Princeton, N.J.: Princeton University Press, 1965), 64–65; Robert E. Park, "The Conflict and Fusion of Cultures with Special Reference to the Negro," *Journal of Negro History* 4, no. 2 (October 1919): 120; Raboteau, *Slave Religion,* 165–172; Stuckey, *Slave Culture,* 38–39.

37. Quoted in Franklin, *Black Self-Determination,* 73.

38. Levine, *Black Culture,* 80.

39. Gilkes, "The Politics of 'Silence,'" 83–84; White, *Ar'n't I a Woman?* 119–141; Webber, *Deep Like the Rivers,* 192–193; Smith, *Conjuring Culture,* 69, 129.

40. Collins, *Black Feminist Thought,* 27.

41. Gilkes, "The Politics of 'Silence,'" 87.

42. Zilpha Elaw, *Memoirs of the Life, Religious Experiences, Ministerial Travels and Labours of Mrs. Zilpha Elaw, An American Female of Colour,* in *Sisters of the Spirit: Three Black Women's Autobiographies of the Nineteenth Century,* ed. William L. Andrews (London: author, 1846; reprint, Bloomington: Indiana University Press, 1986); Gayle T. Tate, "Spiritual Resistance of Early Black Female Evangelists, 1810–1845," *Abafazi* 7, no. 1 (fall/winter 1996): 26.

43. White, *Ar'n't I a Woman?* 125.

44. Ronald E. Brown and Monica L. Wolford, "Religious Resources and African-American Political Action," *National Political Science Review* 4 (1994): 31.

45. "Rose Williams," in Mellon, *Bullwhip Days,* 128.

46. "Miss Caroline Hunter," in Perdue, Barden, and Phillips, *Weevils in the Wheat,* 149.

47. "Nancy Boudry, Ex-Slave," in Rawick, *The American Slave,* Series 2, Georgia Narratives, 12, part 1, vol. 12, 113–114.

48. "Anna Harris," in Perdue, Barden, and Phillips, *Weevils in the Wheat,* 128.

49. "Rosa Starks," in Mellon, *Bullwhip Days,* 136.

50. Harriet Miller," in Rawick, *The American Slave,* Supplement Series 1, Mississippi Narratives, part 4, vol. 9, 1501.

51. Howard W. Odum, *Negro Workaday Songs* (New York: Negro Universities Press, 1969), 117.

52. See, for example, Herbert Aptheker, *American Negro Slave Revolts* (New York: International Publishers, 1963); and Harding, *There Is a River.* Both note slave women's presence in dramatic resistance. See also Peter Wood, *Black Majority* (New York: W. W. Norton, 1974); and Gerald Mullin, *Flight and Rebellion* (New York: Oxford University Press, 1972).

53. See, for example, Darlene Clark Hine and Kate Wittenstein. "Female Slave Resistance: The Economics of Sex," in *The Black Woman Cross-Culturally,* ed. Filomina Chioma Steady (Rochester, N.Y.: Schenkman Books, 1981) 289–299; Gerda Lerner, ed., *Black Women in White America: A Documentary History* (New York: Vintage Books, 1973) 27–45; Raymond A. Bauer and Alice H. Bauer, "Day to Day Resistance to Slavery," *Journal of Negro History* 27, no. 2 (October 1942): 388–419; Terborg-Penn, "Black Women in Resistance," 188–209; and Fox-Genovese, "Strategies and Forms of Resistance," 143–165.

For gender oppression of slave women, see Davis, "Reflections," 3–15; Angela Y. Davis, *Women, Race and Class* (New York: Random House, 1983); White, *Ar'n't I a Woman?*; bell hooks, *Ain't I a Woman: Black Women and Feminism* (Boston: Beacon Press, 1981); and Jones, *Labor of Love.*

54. Hine and Wittenstein, "Female Slave Resistance," 296.

55. Lerner, *Black Women in White America,* 27.

56. Fox-Genovese, "Strategies and Forms of Resistance," 148.

57. Terborg-Penn, "Black Women in Resistance," 188–189.

58. Collins, *Black Feminist Thought,* 11.

59. Ibid., 108.

60. Terborg-Penn, "Black Women in Resistance," 188–189.

61. White, *Ar'n't I a Woman?* 75.

62. Ophelia Settle Egypt, J. Masuoka, Charles S. Johnson, "Unwritten History of Slavery; Autobiographical Accounts of Negro Ex-Slaves," Social Science Document No. 1. Nashville: Fisk University, Social Science Institute, 1945, 284–291.

63. White, *Ar'n't I a Woman?* 121–124, 121–127; Jones, *Labor of Love,* 12–13; Stevenson, "Slavery," 1053–1055. Note the labor and health issues of female slaves in Richard H. Steckel, "Women, Work, and Health Under Plantation Slavery in the United States," in Gaspar and Hine, *More Than Chattel,* 43–60.

64. Jones, *Labor of Love,* 39, 29–32.

65. Blassingame, *The Slave Community,* 151–152.

66. "Narrative of James Curry," 133.

67. Wright, "African American Sisterhood," 35; and see White, *Ar'n't I a Woman?* 119–141.

68. White, *Ar'n't I a Woman?* 94.

69. Ibid., 94–95.

70. Wright, "African American Sisterhood," 35.

71. Jones, *Labor of Love,* 40.

72. "Narrative of James Curry," 131.

73. "Lewis Clarke: Leaves from a Slave's Journal of Life," in Blassingame, *Slave Testimony,* 153.

74. Thomas Jones, *The Experience of Thomas H. Jones, Who Was a Slave for Forty-Three Years* (Boston: Bazin and Chandler, 1862), 15.

75. Lerner, *Black Women in White America,* 26–27; Herbert Aptheker, *One Continual Cry* (New York: Humanities Press, 1965), 48.

76. Susie King Taylor, *Reminiscences of My Life in Camp with the 33rd United States Colored Troops* (Boston: author, 1902), 5.

77. Laura S. Haviland, *A Woman's Life-Work, Labor and Experiences* (Chicago: Publishing Association of Friends, 1881), 300–301. Once Granson's work was discovered, the school was suspended for a while. Granson resumed when she was no longer under the scrutiny of the authorities.

78. Quoted in Sterling, *We Are Your Sisters,* 57; and see Giddings, *When and Where I Enter,* 39.

79. Sterling, *We Are Your Sisters,* 62–64, 67, 72, 178, 343–344; Webber, *Deep Like the Rivers,* 237, 240.

Chapter 3. Weaving the Colors of Oppression: Black Women's Urban Resistance, the Market Economy, and the Cult of Domesticity

1. Jones, *Labor of Love,* 46–47, 53–54, 56.

2. Richard C. Wade, *Slavery in the Cities: The South 1820–1860* (New York: Oxford University Press, 1964), 33–54; Philip S. Foner, *History of Black Americans: From the Emergence of the Cotton Kingdom to the Eve of the Compromise of 1850* (Westport, Conn.: Greenwood Press, 1983), 58–75; Lewis A. Randolph and Gayle T. Tate, *The Rise and Decline of African American Political Power in Richmond: Race, Class, and Gender,* Urban Affairs Annual Review 42 (Thousand Oaks: Sage Publications, 1995), 137–139; and John T. O'Brien Jr., "From Bondage to Citizenship: The Richmond Black Community, 1865–1867" (Ph.D. diss., University of Rochester, 1975), 43–53.

3. Norris W. Preyer, "The Historian, the Slave, and the Ante-Bellum Textile Industry," *Journal of Negro History* 46, no. 2 (April 1961): 73.

4. Rhoda Golden Freeman, *The Free Negro in New York City in the Era before the Civil War* (New York: Garland, 1994), 53–61.

5. *Emancipator,* 2 March 1837.

6. Julie Winch, *Philadelphia's Black Elite: Activism, Accommodation, and the Struggle for Autonomy, 1787–1848* (Philadelphia: Temple University Press, 1988), 130–132; Leon F. Litwack, *North of Slavery: The Negro in the Free States, 1790–1860* (Chicago: University of Chicago Press, 1961), 78–79.

7. George E. Walker, "The Afro-American in New York City, 1827–1860" (Ph.D. diss., Columbia University, 1975), 119; note the efforts of blacks regarding suffrage (116–131).

8. Alexis de Tocqueville, *Democracy in America,* ed. Philips Bradley (New York: Vintage, 1945), 1:373.

9. Frederick Douglass, "Prejudice Against Color," *North Star,* 13 June 1850.

10. Freeman, *The Free Negro in New York City,* 12, 13.

11. Ibid., 155.

12. Karl Deutsch, "Social Mobilization and Political Development," *American Political Science Review* 55, no. 3 (1961), 493.

13. Gayle T. Tate, "Tangled Vines: Ideological Interpretations of Afro-Americans in the Nineteenth Century" (Ph.D. diss., City University of New York, 1984), 1; John Blassingame and Mary Frances Berry, *Long Memory: The Black Experience in America* (New York: Oxford University Press, 1982), 388–393.

14. William Gamson, *The Strategy of Social Protest* (Homewood, Ill.: Dorsey, 1975), 15.

15. Gayraud S. Wilmore, *Black Religion and Black Radicalism: An Interpretation of the Religious History of Afro-American People.* 2nd ed., rev. (Maryknoll, N.Y.: Orbis Books, 1983), 79.

16. Walker, "The Afro-American in New York City," 96; Clarence Taylor, *The Black Churches of Brooklyn* (New York: Columbia University Press, 1994), 10.

17. Ralph Watkins, "A Reappraisal of the Role of Voluntary Associations in the African American Community," *Afro-American in New York Life and History* 14, no. 2 (1990): 51–56; Quarles, *Black Abolitionists,* 101; Daniel Perlman, "Organizations of the Free Negro in New York City, 1800–1860," *Journal of Negro History* 56, no. 3 (July 1971): 182.

18. Perlman, "Organizations of the Free Negro," 186.

19. Sterling, *We Are Your Sisters,* 105–106.

20. Quarles, *Black Abolitionists,* 101

21. James Oliver Horton and Lois E. Horton, *Black Bostonians: Family Life and Community Struggle in the Antebellum North* (New York: Holmes and Meier, 1979), 32.

22. Quarles, *Black Abolitionists,* 102–103.

23. Dorothy Porter, "The Organized Educational Activities of Negro Literary Societies, 1828–1846," *Journal of Negro Education* 5 (October 1936): 555–576; Sterling, *We Are Your Sisters,* 112–113; Bettye Collier-Thomas, "The Role of the Black Woman in the Development and Maintenance of Black Organizations," in *Black Organizations: Issues on Survival Techniques,* ed. Lennox S. Yearwood (Washington, D.C.: University Press of America, 1980), 135; Fifth Annual Report of the New York Committee of Vigilance, (New York, 1842), 38, in Schomburg Center for Research in Black Culture (hereafter cited as Schomburg Center), NYPL.

24. C. Peter Ripley, ed., *Witness for Freedom: African American Voices on Race, Slavery, and Emancipation* (Chapel Hill: University of North Carolina Press, 1993), 135.

25. Foner, *History of Black Americans,* 2:499.

26. Bella Gross, "Freedom's Journal and the Rights of All," *Journal of Negro History* 17, no. 3 (June 1932): 245.

27. Walker, "The Afro-American in New York City," 82.

28. *Freedom's Journal,* 16 March 1827.

29. *Colored American,* 10 October 1840.

30. James McCune Smith, "Citizenship," *Anglo-African Magazine* 1, no. 5 (May 1859): 149.

31. Mari Marsuda, "Looking to the Bottom: Critical Legal Studies and Reparations," in *Critical Race Theory: The Key Writings that Formed the Movement,* ed. Kimberle Crenshaw, Neil Gotanda, Gary Peller, and Kendall Thomas

(New York: New Press, 1995), 65; Smith, "Citizenship"; Tate, "Tangled Vines," 251–253; Frederick Douglass address at the 1853 convention, in *Minutes of the Proceedings of the National Negro Convention Movement, 1830–1864,* ed. Howard Bell (New York: Arno Press, 1969), 28.

32. *Colored American,* 8 July 1837.

33. *Frederick Douglass' Paper,* 16 August 1852.

34. Tate, "Black Nationalism," 43.

35. Maria W. Stewart, *Productions of Mrs. Maria W. Stewart* (Boston: Friends of Freedom and Virtue, 1835), 19.

36. "Call to Negro Teachers' Meeting, 1841," in *A Documentary History of the Negro People in the United States,* ed. Herbert Aptheker (New York: Citadel Press, 1951), 212.

37. Linda Perkins, "Black Women and Racial 'Uplift' Prior to Emancipation," in Steady, *The Black Woman Cross-Culturally,* 317–334.

38. Gilkes, "The Politics of 'Silence,'" 90–97.

39. Karl Marx, *Capital,* trans. Samuel Moore and Edward Aveling (Chicago: C. H. Kerr, 1909), 1:823.

40. W. E. B. DuBois, *The World and Africa* (New York: International Publishers, 1972), 64–65; Franklin and Moss, *From Slavery to Freedom,* 2:36–38.

41. Charles H. Haswell, *Reminiscences of an Octogenarian of the City of New York, 1816–1860* (New York: Harper and Brothers, 1896), 117.

42. Williams, *Capitalism and Slavery,* 128; *New York Times,* 24 January 1855; *New York Tribune,* 31 March 1857.

43. George J. Lankevich and Howard B. Furer, *A Brief History of New York City, 1840–1857* (New York: Columbia University Press, 1981), 77. Note the triangular patterns in Robert G. Albion, *The Rise of the New York Port, 1815–1860* (1939; reprint, New York: Scribner and Sons, 1970), 3; Roi Ottley and William W. Weatherby, eds., *The Negro in New York: An Informal Social History* (New York: Oceana Publications, 1967), 59–60.

44. *De Bow's Review* 23 (1861): 203; James DeBow, *Industrial Resources of the Southern and Western States* (New Orleans, 1853), 3:93; *New York Daily News,* 22 December 1860; Colwell, *The Five Cotton States,* 23–24. See also the reactions from newspapers about Colwell's conservative estimates in the *New York Herald,* 2 February 1860, and the *Newark Post,* 12 April 1861.

45. James De Bow, *Interest in Slavery of the Southern Non-Slaveholders* (Charleston, 1860), 6. See also *Frederick Douglass' Paper,* "The End of All Compromises with Slavery—Now and Forever," 26 May 1854, for the slave connection between the North and South.

46. Peter N. Carroll and David W. Noble, *The Free and the Unfree: A New History of the United States,* 2nd ed. (New York: Penguin Books, 1988), 157.

47. *New York Tribune,* 29 September 1860.

48. *New York Times,* 12 August 1853, 29 September 1855, 7 December 1852, 7 June 1859; Phelps-Dodge Papers, 14 November 1848, 19 July 1853, 23

July 1853, NYPL; *Journal of Commerce*, 24 October 1857; Joseph A. Scoville, *Old Merchants of New York City, by Walter Barrett, Clerk* (1885; reprint, New York: Greenwood Press, 1968), vol. 4, first series, 134–139.

49. *Richmond Enquirer*, 15 April 1856.

50. Samuel J. May, *Some Recollections of the Anti-Slavery Conflict* (Boston, 1869; reprint, New York: Arno Press, 1969), 127–128.

51. David Brion Davis, *The Problem of Slavery in Western Culture* (New York: Oxford University Press, 1966), 9.

52. Foner, *Business and Slavery,* 1; North, *The Economic Growth of the United States*, 159–160, 167.

53. North, *The Economic Growth of the United States,* 167.

54. Ronald Takaki, *Iron Cages: Race and Culture in 19th Century America* (New York: Oxford University Press, 1990), 160–161; North, *The Economic Growth of the United States*, 162.

55. North, *The Economic Growth of the United States,* 161.

56. Ibid., 164; Jeanne Boydston, *Home and Work: Housework, Wages, and the Ideology of Labor in the Early Republic* (New York: Oxford University Press, 1990), 105–107.

57. *Fifth Census; or, Enumeration of the Inhabitants of the United States, 1830* (Washington, D.C.: Duff Green, 1832), 36–37, 50–51; U.S. Census Office, *The Seventh Census of the United States, 1850* (Washington, D.C.: Robert Armstrong, 1853), 52, 67, 92, 96, 97, 99, 102, 158, 179, 221, 474, 612, 830; U.S. Bureau of the Census, *Historical Statistics of the United States: Colonial Times to 1957* (Washington, D.C.: Government Printing Office, 1960), 8, 14.

58. U.S. Census Office, *The Seventh Census*, 67, 92, 96, 99, 158, 179, 221, 234, 612, 662, 830; U.S. Bureau of the Census, *Historical Statistics of the United States,* 8, 14.

59. Irving Lewis Allen, *The City in Slang: New York Life and Popular Speech* (New York: Oxford University Press, 1993), 20–22; Christine Stansell, *City of Women: Sex and Class in New York, 1789–1860* (New York: Alfred A. Knopf, 1986), 5.

60. Takaki, *Iron Cages,* 170.

61. *New York Herald,* 1 November 1860; *DeBow's Review* 21 (1855): 530–538; Stansell, *City of Women,* 4–5; *New York Tribune,* 20 July 1853, 19 August 1850; William E. Dodge, *Old New York* (New York, 1880) 10; Robert R. Russell, *Economic Aspects of Southern Sectionalism, 1840–1861* (Urbana: University of Illinois Press, 1924), 101.

62. George M. Fredrickson, *White Supremacy: A Comparative Study in American and South African History* (New York: Oxford University Press, 1981), 79.

63. Milton D. Morris, *The Politics of Black America* (New York: Harper and Row, 1975), 51.

64. Litwack, *North of Slavery,* 64.

65. Takaki, *Iron Cages,* 78–79, 110, 126–127.

66. Ibid., 112–113.

67. David Potter, *The South and the Sectional Conflict* (Baton Rouge: Louisiana State University Press, 1968), 114.

68. Fredrickson, *White Supremacy,* 151–152. Joel Kovel argues that the distinguishing features of racial attitudes in the North and South were different. While the South was shaped by the forces of dominative racism, or total hegemony over blacks, Northern racial attitudes were more typified by the shunning or exclusionary racial practices that refused blacks entrance into society on any level. See Joel Kovel, *White Racism: A Psychohistory* (New York: Vintage Books, 1970), 32.

69, Kai Erikson, *Wayward Puritans: A Study in the Sociology of Deviance* (New York: Wiley Press, 1966), 13, 64.

70. Allen, *The City in Slang,* 5.

71. Kovel, *White Racism,* 4–5; note a similar argument in Litwack, *North of Slavery,* 156–158.

72. Allen, *The City in Slang,* 21.

73. Minion K. C. Morrison, *Black Political Mobilization: Leadership, Power, and Mass Behavior* (New York: State University of New York Press, 1997), 6.

74. Sterling, *We Are Your Sisters,* 110.

75. James Forman, *The Making of Black Revolutionaries* (New York: Macmillan, 1972), 218.

76. Gary Nash, *Forging Freedom: The Formation of Philadelphia's Black Community, 1720–1840* (Cambridge: Harvard University Press, 1988), 191.

77. Quarles, *Black Abolitionists,* 158.

78. White, *Ar'n't I A Woman?* 119–141; Wright, "African American Sisterhood," 32–33.

79. Horton and Horton, *Black Bostonians,* 20.

80. Jones, *Labor of Love,* 127.

81. Malveaux, " 'Ain't I a Woman,'" 79.

82. Tate, "Political Consciousness and Resistance," 73.

83. Horton and Horton, *Black Bostonians,* 20.

84. Ibid.

85. Emma Jones Lapsansky, "Friends, Wives, and Strivings: Networks and Community Values among Nineteenth-Century Philadelphia Afroamerican Elites," *Pennsylvania Magazine of History and Biography* 58, no. 1 (January 1984): 8; see also Emma Jones Lapsansky, *Black Presence in Pennsylvania: "Making It Home,"* Pennsylvania Historical Studies 21 (University Park: Pennsylvania Historical Association), 7–20.

86. James Oliver Horton, "Freedom's Yoke: Gender Conventions Among Antebellum Free Blacks," *Feminist Studies* 12, no. 1 (spring 1986), 62.

87. Ibid., 64.

88. U.S. Census Office, *The Seventh Census,* 80–81; *Frederick Douglass' Paper,* 4 March 1853; Charles H. Wesley, "The Negroes of New York in the Emancipation Movement," *Journal of Negro History* 24, no. 1 (January 1939): 65–66; Walker, "The Afro-American in New York City," 33–39; Robert Ernst, "The Economic Status of New York City Negroes, 1850–1863," in *The Making of Black America,* ed. August Meier and Elliott Rudwick (New York: Atheneum, 1969), 1:258. The federal census of 1840, although not as reliable as the census of 1850, still indicates the growth of black populations in urban cities.

89. Horton and Horton, *Black Bostonians,* 10.

90. Gary B. Nash, "Forging Freedom: The Emancipation Experience in the Northern Seaport Cities, 1775–1820," in *Slavery and Freedom in the Age of the American Revolution,* ed. Ira Berlin and Ronald Hoffman (Urbana: University of Illinois Press, 1983), 15.

91. Stansell, *City of Women,* 11–18, 120–121; Boydston, *Home and Work,* 58–62; Alice Kessler-Harris, *Out to Work: A History of Wage-Earning Women in the United States* (New York: Oxford University Press, 1982), 45–57.

92. *Fifth Census,* 36–37, 50–51; *McElroy's Philadelphia Directory, for 1852* (Philadelphia: Edward C. and John Biddle, 1852), 164, 200–201; Manuscript Returns of the Seventh Census of the United States (150), Population Schedules, Record Group 29, Microfilm Pub. 432, Reels 281–287. National Archives, Washington, D.C.

93. Foner, *History of Black Americans,* 2:214. Boston's 1840 census data shows a huge increase of the black population, which may indicate that non-white groups as a whole were included in the statistics. Since Boston's Irish population increased by 65,113 persons by the mid-1840s, black workers would not have been encouraged to migrate to the city.

94. Leonard P. Curry, *The Free Black in Urban America, 1800–1850: The Shadow of the Dream* (Chicago: University of Chicago Press, 1981), 250.

95. See *Fifth Census,* 35–38, 50–53; U.S. Census Office, *The Seventh Census,* 52, 66–67, 91–92, 96–102, 158, 179; Jesse Chickering, *A Statistical View of the Population of Massachusetts, 1760–1840* (Boston: C. C. Little and J. Brown, 1846), 128, 151–155; see also John Doggett Jr., *Doggett's New York City Directory, for 1846 and 1847* (New York: John Doggett Jr., 1846).

96. *Frederick Douglass' Paper,* 4 March 1853.

97. W. E. B. DuBois, *The Philadelphia Negro: A Social Study* (1899; reprint, New York: Schocken Books, 1967), 53–55; Nash, *Forging Freedom,* 12–15; Litwack, *North of Slavery,* 165–166; Foner, *History of Black Americans,* 2:213–216.

98. Kessler-Harris, *Out to Work,* 46–47, 55; Edythe Quinn Caro, "The Hills in the Mid-Nineteenth Century: The History of a Rural Afro-American Community in Westchester County" (master's thesis, Herbert H. Lehman College, City University of New York, 1988) 19.

99. Kessler-Harris, *Out to Work*, 20–44; Julie A. Matthaei, *An Economic History of Women in America: Women's Work, the Sexual Division of Labor, and the Development of Capitalism* (New York: Schocken Books, 1982), 143–156; Thomas Dublin, "Women, Work, and the Family: Female Operatives in the Lowell Mills, 1830–1860," *Feminist Studies* 3, nos. 1/2 (fall 1975): 30–39.

100. North, *The Economic Growth of the United States*, 194.

101. Ibid., 199–203.

102. Giddings, *When and Where I Enter*, 47–48.

103. Gerda Lerner, *The Majority Finds Its Past: Placing Women in American History* (New York: Oxford University Press, 1979), 26.

104. Matthaei, *An Economic History of Women in America*, 123–124; Stansell, *City of Women*, 68–74, 130–131.

105. Giddings, *When and Where I Enter*, 48–55; White, *Ar'n't I a Woman?* 28–46; Patricia Morton, *Disfigured Images: The Historical Assault on Afro-American Women* (Westport, Conn.: Praeger, 1991), 1–13.

106. Stansell, *City of Women*, 15–17; Christine Bolt, *The Women's Movements in the United States and Britain from the 1790s to the 1920s* (Amherst: University of Massachusetts Press, 1993), 18–40; Kessler-Harris, *Out to Work*, 46–49.

107. Malveaux, " 'Ain't I a Woman,' " 79.

108. Harley, "Northern Black Female Workers," 10.

109. Kessler-Harris, *Out to Work*, 47.

110. Foner, *History of Black Americans*, 2:68.

111. Ibid., 2:66.

112. Matthaei, *An Economic History of Women in America*, 101–106.

113. Ibid., 22–35.

114. Eric Foner, *Free Soil, Free Men: The Ideology of the Republican Party before the Civil War* (New York: Oxford University Press, 1970), 14–15; Joe I. Dubbert, *A Man's Place: Masculinity in Transition* (Englewood Cliffs, N.J.: Prentice-Hall, 1979), 26–28; see Herbert Gutman, "The Reality of the Rags-to-Riches 'Myth': The Case of the Patterson, New Jersey, Locomotive, Iron, and Machinery Manufacturers, 1830–1880," in *Nineteenth-Century Cities: Essays in the New Urban History*, ed. Stephen Thernstrom and Richard Sennett (New Haven, Conn.: Yale University Press, 1969), 38–45.

115. Matthaei, *An Economic History of Women in America*, 103.

116. There are a number of works that deal with the ideology of domesticity. See, for example, Barbara Welter, "The Cult of True Womanhood, 1820–1860," *American Quarterly* 18 (summer 1966): 151–174; Nancy F. Cott, *The Bonds of Womanhood: "Women's Sphere" in New England, 1780–1835* (New Haven, Conn.: Yale University Press, 1977); Barbara Leslie Epstein, *The Politics of Domesticity: Women, Evangelism and Temperance in Nineteenth-Century America* (Middletown, Conn.: Wesleyan University Press, 1981); and Kessler Harris, *Out to Work*, 45–72.

117. Peter N. Carroll and David W. Noble, *The Free and the Unfree: A New History of the United States,* 2nd ed. (New York: Penguin Books, 1988), 148.

118. Bolt, *The Women's Movements,* 38–39; Caroline Ware, *The Early New England Cotton Manufacture: A Study in Industrial Beginnings* (Boston: Houghton Mifflin, 1931), 43–67.

119. Welter, "The Cult of True Womanhood," 151–174; Bolt, *The Women's Movements,* 38–40; Fox-Genovese, *Within the Plantation Household: Black and White Women of the Old South* (Chapel Hill: University of North Carolina Press, 1988), 192–241.

120. Matthaei, *An Economic History of Women in America,* 112.

121. Bolt, *The Women's Movements,* 38–40.

122. Ibid.

123. Dublin, "Women, Work, and the Family," 30.

124. R. J. Young, *Antebellum Black Activists: Race, Gender, and Self* (New York: Garland, 1996), 125–129; Sterling, *We Are Your Sisters,* 133–144; Dublin, "Women, Work, and the Family," 30–31.

125. Kessler-Harris, *Out to Work,* 54.

126. Stansell, *City of Women,* 109.

127. Mary Frances Berry and John W. Blassingame, *Long Memory: The Black Experience in America* (New York: Oxford University Press, 1982), 34; and note Litwack, *North of Slavery,* 64–112, on the legal repression of Northern blacks, and Harding, *There Is a River,* 117–139.

128. Harley, "Northern Black Female Workers, 10.

129. African Repository, November 1851; and note the intertwining racial prejudice and labor discrimination in Graham Russell Hodges, *New York City Cartmen, 1667–1850* (New York: New York University Press, 1986), 4–5.

130. Nash, "Forging Freedom," 6.

131. Horton and Horton, *Black Bostonians,* 8.

132. Harley, "Northern Black Female Workers," 6–7; Giddings, *When and Where I Enter,* 8; Foner, *History of Black Americans,* 2:211–213.

133. Stansell, *City of Women,* 159.

134. Patricia Hill-Collins, *Black Feminist Thought,* 139–142.

135. Tate, "Political Consciousness and Resistance," 71.

Chapter 4. As Quiet as It's Kept: Black Women's Urban Economic Activity and Empowerment

1. Ernst, "The Economic Status of New York City Negroes," 260.

2. Curry, *The Free Black in Urban America,* 30.

3. Ernst, "The Economic Status of New York City Negroes," 258.

4. Henry M. Minton, M.D. "Early History of Negroes in Business in Philadelphia," 8–9, paper, American Historical Society, March 1913, Historical Society of Pennsylvania.

5. Juliet E. K. Walker, *The History of Black Business in America: Capitalism, Race, Entrepreneurship* (New York: Simon and Schuster Macmillan, 1998), 129–130.

6. Ibid., 32–51; Whittington B. Johnson, *The Promising Years, 1750–1830: The Emergence of Black Labor and Business* (New York: Garland, 1993), 1–2; John Sibley Butler, *Entrepreneurship and Self-Help among Black Americans: A Reconsideration of Race and Economics* (New York: State University of New York Press, 1991), 35–36, 38, 40–41, 47–60.

7. Johnson, *The Promising Years,* 184.

8. Ibid., 122–124, 129–130; Walker, *The History of Black Business in America,* 83–126.

9. Leonard Stavinsky, "The Origins of Negro Craftsmanship in Colonial America," *Journal of Negro History* 32, no. 4 (October 1947), 417–418, 428; P. G. LePage, "Arts and Crafts of the Negro," *International Studio* 78 (March 1924): 477–478; Walker, *The History of Black Business in America,* 2–11; Stevenson, "Slavery," 1050.

10. Johnson, *The Promising Years,* 124; Walker, *The History of Black Business in America,* 83–126.

11. Johnson, *The Promising Years,* 129, 186. Note the list of black urban businesses in the 1850s compiled by Martin Delany in Walker, *The History of Black Business in America,* 84.

12. Johnson, *The Promising Years,* 1–2.

13. Butler, *Entrepreneurship and Self-Help,* 46; and see the full discussion of the business activities of slaves in Walker, *The History of Black Business in America,* 52–82.

14. Juliet E. K. Walker, "Racism, Slavery and Free Enterprise: Black Entrepreneurship in the United States before the Civil War," *Business History Review* 60 (autumn 1986): 364; and note Walker's discussion of the factors that motivated black entrepreneurs (370–377).

15. Johnson, *The Promising Years,* 1–2, 122.

16. Ibid., 122.

17. Ibid., 157.

18. Abram Harris, *The Negro As Capitalist* (New York: Arno Press, 1936), 9–10.

19. Johnson, *The Promising Years,* 1.

20. Ibid., 186.

21. Ibid., 186, 183; and see Audreye Johnson, "Catherine Ferguson," in Hine, *Black Women in America,* 426.

22. Sterling, *We Are Your Sisters,* 103. See the comprehensive discussion of free black women's business activities during the antebellum era in Walker, *The History of Black Business in America,* 127–149.

23. Walker, *The History of Black Business in America,* 137, 92–93.

24. Sterling, *We Are Your Sisters,* 95; Nancy Prince, *A Narrative of the Life and Travels of Mrs. Nancy Prince,* in *Collected Black Women's Narratives,* ed.

Henry Louis Gates Jr., 2nd ed. (Boston, 1853; reprint, New York: Oxford University Press, 1988), 20–21.

25. Prince, *A Narrative*, 23, 39.

26. Ibid., 84.

27. Pennsylvania Abolition Society of Analysis of Census Facts Collected by Bacon and Garner, 1838, Historical Society of Pennsylvania (Philadelphia); "A Register of Trades of Colored People in the City of Philadelphia and Districts" (Philadelphia: Merrihew and Gunn, 1838), Historical Society of Pennsylvania (Philadelphia); and see Walkers's table 5.1 for a more comprehensive listing of black female occupations in Philadelphia in *The History of Black Business in America*, 130.

28. Horton and Horton, *Black Bostonians*, 8, 9, 54.

29. Charles M. Wiltse, introduction to *Appeal to the Coloured Citizens of the World*, by David Walker, ix (1829; reprint, New York: Hill and Wang, 1965).

30. Harris, *The Negro as Capitalist*, 21–22; Butler, *Entrpreneurship and Self-Help*, 40–42; Walker, *The History of Black Business in America*, 87–91, 96–99.

31. Harris, *The Negro as Capitalist*, 22.

32. Jean Matthews, "Race, Sex, and the Dimensions of Liberty in Antebellum America," *Journal of the Early Republic* 6 (fall 1986): 278; Harris, *The Negro as Capitalist*, 24.

33. Walker, "Racism, Slavery and Free Enterprise," 345.

34. For black female occupations in Philadelphia, see *A Statistical Inquiry into the Condition of the People of Colour, of the City and Districts of Philadelphia* (Philadelphia: Kite and Walton, 1849), 17, 18–19, and the Philadelphia city directories from 1840 to 1850, Historical Society of Pennsylvania; for New York City, see the city directories of the 1840s and the U.S. Census of 1840; and for Boston, see the Boston city directories for the 1840s and the U.S. Census of 1850 and 1860.

35. Tate, "Political Consciousness and Resistance," 73.

36. Collins, *Black Feminist Thought*, 92.

37. Judith Rollins, *Between Women: Domestics and Their Employers* (Philadelphia: Temple University Press, 1985), 212.

38. Harley, "Northern Black Female Workers, 6–7, 55. Bogart R. Leashore examines the black female "live-in" domestic workers in Detroit following emancipation in "Black Female Workers: Live-in Domestics in Detroit, Michigan, 1860–1880," *Phylon* 45, no. 2 (June 1984), 111–120.

39. Elizabeth Clark-Lewis, *Living In, Living Out: African American Domestics and the Great Migration* (New York: Kodansha International, 1994), 97, 65–66; David M. Katzman, *Seven Days a Week: Women and Domestic Service in Industrializing America* (New York: Oxford University Press, 1978), 184–222; Stansell, *City of Women*, 156–163; Elizabeth Clark-Lewis, "Domestic Workers in the North," in Hine, *Black Women in America*, 341.

40. Clark-Lewis, *Living In, Living Out*, 65–66; and David M. Katzman, *Seven Days a Week*, 177–179.

41. Clark-Lewis, *Living In, Living Out,* 101. While Clark-Lewis's study deals with Northern domestics during the Great Migration, the attitudes of employers of household laborers appear to be timeless; and see David M. Katzman, *Seven Days a Week,* 184–222.

42. Stansell, *City of Women,* 155–168; Clark-Lewis, *Living In, Living Out,* 106–113; Boydston, *Home and Work,* 79–80.

43. Clark-Lewis, *Living In, Living Out,* 107.

44. Darlene Clark Hine, "Rape and the Inner Lives of Black Women in the Middle West: Preliminary Thoughts on the Culture of Dissemblance," *Signs* 14, no. 4 (1989): 915; and see Collins, *Black Feminist Thought,* 92–96.

45. Boydston, *Home and Work,* 76–88.

46. Ibid.

47. Matthaei, *An Economic History of Women in America,* 157.

48. Stansell, *City of Women,* 13.

49. Clark-Lewis, *Living In, Living Out,* 142.

50. Quoted in Sterling, *We Are Your Sisters,* 215.

51. James McCune Smith, "The Washerwoman," *Frederick Douglass' Paper,* 17 June 1852.

52. Boydston, *Home and Work,* 89.

53. Ibid.

54. Sterling, *We Are Your Sisters,* 216.

55. Elsa Barkley Brown, "Hearing Our Mothers' Lives," 14, Fifteenth Anniversary of African-American and African Studies, Emory University, Atlanta, 1986.

56. Clark-Lewis, *Living In, Living Out,* 141, 1.

57. Sterling, *We Are Your Sisters,* 105–106.

58. Horton and Horton, *Black Bostonians,* 36.

59. Stansell, *City of Women,* 14.

60. Ibid., 133; Richardson Wright, *Hawkers and Walkers in Early America* (1927; reprint, New York: Arno, 1976), 234; Haswell, *Reminiscences of an Octogenarian,* 447.

61. Charles L. Blockson, *Catalogue of the Charles L. Blockson Afro-American Collection, A Unit of the Temple University Libraries* (Philadelphia: Temple University Press, 1990), 132.

62. Sterling, *We Are Your Sisters,* 218–219.

63. Ibid., 216; Foner, *History of Black Americans,* 2:213; Stansell, *City of Women,* 110–114; Boydston, *Home and Work,* 125, 131–132; Kessler-Harris, *Out to Work,* 65–66; *New York Daily Tribune,* 2 August 1845.

64. Butler, *Entrepreneurship and Self-Help,* 40–41.

65. *A Statistical Inquiry into the Condition of the People of Colour, of the City and Districts of Philadelphia,* 18; "A Register of Trades of Colored People in the City of Philadelphia and Districts."

66. Stansell, *City of Women,* 14.

67. Sterling, *We Are Your Sisters*, 95–96.

68. Horton and Horton, *Black Bostonians*, 16; and note the more comprehensive discussion on boardinghouses and boarder (16–18).

69. Stansell, *City of Women*, 13; Sterling, *We Are Your Sisters*, 92–93.

70. Lapsansky, "Friends, Wives, and Strivings," 8.

71. Sterling, *We Are Your Sisters*, 97, 217.

72. Stansell, *City of Women*, 14–15. There were a full range of "bawdy houses" where illicit activities provided the entertainment for the evening. See the description in Ottley and Weatherby, *The Negro in New York*, 76–79.

73. Sterling, *We Are Your Sisters*, 217; *Colored American*, 7 June 1841, Schomburg Center, NYPL.

74. *Weekly Anglo-African*, 12 August 1860, Schomburg Center, NYPL.

75. White, *Ar'n't I a Woman?*, 126–131.

76. Sterling, *We Are Your Sisters*, 103, 97.

77. Quarles, Black Abolitionists, 49.

Chapter 5. Shaking the Tree of Liberty: Alienation and Activism

1. Frances Smith Foster, ed., *A Brighter Coming Day: A Frances Ellen Watkins Harper Reader* (New York: Feminist Press, 1990), 99, 95–96.

2. *Liberator*, 26 March 1831.

3. Anne M. Boylan, "Antislavery Activity among African American Women," in *The Abolitionist Sisterhood: Women's Political Culture in Antebellum America*, ed. Jean Fagan Yellin and John C. Van Horne (Ithaca, N.Y.: Cornell University Press, 1994), 121, 133.

4. Ibid., 129; Quarles, *Black Abolitionists*, 27, 30, 31, 49, 94; Shirley J. Yee, *Black Women Abolitionists: A Study in Activism, 1828–1860* (Knoxville: University of Tennessee Press, 1992), 18–19.

5. Julie Winch, "Philadelphia's Black Female Literary Societies," in Yellin and Van Horne, *The Abolitionist Sisterhood*, 103.

6. Deborah K. King, "Multiple Jeopardy, Multiple Consciousness: The Context of a Black Feminist Ideology" in *Black Women in America: Social Science Perspectives*, ed. Micheline R. Malson, Elisabeth Mudimbe-Boyi, Jean F. O'Barr, and Mary Wyer (Chicago: University of Chicago Press, 1988), 270.

7. Michael Albert et al., *Liberating Theory* (Boston: South End Press, 1986), 6.

8. Anthony Gronowicz, *Race and Class Politics in New York City before the Civil War* (Boston: Northeastern University Press, 1998), 56.

9. Rose M. Brewer, "Theorizing Race, Class and Gender: The New Scholarship of Black Feminist Intellectuals and Black Women's Labor," in James and Busia, *Theorizing Black Feminisms*, 16.

10. Harper to William Still, "On Free Produce," 20 October 1854, in Foster, *A Brighter Coming Day*, 45; and see Bettye Collier-Thomas, "Frances Ellen Watkins Harper: Abolitionist and Feminist Reformer, 1825–1911," in *African-American Women and the Vote, 1837–1965*, ed. Ann D. Gordon, with Bettye Collier-Thomas, John H. Bracey, Arlene Voski Avakian, and Joyce Avrech Berkman (Amherst: University of Massachusetts Press, 1997), 46.

11. Curry, *The Free Black in Urban America*, 82.

12. Daniel Curry, *New York: Historical Sketches of the Rise and Progress of the Metropolitan City of America* (New York: Carlton and Phillips, 1853), 308.

13. Linda Brent, *Incidents in the Life of a Slave Girl* (New York: Harcourt Brace Jovanovich, 1973), 181.

14. Maria W. Stewart, "Lecture Delivered at the Franklin Hall, Boston, September 21, 1832," in *Maria W. Stewart: America's First Black Woman Political Writer*, ed. Marilyn Richardson (Bloomington: Indiana University Press, 1987), 48.

15. Ernst, *Immigrant Life in New York City*, 67.

16. James D. Burn, *Three Years among the Working-Classes in the United States during the War* (London: Smith, Elder, 1865), xiv.

17. Aldon D. Morris, *The Origins of the Civil Rights Movement: Black Communities Organizing for Change* (New York: Free Press, 1984), 1.

18. Gronowicz, *Race and Class Politics in New York*, 31.

19. Brent, *Incidents in the Life of a Slave Girl*, 179.

20. *The First Annual Report of the New York Committee of Vigilance for the Year 1837* (New York: Piercy and Reed, 1837), 3, Schomburg Center, NYPL.

21. Foner, *History of Black Americans*, 2:506.

22. Horton and Horton, *Black Bostonians*, 98; Foner, *History of Black Americans*, 505. Note the account of this slave rescue in Gary Collison, *Shadrach Minkins: From Fugitive Slave to Citizen* (Cambridge: Harvard University Press, 1997), 86–87; and see Leonard W. Levy, "The 'Abolition Riot': Boston's First Slave Rescue," *New England Quarterly* 25 (March 1952): 85–92.

23. Frances Ellen Watkins Harper, "Could We Trace the Record of Every Human Heart," lecture at New York City Anti-Slavery Society, 13 May 1857, in Foster, *A Brighter Coming Day*, 102.

24. James Fenimore Cooper, *Notions of the Americans Picked by a Travelling Batchelor* (1828; reprint, New York: Ungar, 1963), 1:283.

25. Collins, *Black Feminist Thought*, 6.

26. Eric Lott, " 'The Seeming Counterfeit:' Racial Politics and Early Blackface Minstrelsy," *American Quarterly* 43, no. 2 (June 1991): 225.

27. James Oliver Horton and Lois E. Horton, *In Hope of Liberty: Culture, Community, and Protest among Northern Free Blacks, 1700–1860* (New York: Oxford University Press, 1997), 165.

28. Phyllis F. Field, *The Politics of Race in New York: The Struggle for Black Suffrage in the Civil War* (Ithaca, N.Y.: Cornell University Press, 1982), 41.

29. Emma Jones Lapsansky, "The Counterculture of Agitation in Philadelphia," in Yellin and Van Horne, *The Abolitionist Sisterhood*, 92.

30. E. S. Abdy, *Journal of a Residence and Tour in the United States of North America from April 1833, to October 1834* (London: John Murray, 1835), 1:301–302.

31. Quarles, *Black Abolitionists*, 135–136.

32. Gronowicz, *Race and Class Politics in New York*, 60.

33. Horton and Horton, *In Hope of Liberty*, 242.

34. John H. Bracey Jr., August Meier, and Elliott Rudwick, eds., *Black Nationalism in America* (Indianapolis: Bobbs-Merrill Educational Publishing, 1970), xxxvii; Philip S. Foner, *The Life and Writings of Frederick Douglass: Pre-Civil War Decade 1850–1860* (New York: International Publishers, 1950), 66–85; Field, *The Politics of Race in New York*, 93; Quarles, *Black Abolitionists*, 172, 183–188.

35. Field, *The Politics of Race in New York*.

36. Litwack, *North of Slavery*, 268. Although the Democratic Party was branded the more racist party, the Republican Party did not advance any rights for blacks at all; see ibid., 268–274.

37. Gronowicz, *Race and Class Politics in New York*, 60–61.

38. Winch, *Philadelphia's Black Elite*, 131.

39. Field, *The Politics of Race in New York*, 98.

40. Ibid., 68.

41. Morton, *Disfigured Images*, 8–9.

42. *Liberator*, 9 May 1845.

43. Morton, *Disfigured Images*, 7.

44. See Mae King's discussion on the political functioning of stereotypes of black women in "The Politics of Sexual Stereotypes," *Black Scholar* 4 (1973): 12–23; see also Morton, *Disfigured Images*, 6–7.

45. Yee, *Black Women Abolitionists*, 41.

46. Davis, *Women, Race and Class*, 182.

47. David W. Blight, "W. E. B. DuBois and the Struggle for American Historical Memory," in *History and Memory in African-American Culture*, ed. Genevieve Fabre and Robert O'Meally (New York: Oxford University Press, 1994), 50–56.

48. Morris, *The Origins of the Civil Rights Movement*, 3; Guida West and Rhoda Lois Blumberg, eds., *Women and Social Protest* (New York: Oxford University Press, 1990), 31–32.

49. Curry, *The Free Black in Urban America*, 201–205.

50. Horton and Horton, *In Hope of Liberty*, 128.

51. West and Blumberg, *Women and Social Protest*, 28.

52. "D" to the "Females of Color," *Weekly Advocate*, 7 January 1837, Schomburg Center, NYPL.

53. Boylan, "Antislavery Activity," 132.

54. *Colored American,* 17 November 1838, Schomburg Center, NYPL.

55. Quoted in Yee, *Black Women Abolitionists,* 46.

56. Sterling, *We Are Your Sisters,* 118.

57. Maria W. Stewart, "Religion and the Pure Principles of Morality, the Sure Foundation on Which We Must Build," in Richardson, *Maria W. Stewart,* 38.

58. Horton and Horton, *In Hope of Liberty,* 175.

59. Stewart, "Religion and the Pure Principles of Morality," 68–69.

60. Sterling, *We Are Your Sisters,* 222.

61. Horton and Horton, *Black Bostonians,* 65, 221–222.

62. Marguerite Ross Barnett, "A Theoretical Perspective on American Public Policy," in *Public Policy for the Black Community: Strategies and Perspectives,* ed. Marguerite Ross Barnett and James A. Hefner (New York: Alfred Publishing, 1976), 13.

63. Morris, *The Origins of the Civil Rights Movement,* 1–16; Morrison, *Black Political Mobilization,* 23–52; Toni-Michelle C. Travis, "Boston: The Unfinished Agenda," in *Racial Politics in American Cities,* ed. Rufus P. Browning, Dale Rogers Marshall, and David H. Tabb (New York: Longman, 1990), 108–121.

64. Tilly, *From Mobilization to Revolution,* 72.

65. Franklin, *Black Self-Determination,* 87.

66. McAdam, *Political Process,* 2.

67. Temma Kaplan, "Female Consciousness and Collective Action: The Case of Barcelona, 1910–1918," *Signs: Journal of Women in Culture and Society* 7, no. 3 (1982): 545–566; David Snow, Louis A. Zurcher Jr., and Sheldon Eckland-Olson, "Social Networks and Social Movements: A Microstructural Approach to Differential Recruitment," *American Sociological Review* 45, no. 5 (1980): 787–801.

68. Melvin Dixon, "The Black Writer's Use of Memory," in Fabre and O'Meally, *History and Memory,* 26.

69. Note Bettye C. Thomas's argument concerning the historical role played by black women in organizational development in antebellum communities in "The Role of the Black Woman," 135; see also Gerda Lerner, "Early Community Work of Black Club Women," *Journal of Negro History* 59, no. 2 (April 1974): 158.

70. Belinda Robnett, "African-American Women in the Civil Rights Movement, 1954–1965: Gender, Leadership, and Micromobilization," *American Journal of Sociology* 101, no. 6 (May 1996): 1663, 1664–1665.

71. Stewart, "Religion and the Pure Principles of Morality," 40.

72. Clarence Taylor, *The Black Churches of Brooklyn* (New York: Columbia University Press, 1994), 10.

73. Quoted in Yee, *Black Women Abolitionists,* 77.

74. Boylan, "Antislavery Activity," 121.

75. Horton and Horton, *In Hope of Liberty,* 127.

76. Horton and Horton, *Black Bostonians,* 64–65.

77. Yee, *Black Women Abolitionists,* 58.

78. Daughters of Africa Society minutes, 3 June 1823, 5 August 1823, 11 May 1824, 5 June 1832, 3 November 1835, Historical Society of Pennsylvania.

79. Horton and Horton, *In Hope of Liberty,* 151.

80. Ray Allen Billington, *The Journal of Charlotte L. Forten: A Free Negro in the Slave Era* (New York: W. W. Norton, 1953), 55.

81. Janice Sumler-Lewis, "The Forten-Purvis Women of Philadelphia and the American Anti-Slavery Crusade," *Journal of Negro History* 66, no. 4 (winter 1981–82): 281–288.

82. Lapsansky, *Black Presence in Pennsylvania,* 19.

83. Acts 9:36.

84. *Freedom's Journal,* 1 February 1828, 179.

85. Horton and Horton, *Black Bostonians,* 19.

86. Preamble to the constitution of the Women's Association of Philadelphia in Sterling, *We Are Your Sisters,* 117.

87. Ibid., 118.

88. Sterling, *We Are Your Sisters,* 110.

89. Joseph Wilson, *Sketches of the Higher Classes of Colored People in Philadelphia by a Southerner* (Philadelphia, 1841), 109; Porter, "The Organized Educational Activities of Negro Literary Societies," 574; Dorothy Porter, "David Ruggles, an Apostle of Human Rights," *Journal of Negro History* 28, no. 1 (January 1943): 34.

Chapter 6. Hallowed Fire: The Gospel Politics of Black Female Evangelists

1. R. C. Gordon-McCutchan, "The Irony of Evangelical History," *Journal for the Scientific Study of Religion* 20 (December 1981): 309; G. Adolph Koch, *Religion of the American Enlightenment* (New York: Thomas Crowekk, 1968), 244–247.

2. Andrews, *Sisters of the Spirit,* 3.

3. Often the "call to preach the gospel" has been via visions, dreams, or voices that lead individuals to the conviction that God had chosen them for this mission. C. Eric Lincoln and Lawrence H. Mamiya describe the intensity of this feeling and belief in *The Black Church in the African American Experience* (Durham, N.C.: Duke University Press, 1990), 275.

4. Albert J. Raboteau, "The Black Experience in American Evangelicalism: The Meaning of Slavery," in *African-American Religion: Interpretive Essays in History and Culture,* ed. Timothy E. Fulop and Albert J. Raboteau (New York: Routledge, 1997), 93.

5. C. Eric Lincoln, "The Black Heritage in the South," in *Religion in the South,* ed. C. Wilson (Jackson: University Press of Mississippi, 1985), 39.

6. Alan Gallay, "Planters and Slaves in the Great Awakening," in *Masters and Slaves in the House of the Lord: Race and Religion in the American South, 1740–1870,* ed. John R. Boles (Bowling Green: University Press of Kentucky, 1988), 19, 91–92.

7. Lincoln, "The Black Heritage in the South," 39; Collier-Thomas, *Daughters of Thunder,* 11–23.

8. Nellie Y. McKay, "Feminism at Work in the Church: Those Preaching Black Women of the 19th Century," *Abafazi* (fall/winter 1993): 2; Collier-Thomas, *Daughters of Thunder,* 11–37.

9. Andrews, *Sisters of the Spirit,* 4.

10. Jarena Lee, *The Life and Religious Experience of Jarena Lee, a Coloured Lady, Giving an Account of Her Call to Preach the Gospel,* in Andrews, *Sisters of the Spirit,* 27; Zilpha Elaw, *Memoirs of the Life, Religious Experience, Ministerial Travels and Labours of Mrs. Zilpha Elaw, an American Female of Colour; Together with Some Accounts of the Great Religious Revivals in America,* in Andrews, *Sisters of the Spirit,* 55; see Andrews's excellent note regarding Elaw's early period (239–240, n. 2).

11. Nell Irvin Painter, *Sojourner Truth: A Life, a Symbol* (New York: W. W. Norton, 1996), 27.

12. Ibid., 48–61, 79–87.

13. John A. Andrew III, "Betsey Stockton: Stranger in a Strange Land," *Journal of Presbyterian History* 52 (1974): 158–159, 163.

14. Prince, *A Narrative of the Life,* 43.

15. Elaw, *Memoirs of the Life,* 137.

16. Ibid.

17. Elizabeth, *Elizabeth, a Colored Minister of the Gospel, Born in Slavery* (Philadelphia: Tract Association of Friends, 1889), 9.

18. Jualynne Dodson, "Nineteenth-Century A.M.E. Preaching Women," in *Women in New Worlds: Historical Perspectives on the Wesleyan Tradition,* ed. Hilah F. Thomas and Rosemary Skinner Keller (Nashville: Abingdon, 1981), 276–278.

19. McKay, "Feminism at Work in the Church," 2; Collier-Thomas, *Daughters of Thunder,* 11–37.

20. Andrews, *Sisters of the Spirit,* 3.

21. Elaw, *Memoirs of the Life,* 128.

22. Genevieve Fabre, "African-American Commemorative Celebrations in the Nineteenth Century," in Fabre and O'Meally, *History and Memory in African-American Culture,* 77–81.

23. Tate, "Black Nationalism," 42.

24. Gronowicz, *Race and Class Politics,* 89–95; Morton, *Disfigured Images,* 1–13.

25. Lee, *The Life and Religious Experience of Jarena Lee,* 27; Collier-Thomas, *Daughters of Thunder,* 44–46.

26. Elizabeth, *Elizabeth*, 2.

27. Julia A. J. Foote, *A Brand Plucked from the Fire*, in Andrews, *Sisters of the Spirit*, 169.

28. Elizabeth, *Elizabeth*, 2, 3.

29. Foote, *A Brand Plucked from the Fire*, 176.

30. Ibid.

31. Ibid., 176, 3.

32. Ibid., 166.

33. Ibid., 178.

34. Wilmore, *Black Religion and Black Radicalism*, 221.

35. Harold Lindstrom, *Wesley and Sanctification* (London: Epworth, 1950), 100–101, 113–120; see the discussion in Andrews, *Sisters of the Spirit*, 14–15; and Patricia Shecter, "Feminist Spirituality and Radical Political Commitment," *Journal of Women and Religion* 1, no. 1 (spring 1981): 51–54.

36. Lee, *The Life and Religious Experience of Jarena Lee*, 39.

37. Shecter, "Feminist Spirituality," 52

38. Jean McMahon Humez, ed., *Gifts of Power: The Writings of Rebecca Jackson, Black Visionary, Shaker Eldress* (Amherst: University of Massachusetts Press, 1981), 6; Collier-Thomas, *Daughters of Thunder*, 47–48.

39. Elaw, *Memoirs of the Life*, 77.

40. Lee, *The Life and Religious Experience of Jarena Lee*, 29, 34.

41. Foote, *A Brand Plucked from the Fire*, 180. See Collier-Thomas, *Daughters of Thunder*, 3–4, 57–68, for the way that conversion and salvation were woven into Foote's sermons.

42. Lee, *The Life and Religious Experiences of Jarena Lee*, 34.

43. Elaw, *Memoirs of the Life*, 67.

44. Humez, *Gifts of Power*, 20. Note the sanctification experience of Amanda Berry Smith in *An Autobiography: The Story of the Lord's Dealings with Mrs. Amanda Smith the Colored Evangelist* (New York: Oxford University Press, 1988), 73–79.

45. Elaw, *Memoirs of the Life*, 56–57.

46. Ibid., 64.

47. Lee, *The Life and Religious Experience of Jarena Lee*, 35.

48. Elaw, *Memoirs of the Life*, 77, 82.

49. Foote, *A Brand Plucked from the Fire*, 200, 201.

50. Elaw, *Memoirs of the Life*, 66, 67, 42.

51. Ibid., 122.

52. Thomas J. O'Dea, *The Sociology of Religion* (Englewood Cliffs, N.J.: Prentice Hall, 1966), 14; see also Clarence G. Newsome, "Mary McLeod Bethune As Religionist," in Thomas and Keller, *Women in New Worlds*, 102–104; and Dodson, "Nineteenth-Century a.m.E. Preaching Women," 276–280.

53. Raboteau, "The Black Experience in American Evangelicalism," 99.

54. Monroe Fordham, *Major Themes in Northern Black Religious Thought, 1800–1860* (Hicksville, N.Y.: Exposition Press, 1975), 35.

55. Raboteau, "The Black Experience in American Evangelicalism," 99.

56. Ibid., 98.

57. Fordham, *Major Themes in Northern Black Religious Thought*, 35.

58. Painter, *Sojourner Truth*, 45.

59. Elaw, *Memoirs of the Life*, 91; and see Collier-Thomas, *Daughters of Thunder*, 8–9.

60. Andrews, *Sisters of the Spirit*, 9.

61. Elaw, *Memoirs of the Life*, 83.

62. Foner, *History of Black Americans*, 2:201.

63. Quoted in ibid.; Horton and Horton, *Black Bostonians*, 67.

64. Foote, *A Brand Plucked from the Fire*, 219, 216.

65. *Freedom's Journal*, 16 March 1827.

66. Elaw, *Memoirs of the Life*, 133.

67. Prince, *A Narrative of the Life*, 75.

68. Foote, *A Brand Plucked from the Fire*, 215.

69. Olive Gilbert, *Narrative of Sojourner Truth: A Bondswoman of Olden Time* (1850, Boston; reprint, New York: Arno Press, 1968), 185.

70. Elaw, *Memoirs of the Life*, 85.

71. Foote, *A Brand Plucked from the Fire*, 222.

72. Lee, *The Life and Religious Experience of Jarena Lee*, 36; Carolyn De Swarte Gifford, "Women in Social Reform Movements," in *Women and Religion in America: The Nineteenth Century*, ed. Rosemary R. Ruether and Rosemary Skinner Keller (New York: Harper and Row, 1981), 299–302; Rosemary R. Ruether, "Christianity," in Ruether and Keller, *Women in World Religions*, 207–210.

73. Foote, *A Brand Plucked from the Fire*, 207.

74. *Freedom's Journal*, 16 March 1827; *Weekly Advocate*, New York, 7 January 1837; *Colored American*, 4 March 1837, Schomburg Center, NYPL.

75. Elaw, *Memoirs of the Life*, 91, 98. Note Amanda Berry Smith's fear of whites in *An Autobiography*, 80. Even though she was born later than these evangelists, the fear was still pervasive.

76. Elizabeth, *Elizabeth*, 10–11.

77. Prince, *A Narrative of the Life*, 77–79.

78. Gilbert, *Narrative of Sojourner Truth*, 140–141.

79. Quarles, *Black Abolitionists*, 49.

80. Bracey, Meier, and Rudwick, *Black Nationalism*, xxxiii—xxxiv.

81. Prince, *A Narrative of the Life*, 42.

82. Painter, *Sojourner Truth*, 113.

83. Gilbert, *Narrative of Sojourner Truth*, 126–127.

Chapter 7. Rocking the Bastille:
Black Women's Abolitionism

1. Patricia Hill Collins, "The Social Construction of Black Feminist Thought," in Malson, Mudimbe-Boyi, O'Barr, and Wyer, *Black Women in America*, 297–300.

2. Tate, "Black Nationalism," 40.

3. Nancy A. Naples, "Women's Community Activism: Exploring the Dynamic of Politicization and Diversity," in Naples, *Community Activism and Feminist Politics*, 332.

4. Rosalyn Terborg-Penn, *African American Women in the Struggle for the Vote, 1850–1920* (Bloomington: Indiana University Press, 1998), 2, 6–7; Elsa Barkley Brown, "Negotiating and Transforming the Public Sphere: African American Political Life in the Transition from Slavery to Freedom," *Public Culture* 7, no. 1 (fall 1994); Yee, *Black Women Abolitionists*, 87.

5. *North Star,* 9 March 1849, 12 April 1850, Schomburg Center, NYPL.

6. See Merton L. Dillon's discussion on the term "immediate abolitionism" and its multilayered meaning, which contributed to the hostility toward abolitionism, in *The Abolitionists: The Growth of a Dissenting Minority* (New York: W. W. Norton, 1974), 36–39; however, note that black abolitionists did view the term as a philosophical and pragmatic approach to emancipation, particularly by the 1840s when the ideological stance of moral suasion had not ended slavery.

7. Ibid., 70.

8. See Rosalyn Terborg-Penn, "Free Women Entrepreneurs from the 1820s to the 1850s: Nancy Prince and Mary Seacole," in *Crossing Boundaries: Comparative History of Black People in Diaspora,* ed. Darlene Clark Hine and Jacqueline McLeod (Bloomington: Indiana University Press, 1999), 171, for a discussion on how Nancy Prince may have been recruited to the Woman's Rights Convention in Philadelphia in 1854 by the Fortens to ensure a significant black female presence.

9. Quarles, *Black Abolitionists,* 47–50.

10. Dillon, *The Abolitionists,* 71.

11. *Herald of Freedom,* 1 June 1839; *Colored American,* 1 September 1838, Schomburg Center, NYPL; Quarles, *Black Abolitionists,* 49; Foner, *History of Black Americans,* 454–457; "First Colored Convention," *Anglo-American Magazine* 1, no. 10 (October 1859), 305–310, Schomburg Center, NYPL; Howard Holman Bell, ed., *Minutes of the Proceedings of the National Negro Conventions, 1830–1864* (New York: Arno Press and the New York Times, 1969), 28.

12. Jean R. Soderlund, "Priorities and Power: The Philadelphia Female Anti-Slavery Society," in Yellin and Van Horne, *The Abolitionist Sisterhood,* 79–80.

13. Sumler-Lewis, "The Forten-Purvis Women," 283.

14. Ibid.

15. PFASS minutes, 1833–1848, 29 September 1836, Historical Society of Pennsylvania.

16. PFASS minutes, 14 January 1847, Historical Society of Pennsylvania.

17. Sumler-Lewis, "The Forten-Purvis Women," 284.

18. Note a discussion of the ideological strife, divisions, and factionalism within the antislavery movement in Aileen S. Kraditor, *Means and Ends in American Abolitionism; Garrison and His Critics on Strategy and Tactics, 1834–1850* (New York: Pantheon Books, 1969); and note Lewis Perry's argument that anarchism was inherent in all of the components and factions of the antislavery movement. See Lewis Perry, *Radical Abolitionism: Anarchy and the Government of God in Antislavery Thought* (Ithaca, N.Y.: Cornell University Press, 1973). See also Merton L. Dillon, *The Abolitionists: The Growth of a Dissenting Minority* (New York: W. W. Norton, 1974).

19. Sumler-Lewis, "The Forten-Purvis Women," 284.

20. PFASS minutes, 19 May 1842, Historical Society of Pennsylvania.

21. Ibid.

22. Sumler-Lewis, "The Forten-Purvis Women," 283.

23. Yee, *Black Women Abolitionists*, 92.

24. Debra Gold Hansen, "The Boston Female Anti-Slavery Society and the Limits of Gender Politics," in Yellin and Van Horne, *The Abolitionist Sisterhood*, 62, 64.

25. Derrick A. Bell Jr., *Race, Racism, and American Law*, 2nd ed. (Boston: Little, Brown, 1980), 366; for further discussion on the events surrounding the school segregation issue and the subsequent court case, see Horton and Horton, *Black Bostonians*, 70–79.

26. Prince, *A Narrative of the Life*, 42.

27. Quarles, *Black Abolitionists*, 55.

28. Quoted in Hansen, "The Boston Female Anti-Slavery Society," 58.

29. Willi Coleman, "Architects of a Vision: Black Women and Their Antebellum Quest for Political and Social Equality," in Gordon, with Collier-Thomas, Bracey, Avakian, and Berkman, *African American Women and the Vote, 1837–1965*, 27.

30. Tate, "Black Nationalism," 40–48.

31. Stewart, "Religion and the Pure Principles of Morality," 30, 14.

32. Ibid., 40.

33. Ibid., 35.

34. Coleman, "Architects of a Vision," 28.

35. Stewart, "Religion and the Pure Principles of Morality," 30.

36. Ibid., 30, 39–40, 19; and see discussion of Stewart's nationalism in Tate, "Black Nationalism," 40–48.

37. Stewart, "Religion and the Pure Principles of Morality," 16.

38. Ibid., 27.

39. Bogin, "Sarah Parker Remond," 1:124.

40. Dorothy Porter, "Sarah Parker Remond, Abolitionist and Physician," *Journal of Negro History* 20, no. 1 (January 1935): 287.

41. *Warrington Times* 29 January 1859, 5 February 1859; *Liberator,* 11 March 1859, reprint from *Warrington Guardian,* n.d., NYPL; Dorothy B. Porter, "Sarah Parker Remond, Abolitionist and Physician," *Journal of Negro History* 20, no. 1 (January 1935): 290–292.

42. *Anti-Slavery Advocate* 2 (April 1859), 223, NYPL; *Warrington Times* 5 February 1859, NYPL.

43. Bogin, "Sarah Parker Remond," 1:141.

44. Sarah Parker Remond, "The Negroes in the United States of America," *Journal of Negro History* 27, no. 2 (April 1942): 218.

45. Frances Smith Foster, "Frances Ellen Watkins Harper (1825–1911)," in Hine, *Black Women in America,* 1:533; Foster, *A Brighter Coming Day,* 8–9; William Still, *The Underground Railroad* (1871; reprint, Chicago: Johnson Publishing Company, 1970), 783–785.

46. Mary Ann Shadd Cary to Thomas F. Cary, (n.d), Ontario Black History Society, box 2, folder 6, Ontario, Canada.

47. Frances Ellen Watkins Harper, "Liberty for Slaves," *National Anti-Slavery Standard,* 23 May 1857, NYPL.

48. "Miss Watkins and the Constitution," *National Anti-Slavery Standard,* 9 April 1859, NYPL.

49. Harper to William Still, "The Agent of the State Anti-Slavery Society of Maine Travels with Me," in Foster, *A Brighter Coming Day,* 44.

50. Foster, *A Brighter Coming Day,* 15.

51. Harper to William Still, "On Free Produce," in Foster, *A Brighter Coming Day,* 45; and see letter and comments by William Still, *The Underground Railroad,* 787–788.

52. Quarles, *Black Abolitionists,* 76.

53. "An Appeal for the Philadelphia Rescuers," *Weekly Anglo-African,* 23 June 1860, Schomburg Center, NYPL.

54. Harper to William Still, "I Am Able to Give Something," in Still, *The Underground Railroad,* 792.

55. Harper to William Still, "Poor Doomed and Fated Men," 12 December 1859, in Foster, *A Brighter Coming Day,* 51.

56. Harper to William Still, "Breathing the Air of Freedom," 12 September 1856, in Foster, *A Brighter Coming Day,* 45.

57. Quarles, *Black Abolitionists,* 241.

58. Harper to John Brown, "To John Brown," 25 November 1859, in Foster, *A Brighter Coming Day,* 49.

59. Brent, *Incidents in the Life of a Slave Girl,* 164, 165.

60. Horton and Horton, *Black Bostonians,* 65.

61. Sterling, *We Are Your Sisters,* 62.

62. Still, *The Underground Railroad*, 210.

63. Ibid., 382–385, 183, 45.

64. Ibid., 289–292, 217–218.

65. Brent, *Incidents in the Life of a Slave Girl*, 155, 215.

66. Ibid., 311–312.

67. Ibid., 73–84; Quarles, *Black Abolitionists*, 165–166; Sterling, *We Are Your Sisters*, 66.

68. Still, *The Underground Railroad*, 104, 572.

69. Brent, *Incidents in the Life of a Slave Girl*, 196.

70. Horton and Horton, *Black Bostonians*, 65.

71. Quarles, *Black Abolitionists*, 158.

72. Levy, "The 'Abolition Riot,'" 85–92.

73. Hallie Q. Brown, *Homespun Heroines and Other Women of Distinction* (Xenia, Ohio: Aldine, 1926), 71–80; Quarles, *Black Abolitionists*, 147. Note Mary Jones's writings that tell of that meeting and the aftermath of the raid at Harpers Ferry in Sterling, *We Are Your Sisters*, 147–150.

74. Franklin and Moss, *From Slavery to Freedom*, 171.

75. Earl Conrad, *Harriet Tubman, Negro Soldier and Abolitionist* (New York: International Publishers, 1942), 30–43; Harriet Buckmaster, *Let My People Go* (1941; reprint, Boston: Beacon Press, 1966), 213–216; Harding, *There Is a River*, 103, 153, 165, 199, 252.

76. Quarles, *Black Abolitionists*, 150.

77. Ibid., 156.

78. James Oliver Horton, "Generations of Protest: Black Families and Social Reform in Ante-Bellum Boston," *New England Quarterly* 49, no. 2 (June 1976): 242–256; Foner, *History of Black Americans* 2:505–506.

79. Quarles, *Black Abolitionists*, 153.

80. Ibid., 158.

81. PFASS minutes, 1833–1848, 14 October 1841, 9 September 1841, Historical Society of Pennsylvania.

82. PFASS minutes, 1833–1848, 12 June 1845, Historical Society of Pennsylvania.

Conclusion: Sites of Change

1. Jackie Pope, "Women in the Welfare Rights Struggle: The Brooklyn Welfare Action Council," in West and Blumberg, *Women and Social Protest*, 63–72.

2. Robnett, *How Long?* 180, 189.

3. William Gamson and David Meyer, "Framing Political Opportunity," in *Comparative Perspectives on Social Movements: Political Opportunities, Mobilizing Structures, and Cultural Framings*, ed. Doug McAdam, John McCarthy and Mayer Zald, 275–290.

4. These studies include Norman I. Fainstein and Susan S. Fainstein, *Urban Political Movements: The Search for Power by Minority Groups in America* (Englewood Cliffs, N.J.: Prentice-Hall, 1974); Carolyn Howe, "Gender, Race, and Community Activism: Competing Strategies in the Struggle for Public Education," in Naples, *Community Activism and Feminist Politics;* Filomina Chioma Steady, "Women and Collective Action: Female Models in Transition," in James and Busia, *Theorizing Black Feminisms;* and Bookman and Morgen, *Women and the Politics of Empowerment* (New York: Cambridge University Press, 1996).

5. Wright, "African American Sisterhood," 37.

6. Collins, *Black Feminist Thought,* 28–30; Naples, *Community Activism and Feminist Politics,* 3–7.

Bibliography

Brooklyn Historical Society, New York
Fales Library, New York University, New York
Historical Society of Pennsylvania
The Library Company of Philadelphia
Library of Congress, Washington, D.C.
Moorland-Springarn Research Center, Howard University, Washington, D.C.
Museum of the City of New York, New York
New York Historical Society, New York
New York Public Library, New York
Ontario Black Historical Society, Ontario, Canada
Queensboro Public Library, Flushing, New York
Rare Book Room, Special Collections, Columbia University, New York
Schomburg Center for Research in Black Culture, New York Public Library, New York
Virginia Historical Society, Richmond, Virginia

Abdy, E. S. *Journal of a Residence and Tour in the United States of North America from April 1833, to October 1834.* London: John Murray, 1835.
Albert, Michael, et al. *Liberating Theory.* Boston: South End Press, 1986.
Albion, Robert G. *The Rise of the New York Port, 1815–1860.* New York: Scribner and Sons, 1939.
Alexander, Sadie Tanner Mossell. "Negro Women in Our Economic Life." In *Words of Fire: An Anthology of African-American Feminist Thought,* ed. Beverly Guy-Sheftall. New York: New Press, 1995.
Allen, Irving Lewis. *The City in Slang: New York Life and Popular Speech.* New York: Oxford University Press, 1993.
Andrew, John A., III. "Betsey Stockton: Stranger in a Strange Land." *Journal of Presbyterian History* 52 (1974).
Andrews, William L., ed. *Sisters of the Spirit: Three Black Women's Autobiographies of the Nineteenth Century.* Bloomington: Indiana University Press, 1986.
Aptheker Herbert. *American Negro Slave Revolts.* New York: International Publishers, 1963.
———. *One Continual Cry.* New York: Humanities Press, 1965.

————, ed. *A Documentary History of the Negro People in the United States.* New York: Citadel Press, 1951.

Barnett, Marguerite Ross. "A Theoretical Perspective on American Public Policy." In *Public Policy for the Black Community: Strategies and Perspectives.* ed. Marguerite Ross Barnett and James A. Hefner. New York: Alfred, 1976.

Bauer, Raymond A., and Alice H. Bauer. "Day to Day Resistance to Slavery." *Journal of Negro History* 27, No. 3 (October 1942).

Berry, Mary Frances, and John W. Blassingame. *Long Memory: The Black Experience in America.* New York: Oxford University Press, 1982.

Billington, Ray Allen. *The Journal of Charlotte L. Forten: A Free Negro in the Slave Era.* New York: W. W. Norton, 1953.

Blassingame, John W. *The Slave Community: Plantation Life in the Antebellum South.* Rev. ed. New York: Oxford University Press, 1979.

————. "Status and Social Structure in the Slave Community." In *Perspectives and Irony in American Slavery,* ed. Harry P. Owens. Jackson: University Press of Mississippi, 1976.

————, ed. *Slave Testimony: Two Centuries of Letters, Speeches, Interviews, and Autobiographies.* Baton Rouge: Louisiana State University Press, 1977.

Blassingame, John, and Mary Frances Berry. *Long Memory: The Black Experience in America.* New York: Oxford University Press, 1982.

Blauner, Herbert. "Internal Conflict and Ghetto Revolt." In *Racial Conflict,* ed. Gary Marx. Boston: Little, Brown, 1971.

Blight, David W. "W. E. B. DuBois and the Struggle for American Historical Memory." In *History and Memory in African-American Culture,* ed. Genevieve Fabre and Robert O'Meally. New York: Oxford University Press, 1994.

Blockson, Charles L. Catalogue of the Charles L. Blockson Afro-American Collection, A Unit of the Temple University Libraries. Philadelphia: Temple University Press, 1990.

Bogin, Ruth. "Sarah Parker Remond: Black Abolitionist from Salem." In *Black Women in American History: From Colonial Times through the Nineteenth Century,* ed. Darlene Clark Hine. Brooklyn: Carlson Publishing, 1990.

Bolt, Christine. *The Women's Movements in the United States and Britain from the 1790s to the 1920s.* Amherst: University of Massachusetts Press, 1993.

Boydston, Jeanne. *Home and Work: Housework, Wages, and the Ideology of Labor in the Early Republic.* New York: Oxford University Press, 1990.

Boylan, Anne M. "Antislavery Activity among African American Women." In *The Abolitionist Sisterhood: Women's Political Culture in Antebellum America,* ed. Jean Fagan Yellin and John C. Van Horne. Ithaca, N.Y.: Cornell University Press, 1994.

Bracey, John H., Jr., August Meier, and Elliott Rudwick, eds. *Black Nationalism in America.* Indianapolis, Ind.: Bobbs-Merrill Educational Publishing, 1970.

Brent, Linda. *Incidents in the Life of a Slave Girl.* New York: Harcourt Brace Jovanovich, 1973.

Brewer, Rose M. "Theorizing Race, Class and Gender: The New Scholarship of Black Feminist Intellectuals and Black Women's Labor." In *Theorizing Black Feminisms: The Visionary Pragmatism of Black Women,* ed. Stanlie M. James and Abena P. A. Busia. New York: Routledge, 1993.

Brown, Elsa Barkley. *"Hearing Our Mothers' Lives."* (unpublished)Fifteenth Anniversary of African-American and African Studies. Atlanta: Emory University, 1986. (speech)

———. "Negotiating and Transforming the Public Sphere: African American Political Life in the Transition from Slavery to Freedom," *Public Culture* 7 (Fall 1994).

Brown, Ronald E., and Monica L. Wolford. "Religious Resources and African-American Political Action." *National Political Science Review* 4 (1994).

Burn, James D. *Three Years among the Working-Classes in the United States during the War.* London: Smith, Elder, 1865.

Burnham, Dorothy. "The Life of the Afro-American Woman in Slavery." *International Journal of Women's Studies* 1, no. 4 (July/August 1978).

Butler, John Sibley. *Entrepreneurship and Self-Help among Black Americans: A Reconsideration of Race and Economics.* New York: State University of New York Press, 1991.

Butler, Kim D. *Freedoms Given, Freedoms Won: Afro-Brazilians in Post-Abolition São Paulo and Salvador.* New Brunswick, N.J.: Rutgers University Press, 1998.

Caro, Edythe Quinn. "The Hills in the Mid-Nineteenth Century: The History of a Rural Afro-American Community in Westchester County." Master's thesis, Herbert H. Lehman College, City University of New York, 1988.

Carroll, Peter N., and David W. Noble. *The Free and the Unfree: A New History of the United States.* 2nd ed. New York: Penguin Books, 1988.

Chickering, Jesse. *A Statistical View of the Population of Massachusetts, 1760–1840.* Boston: C. C. Little and J. Brown, 1846.

Clark-Lewis, Elizabeth. "Domestic Workers in the North." In *Black Women in America: An Historical Encyclopedia,* ed. Darlene Clark Hine. Brooklyn: Carlson Publishing, 1993.

———. *Living In, Living Out: African American Domestics and the Great Migration.* New York: Kodansha International, 1994.

Collier-Thomas, Bettye. *Daughters of Thunder: Black Women Preachers and Their Sermons, 1850–1979.* San Francisco: Jossey-Bass, 1998.

———. "Frances Ellen Watkins Harper: Abolitionist and Feminist Reformer, 1825–1911." In *African-American Women and the Vote, 1837–1965,* ed. Ann D. Gordon, with Bettye Collier-Thomas, John H. Bracey, Arlene Voski Avakian, and Joyce Avrech Berkman. Amherst: University of Massachusetts Press, 1997.

———. "The Role of the Black Woman in the Development and Maintenance of Black Organizations." In *Black Organizations: Issues on Survival Techniques*, ed. Lennox S. Yearwood. Washington, D.C.: University Press of America, 1980.

Collins, Patricia Hill. *Black Feminist Thought: Knowledge, Consciousness, and the Politics of Empowerment*. New York: Routledge, 1991.

Collison, Gary. *Shadrach Minkins: From Fugitive Slave to Citizen*. Cambridge: Harvard University Press, 1997.

Colwell, Stephen. *The Five Cotton States and New York*. Philadelphia, 1861.

Cooper, James Fenimore. *Notions of the Americans Picked by a Travelling Batchelor*. New York: Ungar, 1963.

Cott, Nancy F. *The Bonds of Womanhood: "Women's Sphere" in New England, 1780–1835*. New Haven, Conn.: Yale University Press 1977.

Curry, Daniel. *New York: Historical Sketches of the Rise and Progress of the Metropolitan City of America*. New York: Carlton and Phillips, 1853.

Curry, Leonard P. *The Free Black in Urban America, 1800–1850: The Shadow of the Dream*. Chicago: University of Chicago Press, 1981.

" 'D' to the 'Females of Color.' " *Weekly Advocate*, 7 January 1837.

Davis, Angela Y. "Reflections on the Black Woman's Role in the Community of Slaves." *Black Scholar* (December 1971).

———. *Women, Race and Class*. New York: Vintage Books, 1983.

Davis, David Brion. *The Problem of Slavery in Western Culture*. New York: Oxford University Press, 1966.

DeBow, James. *Industrial Resources of the Southern and Western States*. Vol. 3. New Orleans, 1853.

———. *Interest in Slavery of the Southern Non-Slaveholders*. Charleston, 1860.

Delaney, Lucy A. "From the Darkness Cometh the Light or Struggles for Freedom." In *The Schomburg Library of Nineteenth-Century Black Women Writers: Six Women's Slave Narratives*, ed. Henry Louis Gates Jr. New York: Oxford University Press, 1988.

Delaney, Martin R. *The Condition, Elevation, Emigration and Destiny of the Colored People of the United States*. 1852. Reprint, New York: Arno Press, 1968.

Deutsch, Karl. "Social Mobilization and Political Development." *American Political Science Review* 55, no. 3 (1961).

Dillon, Merton L. *The Abolitionists: The Growth of a Dissenting Minority*. New York: W. W. Norton, 1974.

Dixon, Melvin. "The Black Writer's Use of Memory." In *History and Memory in African-American Culture*, ed. Genevieve Fabre and Robert O'Meally. New York: Oxford University Press, 1994.

Dodge, William E. *Old New York*. New York, 1880.

Dodson, Jualynne. "Nineteenth-Century A.M.E. Preaching Women." In *Women in New Worlds: Historical Perspectives on the Wesleyan Tradition*, ed. Hilah F. Thomas and Rosemary Skinner Keller. Nashville: Abingdon, 1981.

Doggett. John, Jr. *Doggett's New York City Directory, for 1846 and 1847.* New York: John Doggett Jr., 1846.

Douglass, Frederick. "Address at the 1853 Convention." In *Minutes of the Proceedings of the National Negro Convention Movement, 1830–1864,* ed. Howard Bell. New York: Arno Press, 1969.

———. *Life and Times of Frederick Douglass.* Rev. ed. 1892. Reprint, New York: Collier Books, 1962.

———. "Prejudice Against Color." *North Star,* 13 June 1850.

Dubbert, Joe I. *A Man's Place: Masculinity in Transition.* Englewood Cliffs, N.J.: Prentice-Hall, 1979.

Dublin, Thomas. "Women, Work, and the Family: Female Operatives in the Lowell Mills, 1830–1860." *Feminist Studies* 3, nos. 1/2 (fall 1975).

DuBois, W. E.B. *The Philadelphia Negro: A Social Study.* 1899. Reprint, New York: Schocken Books, 1967.

———. "The Religion of the American Negro." *New World* 9 (December 1900).

———. *The World and Africa.* New York: International Publishers, 1972.

Egypt, Ophelia Settle, J. Masuoka, and Charles S. Johnson. "Unwritten History of Slavery, Autobiographical Accounts of Negro Ex-Slaves." Social Science Document No. 1. Nashville: Fisk University, Social Science Institute, 1945.

Elaw, Zilpha. *Memoirs of the Life, Religious Experience, Ministerial Travels and Labours of Mrs. Zilpha Elaw, An American Female of Colour; Together with Some Accounts of the Great Religious Revivals in America.* In *Sisters of the Spirit: Three Black Women's Autobiographies of the Nineteenth Century,* ed. William L. Andrews. Bloomington: Indiana University Press, 1986.

Elizabeth. *Elizabeth, a Colored Minister of the Gospel, Born in Slavery.* Philadelphia: Tract Association of Friends, 1889.

Epstein, Barbara Leslie. *The Politics of Domesticity: Women, Evangelism and Temperance in Nineteenth-Century America.* Middletown, Conn.: Wesleyan University Press 1981.

Erikson, Kai. *Wayward Puritans: A Study in the Sociology of Deviance.* New York: Wiley Press, 1966.

Ernst, Robert. "The Economic Status of New York City Negroes, 1850–1863." In *The Making of Black America,* ed. August Meier and Elliott Rudwick. New York: Atheneum, 1969.

———. *Immigrant Life in New York City, 1825–1863.* New York: King's Crown Press, 1949.

Escott, Paul D. *Slavery Remembered: A Record of Twentieth-Century Slave Narratives.* Chapel Hill: University of North Carolina Press, 1979.

Fabre, Genevieve. "African-American Commemorative Celebrations in the Nineteenth Century." In *History and Memory in African-American Culture,* ed. Genevieve Fabre and Robert O'Meally. New York: Oxford University Press, 1994.

Fashole-Luke, E. W. "Ancestor Veneration and the Communion of Saints." In *New Testament Christianity for Africa and the World,* ed. Mark E. Glasswell and Edward W. Fashole-Luke. London: S.P.C.K., 1974.

Field, Phyllis F. *The Politics of Race in New York: The Struggle for Black Suffrage in the Civil War.* Ithaca, N.Y.: Cornell University Press, 1982.

Fifth Annual Report of the New York Committee of Vigilance. New York, 1842.

The First Annual Report of the New York Committee of Vigilance for the Year 1837. New York: Piercy and Reed, 1837.

Foner, Eric. *Free Soil, Free Men: The Ideology of the Republican Party before the Civil War.* New York: Oxford University Press, 1970.

Foner, Philip S. *Business and Slavery: The New York Merchants and the Irrepressible Conflict.* Chapel Hill: University of North Carolina Press, 1941.

———. *History of Black Americans: From the Emergence of the Cotton Kingdom to the Eve of the Compromise of 1850.* Westport, Conn.: Greenwood Press, 1983.

———. *The Life and Writings of Frederick Douglass: Pre-Civil War Decade 1850–1860.* New York: International Publishers, 1950.

Foote, Julia A. J. *A Brand Plucked from the Fire.* In *Sisters of the Spirit,* ed. William L. Andrews. Bloomington: Indiana University Press, 1986.

Fordham, Monroe. *Major Themes in Northern Black Religious Thought, 1800–1860.* Hicksville, N.Y.: Exposition Press, 1975.

Forman, James. *The Making of Black Revolutionaries.* New York: Macmillan, 1972.

Foster, Frances Smith, ed. *A Brighter Coming Day: A Frances Ellen Watkins Harper Reader.* New York: Feminist Press, 1990.

Fox-Genovese, Elizabeth. "Strategies and Forms of Resistance: Focus on Slave Women in the United States." In *In Resistance: Studies in African, Caribbean, and Afro-American History,* ed. Gary Y. Okihiro. Amherst: University of Massachusetts Press, 1986.

———. *Within the Plantation Household: Black and White Women of the Old South.* Chapel Hill: University of North Carolina Press, 1988.

Franklin, John Hope, and Alfred A. Moss Jr. *From Slavery to Freedom: A History of Negro Americans.* 6th ed. New York: Alfred A. Knopf, 1988.

Franklin, V. P. *Black Self-Determination: A Cultural History of African-American Resistance.* Rev. ed. New York: Lawrence Hill Books, 1992.

Fredrickson, George M. *White Supremacy: A Comparative Study in American and South African History.* New York: Oxford University Press, 1981.

Freeman, Rhoda Golden. *The Free Negro in New York City in the Era before the Civil War.* New York: Garland, 1994.

Frucht, Richard, ed. *Black Society in the New World*. New York: Random House, 1971.

Gallay, Alan. "Planters and Slaves in the Great Awakening." In *Masters and Slaves in the House of the Lord: Race and Religion in the American South, 1740–1870*, ed. John R. Boles. Bowling Green: University Press of Kentucky, 1988.

Gamson, William. *The Strategy of Social Protest*. Homewood, Ill.: Dorsey, 1975.

Gates, Henry Louis, Jr. *Collected Black Women's Narratives*. New York: Oxford University Press, 1988.

Genovese, Eugene. *Roll, Jordan, Roll: The World the Slaves Made*. New York: Pantheon Books, 1974.

———. *The World the Slaveholders Made*. New York: Vintage Books, 1969.

Giddings, Paula. *When and Where I Enter: The Impact of Black Women on Race and Sex in America*. New York: Bantam Books, 1984.

Gifford, Carolyn De Swarte. "Women in Social Reform Movements." In *Women and Religion in America: The Nineteenth Century*, ed. Rosemary R. Ruether and Rosemary Skinner Keller. New York: Harper and Row, 1981.

Gilbert, Olive. *Narrative of Sojourner Truth: A Bondswoman of Olden Time*. 1850. Reprint, New York: Arno Press, 1968.

Gilkes, Cheryl Townsend. "The Politics of 'Silence': Dual-Sex Political Systems and Women's Traditions of Conflict in African-American Religion." In *African-American Christianity: Essays in History*, ed. Paul E. Johnson. Berkeley: University of California Press, 1994.

Gordon-McCutchan, R. C. "The Irony of Evangelical History." *Journal for the Scientific Study of Religion* 20 (December 1981).

Gronowicz, Anthony. *Race and Class Politics in New York before the Civil War*. Boston: Northeastern University Press, 1998.

Gross, Bella. "Freedom's Journal and the Rights of All." *Journal of Negro History* 17, no. 3 (June 1932).

Gutman, Herbert. "The Reality of the Rags-to-Riches 'Myth': The Case of the Patterson, New Jersey, Locomotive, Iron, and Machinery Manufacturers, 1830–1880." In *Nineteenth-Century Cities: Essays in the New Urban History*, ed. Thernstrom Stephen and Richard Sennett. New Haven, Conn.: Yale University Press, 1969.

Hall, Kermit L., William M. Wiecek, and Paul Finkelman. *American Legal History: Cases and Materials*. New York: Oxford University Press, 1991.

Handlin, Oscar. *Boston's Immigrants: A Study of Acculturation*. Cambridge: Belknap Press of Harvard University Press, 1959.

Harding, Vincent. *There Is a River: The Black Struggle for Freedom in America*. New York: Harcourt Brace Jovanovich, 1981.

Harley, Sharon. "Northern Black Female Workers: Jacksonian Era." In *The Afro-American Woman: Struggles and Images*, ed. Sharon Harley and Rosalyn Terborg-Penn. Port Washington, N.Y.: Kennikat Press, 1978.

Harms, Robert. "Sustaining the System: Trading Towns along the Middle Zaire." In *Women and Slavery in Africa,* ed. Claire C. Robertson and Martin A. Klein. Madison: University of Wisconsin Press, 1983.

Harper, Francis Ellen Watkins. "Could We Trace the Record of Every Human Heart." In *A Brighter Coming Day: A Frances Ellen Watkins Harper Reader,* ed. Frances Smith Foster. New York: Feminist Press, 1990.

Harris, Abram. *The Negro as Capitalist.* New York: Arno Press, 1936.

Harris, Joseph E., ed. *Global Dimensions of the African Diaspora.* Washington, D.C.: Howard University Press, 1982.

Haswell, Charles H. *Reminiscences of an Octogenarian of the City of New York, 1816–1860.* New York: Harper and Brothers, 1896.

Haviland, Laura S. *A Woman's Life-Work, Labor and Experiences.* Chicago: Publishing Association of Friends, 1881.

Haywoode, Terry. "Working Class Feminism: Creating a Politics of Community, Connection, and Concern." Ph.D. diss., City University of New York, 1991.

Henn, Jeanne K. "Women in the Rural Economy: Past, Present, and Future." In *African Women South of the Sahara,* ed. Margaret Jean Hay and Sharon Stichter. New York: Longman, 1984.

Higginbotham, Evelyn Brooks. "African-American Women's History and the Metalanguage of Race." *Signs: Journal of Women in Culture and Society* 17, no. 2 (1992).

Hine, Darlene Clark, ed. *Black Women in America: An Historical Encyclopedia.* Brooklyn: Carlson Publishing, 1993.

Hine, Darlene Clark, and Kate Wittenstein. "Female Slave Resistance: The Economics of Sex." In *The Black Woman Cross-Culturally,* ed. Filomina Chioma Steady. Rochester, N.Y.: Schenkman Books, 1981.

———. "Rape and the Inner Lives of Black Women in the Middle West: Preliminary Thoughts on the Culture of Dissemblance." *Signs: Journal of Women in Culture and Society* 14, no. 4 (1989).

Hodges, Graham Russell. *New York City Cartmen, 1667–1850.* New York: New York University Press, 1986.

———. *Root and Branch: African Americans in New York and East Jersey, 1613–1863.* Chapel Hill: University of North Carolina Press, 1999.

hooks, bell. *Ain't I A Woman: Black Women and Feminism.* Boston: Beacon Press, 1981.

Horton, James Oliver. "Freedom's Yoke: Gender Conventions among Antebellum Free Blacks." *Feminist Studies* 12, no. 1 (spring 1986).

Horton, James Oliver, and Lois E. Horton. *Black Bostonians: Family Life and Community Struggle in the Antebellum North.* New York: Holmes and Meier, 1979.

———. *In Hope of Liberty: Culture, Community, and Protest among Northern Free Blacks, 1700–1860.* New York: Oxford University Press, 1997.

Humez, Jean McMahon, ed. *Gifts of Power: The Writings of Rebecca Jackson,*

Black Visionary, Shaker Eldress. Amherst: University of Massachusetts Press, 1981.

Johnson, Audreye. "Catherine Ferguson." In *Black Women in America: An Historical Encyclopedia,* ed. Darlene Clark Hine. Brooklyn: Carlson Publishing, 1993.

Johnson, Paul E., ed. *African-American Christianity: Essays in History.* Berkeley: University of California Press, 1994.

Johnson, Whittington B. *The Promising Years, 1750–1830: The Emergence of Black Labor and Business.* New York: Garland, 1993.

Jones, Jacqueline. *Labor of Love, Labor of Sorrow: Black Women, Work and the Family, from Slavery to the Present.* New York: Vintage Books, 1985.

Jones, Thomas. *The Experience of Thomas H. Jones, Who Was a Slave for Forty-Three Years.* Boston: Bazin and Chandler, 1862.

Joyner, Charles. " 'Believer I Know': The Emergence of African-American Christianity." In *African-American Christianity: Essays in History,* ed. Paul E. Johnson. Berkeley: University of California Press, 1994.

Kaplan, Temma. "Female Consciousness and Collective Action: The Case of Barcelona, 1910–1918." *Signs: Journal of Women in Culture and Society* 7 no. 3 (1982).

Katzman, David M. *Seven Days A Week: Women and Domestic Service in Industrializing America.* New York: Oxford University Press, 1978.

Kelly, Joan. "The Doubled Vision of Feminist Theory: A Postscript to the 'Women and Power' Conference." *Feminist Studies* 5 (spring 1979).

Kessler-Harris, Alice. *Out to Work: A History of Wage-Earning Women in the United States.* New York: Oxford University Press, 1982.

King, Deborah K. "Multiple Jeopardy, Multiple Consciousness: The Context of a Black Feminist Ideology." In *Black Women in America: Social Science Perspectives,* ed. Micheline R. Malson, Elisabeth Mudimbe-Boyi, Jean F. O'Barr, and Mary Wyer. Chicago: University of Chicago Press, 1988.

King, Mae. "The Politics of Sexual Stereotypes." *Black Scholar* 4 (1973).

King, Wilma. *Stolen Childhood: Slave Youth in Nineteenth Century in America.* Bloomington: Indiana University Press, 1995.

Klandermans, Bert, and Sidney Tarrow. "Mobilization into Social Movements: Synthesizing European and American Approaches." In *From Structure to Action: Comparing Social Movement Research across Cultures,* ed. Bert Klandermans, Hanspeter Kriesi, and Sidney Tarrow. International Social Movement Research, vol. 1. Greenwich, Conn.: JAI Press, 1988.

Klein, Martin A. "Women in Slavery in the Western Sudan." In *Women and Slavery in Africa,* ed. Claire C. Robertson and Martin A. Klein. Madison: University of Wisconsin Press, 1983.

Koch, G. Adolph. *Religion of the American Enlightenment.* New York: Thomas Crowekk, 1968.

Kovel, Joel. *White Racism: A Psychohistory.* New York: Vintage Books, 1970.

Lankevich, George J., and Howard B. Furer, *A Brief History of New York City, 1840–1857*. New York: Columbia University Press, 1981.

Lapsansky, Emma Jones. *Black Presence in Pennsylvania: "Making It Home."* Pennsylvania Historical Studies 21. University Park: Pennsylvania Historical Association, 1990.

———. "Friends, Wives, and Strivings: Networks and Community Values among Nineteenth-Century Philadelphia Afroamerican Elites." *Pennsylvania Magazine of History and Biography* 108, no. 1 (January 1984).

———. " 'Since They Got Those Separate Churches': Afro-Americans and Racism in Jacksonian Philadelphia." In *African Americans in Pennsylvania: Shifting Historical Perspectives*, ed. Joe William Trotter Jr. and Eric Ledell Smith. University Park: Pennsylvania State University Press, 1997.

Leashore, Bogart R. "Black Female Workers: Live-in Domestics in Detroit, Michigan, 1860–1880." *Phylon* 45, no. 2 (June 1984).

Lee, Jarena. *The Life and Religious Experience of Jarena Lee, a Coloured Lady, Giving an Account of Her Call to Preach the Gospel.* In *Sisters of the Spirit: Three Black Women's Autobiographies of the Nineteenth Century*, ed. William L. Andrews. Bloomington: Indiana University Press, 1986.

LePage, P. G. "Arts and Crafts of the Negro." *International Studio* 78 (March 1924).

Lerner, Gerda. "Early Community Work of Black Club Women." *Journal of Negro History* 59, no. 2 (April 1974).

———. *The Majority Finds Its Past: Placing Women in American History.* New York: Oxford University Press, 1979.

———, ed. *Black Women in White America: A Documentary History.* New York: Vintage Books, 1973.

Levine, Lawrence W. *Black Culture and Black Consciousness.* New York: Oxford University Press, 1977.

Levy, Leonard W. "The 'Abolition Riot': Boston's First Slave Rescue." *New England Quarterly* 25 (March 1952).

Lincoln, C. Eric. "The Black Heritage in the South." In *Religion in the South*, ed. C. Wilson. Jackson: University Press of Mississippi, 1985.

———, ed. *The Black Experience in Religion.* New York: Anchor Press, 1974.

Lincoln, C. Eric, and Lawrence H. Mamiya. *The Black Church in the African American Experience.* Durham, N.C.: Duke University Press, 1990.

Lindstrom, Harold. *Wesley and Sanctification.* London: Epworth, 1950.

Litwack, Leon F. *North of Slavery: The Negro in the Free States, 1790–1860.* Chicago: University of Chicago Press, 1961.

Lott, Eric. " 'The Seeming Counterfeit': Racial Politics and Early Blackface Minstrelsy." *American Quarterly* 43, no. 2 (June 1991).

MacCormack, Carol P. "Slaves, Slave Owners, and Slave Dealers: Sherbro Coast and Hinterland." In *Women and Slavery in Africa*, ed. Claire C. Robertson and Martin A. Klein. Madison: University of Wisconsin Press, 1983.

Malveaux, Julianne. " 'Ain't I a Woman': Differences in the Labor Market Status of Black and White Women." In *Racism and Sexism: An Integrated Study,* ed. Paula S. Rothenberg. New York: St. Martin's Press, 1988.

Marsuda, Mari. "Looking to the Bottom: Critical Legal Studies and Reparations." In *Critical Race Theory: The Key Writings That Formed the Movement,* ed. Kimberle Crenshaw, Neil Gotanda, Gary Peller, and Kendall Thomas. New York: New Press, 1995.

Marx, Karl. *Capital.* Trans. Samuel Moore and Edward Aveling. Chicago: C. H. Kerr, 1909.

Matthaei, Julie A. *An Economic History of Women in America: Women's Work, the Sexual Division of Labor, and the Development of Capitalism.* New York: Schocken Books, 1982.

Matthews, Donald G. *Slavery and Methodism: A Chapter in American Morality.* Princeton, N.J.: Princeton University Press, 1965.

Matthews, Jean. "Race, Sex, and the Dimensions of Liberty in Antebellum America." *Journal of the Early Republic* 6 (fall 1986).

May, Samuel J. *Some Recollections of the Anti-Slavery Conflict.* 1869. Reprint, New York: Arno Press, 1969.

Mbiti, John S. *African Religions and Philosophy.* 1969. Reprint, London: Heinemann, 1988.

McAdam, Doug. *Political Process and the Development of Black Insurgency.* Chicago: University of Chicago Press, 1985.

McClain, William B. "Free Style and a Closer Relationship to Life." In *The Black Experience in Religion,* ed. C. Eric Lincoln. New York: Anchor Press, 1974.

McDougald, Elise Johnson. "The Survey 53, March 1, 1925." In *Harlem's Glory: Black Women Writing, 1900–1950,* ed. Lorraine Elena Ross and Ruth Elizabeth Randolph. Cambridge: Harvard University Press, 1996.

McKay, Nellie Y. "Feminism at Work in the Church: Those Preaching Black Women of the 19th Century." *Abafazi* (fall/winter 1993).

McLaurin, Melton A. *Celia, a Slave.* New York: Avon Books, 1993.

Mellon, James, ed. *Bullwhip Days: The Slaves Remember.* New York: Weidenfeld and Nicolson, 1988.

Miller, Kerby A. "Class, Culture, and Immigrant Group Identity in the United States: The Case of Irish-American Ethnicity." In *Immigration Reconsidered: History, Sociology, and Politics,* ed. Virginia Yans-McLaughlin. New York: Oxford University Press, 1990.

Morgan, Philip D. *Slave Counterpoint: Black Culture in the Eighteenth-Century Chesapeake and Lowcountry.* Chapel Hill: University of North Carolina Press, 1998.

Morris, Aldon D. *The Origins of the Civil Rights Movement: Black Communities Organizing for Change.* New York: Free Press, 1984.

Morris, Milton D. *The Politics of Black America.* New York: Harper and Row, 1975.

Morrison, Minion K. C. *Black Political Mobilization: Leadership, Power and Mass Behavior.* New York: State University of New York Press, 1987.

Morrissey, Marietta. *Slave Women in the New World: Gender Stratification in the Caribbean.* Lawrence: University Press of Kansas, 1989.

Morton, Patricia. *Disfigured Images: The Historical Assault on Afro-American Women.* Westport, Conn.: Praeger, 1991.

Mullin, Gerald. *Flight and Rebellion.* New York: Oxford University Press, 1972.

Mullings, Leith. "Women and Economic Change in Africa." In *Women in Africa: Studies in Social and Economic Change,* ed. Nancy J. Hafkin and Edna G. Bay. Stanford, Calif.: Stanford University Press, 1976.

Naples, Nancy A., ed. *Community Activism and Feminist Politics: Organizing Across Race, Class, and Gender.* New York: Routledge, 1998.

"Narrative of James Curry." In *Slave Testimony: Two Centuries of Letters, Speeches, Interviews, and Autobiographies,* ed. John W. Blassingame. Baton Rouge: Louisiana State University Press, 1977.

Nash, Gary B. "Forging Freedom: The Emancipation Experience in the Northern Seaport Cities, 1775–1820." In *Slavery and Freedom in the Age of the American Revolution,* ed. Ira Berlin and Ronald Hoffman. Urbana: University of Illinois Press, 1983.

———. *Forging Freedom: The Formation of Philadelphia's Black Community, 1720–1840.* Cambridge: Harvard University Press, 1988.

Newsome, Clarence G. "Mary McLeod Bethune As Religionist." In *Women in New Worlds: Historical Perspectives on the Wesleyan Tradition,* ed. Hilan F. Thomas and R. S. Keller. Nashville: Abingdon, 1981.

North, Douglass C. *The Economic Growth of the United States 1790–1860.* New York: W. W. Norton, 1966.

Northup, Solomon. *Twelve Years a Slave.* Ed. Sue Eakin and Joseph Logsdon. Baton Rouge: Louisiana State University Press, 1968.

Oakes, James. *The Ruling Race: A History of American Slaveholders.* New York: Vintage Books, 1982.

Oberschall, Anthony. *Social Conflict and Social Movements.* Englewood Cliffs, N.J.: Prentice-Hall, 1973.

O'Brien, John T., Jr. "From Bondage to Citizenship: The Richmond Black Community, 1865–1867." Ph.D. diss., University of Rochester, 1975.

Obtiko, Mary Ellen. " 'Custodians of a House of Resistance': Black Women Respond to Slavery." In *Women and Men: The Consequences of Power,* ed. Dana V. Hiller and Robin Ann Sheets. Cincinnati: University of Cincinnati, Office of Women's Studies, 1977.

O'Dea, Thomas J. *The Sociology of Religion.* Englewood Cliffs, N.J.: Prentice Hall, 1966.

Odum, Howard W., and Guy B. Johnson. *Negro Workaday Songs.* New York: Negro Universities Press, 1969.

Ottley, Roi, and William W. Weatherby, eds. *The Negro in New York: An Informal Social History*. New York: Oceana Publications, 1967.

Painter, Nell Irvin. *Sojourner Truth: A Life, a Symbol*. New York: W. W. Norton, 1996.

Park, Robert E. "The Conflict and Fusion of Cultures with Special Reference to the Negro." *Journal of Negro History* 4, no. 2.(April 1919).

Perdue, Charles L., Jr., Thomas E. Barden, and Robert K. Phillips, eds. *Weevils in the Wheat: Interviews with Virginia Ex-Slaves*. Charlottesville: University Press of Virginia, 1976.

Perkins, Linda. "Black Women and Racial 'Uplift' Prior to Emancipation." In *The Black Woman Cross-Culturally*, ed. Filomina Chioma Steady. Rochester, N.Y.: Schenkman Books, 1985.

Perlman, Daniel. "Organizations of the Free Negro in New York City, 1800–1860." *Journal of Negro History* 56, no. 3. (July 1971).

Peterson, Carla L. *"Doers of the Word": African-American Women Speakers and Writers in the North, 1830–1880*. New York: Oxford University Press, 1995.

Porter, Dorothy. "David Ruggles, an Apostle of Human Rights." *Journal of Negro History* 28, no. 1 (January 1943).

———. "The Organized Educational Activities of Negro Literary Societies, 1828–1846." *Journal of Negro Education* 5 (October 1936).

Potter, David. *The South and the Sectional Conflict*. Baton Rouge: Louisiana State University Press, 1968.

"Preamble to the Constitution of the Women's Association of Philadelphia." In *We Are Your Sisters: Black Women in the Nineteenth Century*, ed. Dorothy Sterling. New York: W. W. Norton & Company, 1984.

The Present State and Conditions of the Free People of Color of the City of Philadelphia and adjoining districts, as exhibited by the Report of a Committee of the Pennsylvania Society for Promoting the Abolition of Slavery. Philadelphia: Merrihew & Gunn, 1838.

Preyer, Norris W. "The Historian, the Slave, and the Ante-Bellum Textile Industry." *Journal of Negro History* 46, no. 2 (April 1961).

Prince, Nancy. *A Narrative of the Life and Travels of Mrs. Nancy Prince*. In *Collected Black Women's Narratives*, ed. Henry Louis Gates Jr. New York: Oxford University Press, 1988.

Quarles, Benjamin. *Black Abolitionists*. New York: Oxford University Press, 1969.

Raboteau, Albert J. "The Black Experience in American Evangelicalism: The Meaning of Slavery." In *African-American Religion: Interpretive Essays in History and Culture*, ed. Timothy E. Fulop and Albert J. Raboteau. New York: Routledge, 1997.

———. *Slave Religion: The "Invisible Institution" in the Antebellum South*. New York: Oxford University Press, 1978.

Radin, Paul. Foreword to *God Struck Me Dead: Religious Conversion Experiences and Autobiographies of Ex-Slaves,* ed. Clifton H. Johnson. Philadelphia: Pilgrim Press, 1969.

Randolph, Lewis A., and Gayle T. Tate. *The Rise and Decline of African American Political Power in Richmond: Race, Class, and Gender.* Urban Affairs Annual Review 42. Thousand Oaks: Sage Publications, 1995.

Rawick, George P. *The American Slave: A Composite Autobiography.* Westport, Conn.: Greenwood Press, 1977.

"A Register of Trades of Colored People in the City of Philadelphia and Districts." Philadelphia: Society of Friends, 1838.

Ripley, C. Peter, ed. *Witness for Freedom: African American Voices on Race, Slavery, and Emancipation.* Chapel Hill: University of North Carolina Press, 1993.

Robertson, Claire. "Africa into the Americas? Slavery and Women, the Family and the Gender Division of Labor." In *More Than Chattel: Black Women and Slavery in the Americas,* ed. David Barry Gaspar and Darlene Clark Hine. Bloomington: Indiana University Press, 1996.

Robnett, Belinda. "African-American Women in the Civil Rights Movement, 1954–1965: Gender, Leadership, and Micromobilization." *American Journal of Sociology* 101, no. 6 (May 1996).

———. *How Long? How Long?: African-American Women in the Struggle for Civil Rights.* New York: Oxford University Press, 1997.

Rollins, Judith. *Between Women: Domestics and Their Employers.* Philadelphia: Temple University Press, 1985.

Ruether, Rosemary R. "Christianity." In *Women in World Religions,* ed. Arvind Sharma. New York: State University of New York Press, 1987.

Rush, Barbara. " 'The Family Tree Is Not Cut': Women and Cultural Resistance in Slave Family Life in the British Caribbean." In *In Resistance: Studies in African, Caribbean, and Afro-American History,* ed. Gary Y. Okihiro. Amherst: University of Massachusetts Press, 1986.

Russell, Robert R. *Economic Aspects of Southern Sectionalism, 1840–1861.* Urbana: University of Illinois Press, 1924.

Sacks, Karen Brodkin. "Gender and Grassroots Leadership." In *Women and the Politics of Empowerment,* ed. Ann Bookman and Sandra Morgen. Philadelphia: Temple University Press.

Scoville, Joseph A. *Old Merchants of New York City, by Walter Barrett, Clerk.* 1885. Reprint, New York: Greenwood Press, 1968.

Shecter, Patricia. "Feminist Spirituality and Radical Political Commitment." *Journal of Women and Religion* 1, no. 1 (spring 1981).

Smith, Amanda Berry. *An Autobiography: The Story of the Lord's Dealings with Mrs. Amanda Smith, the Colored Evangelist.* New York: Oxford University Press, 1988.

Smith, James McCune. "Citizenship." *Anglo-African Magazine* 1, no. 5 (May 1859).

Smith, Theophus H. *Conjuring Culture: Biblical Formations of Black America.* New York: Oxford University Press, 1994.

Snow, David, Louis A. Zurcher Jr., and Sheldon Eckland-Olson. "Social Networks and Social Movements: A Microstructural Approach to Differential Recruitment." *American Sociological Review* 45, no. 5 (1980).

Stansell, Christine. *City of Women: Sex and Class in New York, 1789–1860.* New York: Alfred A. Knopf, 1986.

Stanton, Lucy. "A Plea for the Oppressed." In *The Three Sarahs: Documents of Antebellum Black College Women,* ed. Ellen NicKenzie Lawson with Marlene D. Merrill. New York: Edwin Mellen Press, 1984.

A Statistical Inquiry into the Condition of the People of Colour, of the City and Districts of Philadelphia. Philadelphia: Kite and Walton, 1849.

Stavinsky, Leonard. "The Origins of Negro Craftsmanship in Colonial America." *Journal of Negro History* 32, no. 4 (October 1947).

Steckel, Richard H. "Women, Work, and Health under Plantation Slavery in the United States." In *More Than Chattel: Black Women and Slavery in the Americas,* ed. David Barry Gaspar and Darlene Clark Hine. Bloomington: Indiana University Press, 1996.

Sterling, Dorothy, ed. *We Are Your Sisters: Black Women in the Nineteenth Century.* New York: W. W. Norton, 1984.

Stevenson, Brenda. "Slavery." In *Black Women in America: An Historical Encyclopedia,* ed. Darlene Clark Hine. Brooklyn: Carlson Publishing, 1993.

Steward, Austen. *Twenty-Two Years a Slave and Forty Years a Freeman, Embracing a Correspondence of Several Years While President of the Wilberforce Colony.* New York: W. Alling, 1857.

Stewart, Maria W. "Lecture Delivered at the Franklin Hall, Boston, September 21, 1832." In *Maria W. Stewart, America's First Black Woman Political Writer,* ed. Marilyn Richardson. Bloomington: Indiana University Press, 1987.

———. *Productions of Mrs. Maria W. Stewart.* Boston: Friends of Freedom and Virtue, 1835.

———. "Religion and the Pure Principles of Morality, the Sure Foundation on Which We Must Build." In *Maria W. Stewart, America's First Black Woman Political Writer,* ed. Marilyn Richardson. Bloomington: Indiana University Press, 1987.

Still, William. *The Underground Railroad.* 1872. Reprint, Chicago: Johnson Publishing, 1970.

Stuckey, Sterling. *Going through the Storm.* New York: Oxford University Press, 1994.

———. *Slave Culture: Nationalist Theory and the Foundations of Black America.* New York: Oxford University Press, 1987.

Sumler-Lewis, Janice. "The Forten-Purvis Women of Philadelphia and the American Anti-Slavery Crusade." *Journal of Negro History* 66, no. 4.

Takaki, Ronald, *Iron Cages: Race and Culture in 19th-Century America*. New York: Oxford University Press, 1990.

Tate, Gayle T. "Black Nationalism and Spiritual Redemption." *Western Journal of Black Studies* 15, no. 4 (fall 1991).

———. "Political Consciousness and Resistance among Black Antebellum Women." *Women and Politics* 13, no. 1 (1993).

———. "Spiritual Resistance of Early Black Female Evangelists, 1810–1845." *Abafazi* 7, no. 1 (fall/winter 1996).

———. "Tangled Vines: Ideological Interpretations of Afro-Americans in the Nineteenth Century." Ph.D. diss., City University of New York, 1984.

Taylor, Clarence. *The Black Churches of Brooklyn*. New York: Columbia University Press, 1994.

Taylor, Susie King. *Reminiscences of My Life in Camp with the 33rd United States Colored Troops*. Boston: Susie King Taylor, 1902.

Terborg-Penn, Rosalyn. *African-American Women in the Struggle for the Vote, 1850–1920*. Bloomington: Indiana University Press, 1998.

———. "Black Women in Resistance: A Cross-Cultural Perspective." In *In Resistance: Studies in African, Caribbean, and Afro-American History*, ed. Gary Y. Okihiro. Amherst: University of Massachusetts Press, 1986.

Thompson, Vincent Bakpetu. *The Making of the African Diaspora in the Americas 1441–1900*. New York: Longman, 1987.

Tilly, Charles. *From Mobilization to Revolution*. Reading, Mass: Addison-Wesley, 1978.

Tocqueville, Alexis de. *Democracy in America*. Ed. Philips Bradley. New York: Vintage Books, 1945.

Travis, Toni-Michelle C. "Boston: The Unfinished Agenda." In *Racial Politics in American Cities*, ed. Rufus P. Browning, Dale Rogers Marshall, and David H. Tabb. New York: Longman, 1990.

Wade, Richard C. *Slavery in the Cities: The South 1820–1860*. New York: Oxford University Press, 1964.

Walker, David. *Appeal to the Coloured Citizens of the World*. 1829. Reprint, New York: Hill and Wang, 1965.

Walker, George C. "The Afro-American in New York City, 1827–1860." Ph.D. diss., Columbia University, 1975.

Walker, Juliet E. K. *The History of Black Business in America: Capitalism, Race, Entrepreneurship*. New York: Simon and Shuster Macmillan, 1998.

———. "Racism, Slavery and Free Enterprise: Black Entrepreneurship in the United States Before the Civil War." *Business History Review* 60 (autumn 1986).

Walton, Hanes, Jr. *Invisible Politics: Black Political Behavior*. New York: State University of New York Press, 1985.

Ware, Caroline. *The Early New England Cotton Manufacture: A Study in Industrial Beginnings*. Boston: Houghton Mifflin, 1931.

Watkins, Ralph. "A Reappraisal of the Role of Voluntary Associations in the African American Community." *Afro-American in New York Life and History* 14, no. 2 (1990).

Webber, Thomas L. *Deep Like the Rivers: Education in the Slave Quarter Community, 1831–1865.* New York: W. W. Norton, 1978.

Welter, Barbara. "The Cult of True Womanhood, 1820–1860." *American Quarterly* 18 (summer 1964).

Wesley, Charles H. "The Negroes of New York in the Emancipation Movement." *Journal of Negro History* 24, no. 1 (January 1939).

West, Guida, and Rhoda Lois Blumberg, eds. *Women and Social Protest.* New York: Oxford University Press, 1990.

White, Deborah Gray. *Ar'n't I a Woman?: Female Slaves in the Plantation South.* New York: W. W. Norton, 1985.

Williams, Eric. *Capitalism and Slavery.* New York: Capricorn Books, 1966.

Wilmore, Gayraud S. *Black Religion and Black Radicalism: An Interpretation of the Religious History of Afro-American People.* 2nd ed., rev. Maryknoll, N.Y.: Orbis Books, 1983.

Wilson, Joseph. *Sketches of the Higher Classes of Colored People in Philadelphia by a Southerner.* Philadelphia, 1841.

Winch, Julie. *Philadelphia's Black Elite: Activism, Accommodation, and the Struggle for Autonomy, 1787–1848.* Philadelphia: Temple University Press, 1988.

———. "Philadelphia's Black Female Societies." In *The Abolitionist Sisterhood: Women's Political Culture in Antebellum America,* ed. Jean Fagan Yellin and John C. Van Horne (Ithaca: Cornell University Press, 1994).

Wood, Peter. *Black Majority.* New York: W. W. Norton, 1974.

———. "Strange New Land 1619–1776." In *To Make Our World Anew: A History of African Americans,* ed. Robin D. G. Kelley and Earl Lewis. New York: Oxford University Press, 2000.

Wright, Michelle D. "African American Sisterhood: The Impact of the Female Slave Population on American Political Movements." *Western Journal of Black Studies* (spring 1991).

Wright, Richardson. *Hawkers and Walkers in Early America* (Philadelphia, 1927). New York: Arno Press, 1976.

Yee, Shirley J. *Black Women Abolitionists: A Study in Activism, 1828–1860.* Knoxville: University of Tennessee Press, 1992.

Young, Josiah U. *Black and African Theologies: Siblings or Distant Cousins?* Maryknoll, N.Y.: Orbis Books, 1986.

Young, R. J. *Antebellum Black Activists: Race, Gender, and Self.* New York: Garland, 1996.

Index